American Avant-garde Theatre

This stunning contribution to the field of theatre history is the first in-depth look at avant-garde theatre in the United States from the early 1950s to the 1990s. *American Avant-Garde Theatre: A History* offers a definition of the avant-garde, and looks at its origins and theoretical foundations by examining:

- Gertrude Stein
- John Cage
- the Beat writers
- avant-garde cinema
- abstract expressionism
- minimalism

There are fascinating discussions and illustrations of the productions of the Living Theatre, the Wooster Group, Open Theatre, Ontological-Hysteric Theatre and Performance Group, among many others. Aronson also examines why avant-garde theatre declined and virtually disappeared at the end of the twentieth century.

Arnold Aronson is Professor of Theatre at Columbia University. He is author of *American Set Design* and *The History and Theory of Environmental Scenography*, and he served as editor of *Theatre Design and Technology* from 1978 to 1988.

Theatre production studies
Edited by John Russell Brown

[This series] will be welcomed by students and teachers alike.

New Theatre Quarterly

To progress today's theatre into tomorrow's, we need to understand yesterday's, and John Russell Brown's admirable detective series ... continues reconstructing what it was like to go to the theatre in the past.

Cue

Designed to span Western theatre from the Greeks to the present day, each book in this path-breaking series explores a period or genre, drawing together aspects of production from staging, wardrobe and acting styles to the management of a theatre, its artistic team and technical crew. Each volume focuses on several texts of exceptional achievement and is well illustrated with contemporary material.

Shakespeare's Theatre (second edition)
Peter Thomson

Jacobean Public Theatre
Alexander Leggatt

Broadway Theatre
Andrew Harris

Greek Tragic Theatre
Rush Rehm

Moscow Art Theatre
Nick Worrall

American Avant-Garde Theatre: A History
Arnold Aronson

American Avant-garde Theatre

A history

Arnold Aronson

London and New York

First published 2000
by Routledge
11 New Fetter Lane, London EC4P 4EE

Simultaneously published in the USA and Canada
by Routledge
29 West 35th Street, New York, NY 10001

Routledge is an imprint of the Taylor & Francis Group

© 2000 Arnold Aronson

Typeset in 10/12 pt Galliard by Taylor & Francis Books Ltd
Printed and bound in Great Britain by Biddles Ltd, Guildford and
King's Lynn

British Library Cataloguing in Publication Data
A catalogue record for this book is available
from the British Library

Library of Congress Cataloging in Publication Data
Aronson, Arnold.
American avant-garde theatre: a history / Arnold Aronson.
p. cm. – (Theatre production studies)
Includes bibliographical references and index.
1. Experimental theater–United States–History–20th
century. 2. American drama–20th century–History and criticism.
I. Title. II. Series.
PN2193.E86 A88 2000
792'.022–dc21 00–032215

ISBN 0–415–02580–X (hbk)
ISBN 0–415–24139–1 (pbk)

For Isaac

Contents

Plates

Preface

In his famous 1939 essay on avant-garde and kitsch, an essay that some have suggested signaled the start of the American avant-garde,[1] art critic Clement Greenberg marveled at a contemporary Western culture that could produce simultaneously T.S. Eliot and Tin Pan Alley lyricist Eddie Guest, or the art of Georges Braque and *Saturday Evening Post* covers. "What perspective of culture," he wondered, "is large enough to enable us to situate them in an enlightening relation to each other?"[2] We might marvel similarly at the theatrical culture of the 1950s. If Greenberg was amazed at the seeming contradictions and disparities within the broad scope of Western society – even though high and low art have dwelt in an almost nurturing symbiosis throughout history – what are we to make of the relatively narrow discipline of American theatre, which, within a single decade, could give birth to *My Fair Lady* and *18 Happenings in 6 Parts, Gypsy* and *The Marrying Maiden*, or *Picnic* and the John Cage performance piece at Black Mountain College? Having acknowledged that they are all species of theatre in that they involve performers, discrete performance spaces, temporal structures, scenic design, props, costumes, and scripts of some sort, it is nonetheless hard to comprehend them as part of the same art form, let alone to envision them emerging from the same culture.

In those societies that have spawned organized forms of theatre, performance can generally be divided into three broad categories:

- All societies have had a theatre of popular entertainment – the theatre of the marketplace and music halls, which combined physical virtuosity, individual talent, and comic invention.
- Most societies have had some version of bourgeois entertainment, such as boulevard theatre or the West End – the mainstream

narrative theatre that reflected, reinforced, and sometimes shaped
societal attitudes and popular tastes.

- And some cultures have developed elitist theatres such as masques
  and other court entertainments – rarefied forms of performance
  available to limited segments of the populace and whose understanding and appreciation required some degree of training or
  special knowledge.

In some periods, such as Elizabethan England, the forms have intertwined and overlapped. The late twentieth-century United States
contained all three forms: the popular theatre was subsumed by television; bourgeois theatre existed on Broadway, Off Broadway, and to an
extent in the movies; and the elitist theatre was represented by the
avant-garde.

Because the avant-garde often contains within itself the intentionally
shocking and provocative, and because – by definition – it constitutes
an attack upon the established practices of mainstream culture and
society, it has been regarded with suspicion and has often been poorly
understood. Somewhat like the term "modern art," "avant-garde" has
been applied indiscriminately, almost as an epithet, to a wide range of
performance that falls outside the boundaries of naturalism or realism –
that is, narrative, psychological, melodramatic theatre. It is applied to
almost any form of performance that is in some way confusing, difficult, or aesthetically displeasing by some received standard of Western
culture. The absurdity of such an approach can be seen in the extreme
in critic Louis Kronenberger's description of the 1952 musical *Wish
You Were Here* as "a wistful comedy of manners ... in the bold *avant-
garde* manner of David Belasco." This "manner," according to
Kronenberger, consisted of "a real swimming pool, real hot dogs, and
what appeared to be real rain."[3] If the André Antoine–David Belasco
school of naturalism – a more than sixty-year-old tradition by the time
of Kronenberger's review – could be labeled as "avant-garde," then
any useful definition of the term will be problematic.

I have proposed a narrower definition in the following pages and
have attempted to show the origins, development, and ultimate decline
of the very vital American avant-garde theatre in the decades following
World War II. Although the avant-garde theatre – both broadly and
narrowly defined – has received a great deal of critical attention, there
have been surprisingly few books devoted to a larger overview of the
phenomenon. This book is an attempt to provide that overview and
place the avant-garde within a critical context. Even so, this book is

not a comprehensive study of American avant-garde theatre. I have had to make some difficult choices. Some groups and individuals who are mentioned here only in passing or not at all – Bread and Puppet Theatre, Mabou Mines, Playhouse of the Ridiculous and the Ridiculous Theatrical Company, Martha Clarke, and Meredith Monk; a whole host of Happening and Fluxus artists, including Red Grooms, Robert Whitman, Dick Higgins, Claes Oldenburg, George Maciunas, and Yoko Ono; California groups including Soon 3, Snake Theatre, San Francisco Mime Troupe, El Teatro Campesino; postmodern dancers Ann Halprin, Yvonne Rainer, Trisha Brown, Steve Paxton, David Gordon, and others; and performance artists Eleanor Antin, Suzanne Lacy, and others too numerous to list – were significant contributors to the ongoing development of the avant-garde and deserve greater attention. I have chosen to focus on those who I felt broke new ground or had the greatest impact on the evolution of the avant-garde. For that reason, I have often concentrated on the early work of these artists rather than later developments. Someone constructing a different narrative might make other choices.

I have also tried to strike a balance between description and explication. All theatre is a performative medium, a visual medium; but in much of the avant-garde theatre performative and visual elements are foregrounded. Photos or fragments of a script alone cannot convey the impact or meaning of a production. Therefore, I have tried to describe what an audience saw on the stage. In many cases I have turned to contemporary observers or the participants themselves to capture a sense of the sometimes electrifying, sometimes shocking, almost always revelatory impact of these works in their initial presentations. I hope that it will provide at least a hint of the excitement for those who were not there.

Acknowledgments

I owe thanks to many people who contributed in various ways to the writing of this book. First, I must thank several of the artists discussed herein whom I have interviewed over the years and who provided me with information and insight. And I thank the theatre companies, organizations, and individuals who provided assistance during my research and writing. The time and support for completing this work was made possible by colleagues at the Columbia University School of the Arts: Bob Fitzpatrick, Grafton Nunes, and Dan Kleinman. I am also grateful to Columbia colleague Austin Quigley and NYU colleague Brooks McNamara for their support and advice. Some of the research that found its way into these pages was done in preparation for my essay in the *Cambridge History of American Theatre*, and I thank editors Don Wilmeth and Christopher Bigsby of that enterprise for their input. Research and manuscript preparation was assisted by former and current students David Leichtman, Colette Boudreau, and Nina Hein. Help in locating sources was provided by Frantisek Deak, Ted Shank, and especially Mimi Smith. I am particularly indebted to my editors at Routledge, Rosie Waters and Talia Rodgers.

I owe an almost unrepayable debt of gratitude to John Russell Brown, not merely for commissioning this volume but also for his endless supply of patience, for his careful reading of every draft of the manuscript, and for his encouragement, keen insight, and persever-ance, which brought this book to fruition. Much of my understanding of the avant-garde was shaped by the teaching and friendship of the late Michael Kirby, who, in his books and articles and long editorship of *The Drama Review*, virtually defined the American avant-garde while resurrecting its historical roots. My first introduction to several of the individuals and groups in this book was through Michael when I was a student at New York University, and my first writings on avant-garde theatre were done under his guidance in the pages of *The Drama Review*. Michael read an early outline of this book, and his comments and criticisms helped to shape the current results. I regret that I did not complete this work before his death.

Finally, I must thank my wife, Ruth Bayard Smith, who was my tireless editor and sounding board and who patiently read each draft while providing unstinting encouragement, and whose love and support made this book possible.

Chapter 1

Origins of the avant-garde

> Actually America has an intellectual climate suitable for radical experimentation. We are, as Gertrude Stein said, the oldest country of the twentieth century.
>
> John Cage[1]

To some observers, the postwar era in American theatre was a period of steady and ineluctable decline. If the American theatre is equated with Broadway – and it was and still is for many commentators and audiences – then statistically at least, it could be argued that the theatre *was* in fact deteriorating at a fairly precipitous pace. The number of new productions decreased with each season, the range of theatre produced narrowed alarmingly, the financial burdens grew more overwhelming, and audiences stayed home to watch television. But if one shifted one's focus away from Broadway (and its low-budget clone, Off Broadway), it became clear that the theatre was not dying at all. What was in decline was an institution – a particular means of creating and producing theatre – and the style of theatre it generated. In fact, American theatre was heading into one of the most vibrant, creative, and productive periods in its history. An evolutionary process was occurring, and the American theatre was transforming into something different from what it had ever been, something that reflected the changing needs of artists and audiences alike and that could adapt more readily to a new world.

In the roughly thirty-year period from the mid-1950s to the mid-1980s, there was an eruption of theatrical activity in the United States that would ultimately reshape every aspect of performance and have significant influences both at home and abroad. The alternatives to Broadway were bursting with energy, talent, and new ideas. The myth of declining theatrical activity was easily belied by looking at the weekly theatre listings of the time, especially in a newspaper such as the then counterculture *Village Voice*. By the late 1960s, on any given weekend in New York, it was possible to choose from over 250 events covering the whole range and gamut of theatre. The most significant of these performances were forging new paths in acting, directing, staging, and design, and were redefining the very notion of theatre. In the words of critic Stanley Kauffmann, "there was a sense of bursting creativity, of things rushing into life. Some cheery souls even called it a new Elizabethan age."[2] Never before in American theatre history had the foundations of the art been examined so minutely, been so challenged, and been so radically altered. The driving force at the center of this activity was the *avant-garde*.

The concept of an avant-garde was something new in American theatre. The European theatre (and art, music, and literature) had experienced waves of avant-garde activity since the emergence of symbolism in the 1880s, but there was no equivalent in the United States. Granted, the American theatre had experienced its own rebellions since the early years of the twentieth century, notably in the Little or Art Theatre movement, which flourished in the teens and twenties, introduced new European works to American audiences and gave birth to Eugene O'Neill and the New Stagecraft, and again in the alternative theatre of the 1930s, which included agitprop performance and the Federal Theatre Project's Living Newspapers as well as the political dramas of the Theatre Union, which was among the first to produce Bertolt Brecht in America. And it is true that by the second decade of the twentieth century American playwrights were beginning to incorporate avant-garde elements from European models: aspects of symbolism, expressionism, and surrealism found their way into the plays of Zona Gale, Susan Glaspell, Alfred Kreymborg, John Howard Lawson, Elmer Rice, and, of course, O'Neill, and would emerge in more sophisticated forms later in the century in the works of William Saroyan, Arthur Miller, Tennessee Williams, and others who employed Strindberg-like inner landscapes, dream sequences, flashbacks, poetic language, lyric realism, symbolic settings, and archetypal characters. But all these writers continued to work within a basically realistic framework and psychological character structure. Themes that would have been easily recognizable to Ibsen – questions of morality, social responsibility, the individual versus society at large, and familial relationships – remained clear and dominant; the exploration and pursuit of the elusive American dream informed most of these plays or lurked just below the surface. Avant-garde elements could be found *within* the new plays, not as a *basis* for creating the plays. The fundamental building blocks of a radical European avant-garde became mere stylistic conceits in the hands of most American playwrights. As a result, the works by these playwrights remained within the establishment; Broadway welcomed every new generation and easily absorbed what changes or permutations each had to offer.

The general thrust and tenor of pre-World War II experimental theatre was summed up by Lee Strasberg, one of the founders of the Group Theatre and later head of the Actors Studio. Writing in 1962, Strasberg declared that

> the theatre generation after the First World War felt itself to be part of a new dream which it hoped would lead to a new theatre. It was not to be words, scenery, and acting as separate elements uniting into a somewhat mechanical entity. It was to be the word transfigured from its purely logical and literary meaning on a page by the living presence of the actor whose creation of the moment the event, the situation, brought out or added dramatic meaning to the word.[3]

Although he went on to cite Edward Gordon Craig and "the art of the theatre," Strasberg saw the problem not with the existing drama *per se* but with contemporary production practices. "This dream was shattered ...," he continued, "by the fact that the central element for the creation of the art of the theatre – a coherent unified company of actors with artistic leadership to express its vision of the dramatist's intention – was missing."[4] Strasberg was advocating neither a new form of theatre nor a radically new dramatic content; he was simply advocating the need for art to take precedence over commerce.

What began to emerge in the 1950s, however, was something quite different. There was a bold spirit of experimentation – a rebellion against the mainstream commercial system and the utter rejection of the *status quo*. What happened in the postwar era was the evolution of a theatre diametrically opposed to the conventions of dramatic practice common in the West since the Renaissance; it was an approach that rejected the beliefs and expectations of traditional audiences and radically altered both the aesthetic and organizational basis upon which performance was created. And because the traditional theatre provided little in the way of precedent, this new theatre drew heavily upon iconoclastic movements within the plastic arts, with the result that traditional barriers between theatre, dance, music, and art began to crumble.

Historically, the function of the avant-garde, as art historian Thomas Crow has suggested, has been to serve "as a research and development arm of the culture industry."[5] But as the 1965 Rockefeller Panel Report on the state of the arts astutely observed, Broadway, through the first half of the twentieth century or so, was sufficiently successful, productive, and financially solvent that it could accommodate and support experimentation within its own confines.[6] Broadway, in other words, served as its own research and development laboratory. O'Neill's investigations of expressionism, for instance, or Tennessee Williams' memory plays, with their stylistic and structural echoes of symbolism, and even the Federal Theatre Project's Living Newspapers, resided quite peacefully within the Broadway milieu of melodrama, social drama, and the well-made play. These experiments were part of a larger institution – demonstrated by the fact that, almost always, the organizations or individuals who rebelled against or critiqued the traditional theatre were nonetheless absorbed into the onrushing mainstream. But by the 1950s, this process of absorption was being disrupted. The avant-garde theatre that emerged in the 1950s could not coexist within the larger framework because it had never been, in conception or execution, part of it. Its relation to conventional theatre consisted of its use of structural components common to all performance, but the compositional attributes that accrued to Western drama, from the neoclassicism of the Renaissance through the absurdism of the mid-twentieth century were virtually absent from the avant-garde of Happenings and chance theatre and the later formalist inventions of Richard Foreman or the Wooster Group. As composer and theoretician John Cage understood, the new spirit of experimentation was "not bound to the past [or] traditions."[7]

In a 1944 essay, artist Robert Motherwell noted that painting "has always been a species of abstraction: the painter has selected from the world he knows, a world which is not entirely the same in each epoch, the forms and relations which interested him, and then employed them as he pleased ... The art of Picasso has differed in the degree of abstraction, but not the kind of abstraction, from the art of the Renaissance tradition of which he is the bitter finale."[8] Motherwell went on to declare that in the twentieth century something quite new had begun to happen: "the external world is totally rejected as the painter's model," and as such, non-objective art "differs fundamentally, differs epistemologically, one might say, from other modes of art."[9] In theatre too, a "non-objective" form emerged that was not simply a subspecies of the post-Renaissance narrative-psychological tradition.

Historically, the theatre artist, like the painter, had selected elements – that is, abstracted – from the known surrounding world in order to create a play. Conventional forms and structures were used to evoke the physical and emotional properties of the experiential world. In early twentieth-century modernism, this process simply moved inward, creating a conventionalized reality based on an understanding of an inner world of emotion and the subconscious workings of the mind. Thus we may look at, say, Samuel Beckett in the same manner that Motherwell looked at Picasso. Beckett's world may be initially less recognizable to the average spectator than that of Ibsen, for example, yet Beckett too marks the end of a tradition stretching back to the Renaissance; he is not, as some would have it, the epitome of the avant-garde but an end point of the modern (i.e., post-Renaissance) theatre. The avant-garde theatre that emerged in New York and else-where in the 1950s, however, created neither an abstraction nor a distillation of the concrete world; in a sense it did not create a world at all, at least in any common understanding of the term. It created an art in which the reference points were other forms of art, the creative process of the artist, and the theatrical experience itself – not the external or so-called "real" world. As Jean-François Lyotard said in discussing the aesthetic developments engendered by Denis Diderot, "Art would no longer imitate nature but would create a whole other world, *eine Zwischenwelt* [a between world] as Paul Klee would later say."[10] To borrow from Michael Kirby's definition of Happenings, avant-garde theatre, by and large, created a structure and experience that was neither logical nor illogical but, rather, "alogical."[11]

In stating that this new theatre did not evolve from neoclassical and Renaissance models – that it did not create a world – I am suggesting that this theatre was not fundamentally linear, illusionistic, thematic, or psychological, certainly not in any conventional sense. It was a non-literary theatre – meaning not that it lacked language but that it could not be *read* in the way a work of literature could be. Avant-garde theatre was primarily formal, schematic, intellectually derived, and dependent upon aesthetic rather than visceral emotion. The American avant-garde theatre that made its first appearance with a production of Erik Satie's *Ruse of the Medusa* at Black Mountain College in 1948 and evolved slowly over the next ten years drew its energy and inspiration from the compositions and theories of John Cage, the writings of Gertrude Stein, action painting, the work of Antonin Artaud, and a dash of Bertolt Brecht. And from those artists who sought refuge in the United States from the ravages of Nazism and World War II came the ideas of symbolism, expressionism, futurism, surrealism, and espe-cially Dada. These influences intermingled in the American artistic melting pot to create a new avant-garde theatre.

*   *   *

The historical roots of the term "avant-garde" lie in French military terminology. The term was apparently first tied to art by Henri de Saint-Simon (1760–1825), whose writings were to exert a profound influence on Karl Marx and who, together with Auguste Comte, was a founder of sociology.[12] In his last major work, *Opinions littéraires, philosophiques et industrielles* (1825), Saint-Simon proposed a utopian society to be led by a triumvirate of scientists, industrialist-artisans, and artists, with the last constituting an elite force within this group of leaders.[13] "It is we, artists," says a speaker in Saint-Simon's Platonic dialogue, sounding not unlike one of the romantic poets, "who will serve you as avant-garde." Saint-Simon goes on to rejoice in the role of the arts in this new society:

> What a most beautiful destiny for the arts, that of exercising over society a positive power, a true priestly function, and of marching forcefully in the van of all the intellectual faculties, in the epoch of their greatest development. This is the duty of artists, this their mission.[14]

Thus, from the very beginning – from the instant that the military term became descriptive of artists seeking new paths in the cultural landscape – it carried with it a sense of missionary zeal as well as polit-ical and sociological implications. Because of the self-referential and formalistic tendencies of much of the avant-garde throughout its history, it is often forgotten that initially the avant-garde was meant to transform society, that it was seen initially as a utopian program for creating an idealistic world for the future. The tensions and contradic-tions between art as a socially transformative tool and art as aesthetic exploration would present an ongoing struggle for avant-garde artists. For these artists, the challenge was to transform society while standing apart from it.

In fact, a true avant-garde theatre must seek an essential change in audience perceptions that, in turn, will have a profound impact on the relationship of the spectator to the world. "A primary function of art and thought," as critic Lionel Trilling has pointed out, "is to liberate the individual from the tyranny of his culture in the environmental sense and to permit him to stand beyond it in an autonomy of perception and judgment."[15] The American avant-garde theatre that emerged in the 1950s was firmly in this modern tradition of liberation and enlightenment. Even without a specific political agenda, successful avant-garde theatre has political, social, and personal implications for its viewers. But this alteration of audience perceptions comes through the experience of the work, not through the mere presentation of ideas, as is the case with much social drama. An axiomatic precept of the avant-garde is the substitution of experience for "aboutness." "The world doesn't fear a new idea," D.H. Lawrence observed. "It can pigeonhole any idea. But it can't pigeonhole a new experience."[16] Ideas alone can be subsumed into a passive response, but the avant-garde requires engagement on some level. In a conventional work of theatre or literature, certain elements – plot, for example, or theme – can be extracted and stand on their own, thereby allowing a discussion of the ideas of a traditional work of art separately from its presentation. The work thus has a meaning that exists independently of the execution or observation of the work itself. In the avant-garde, though, the meaning is inherent in the work and cannot be separated from it without destroying both sense and art. The avant-garde embodies ideas within the performance or work of art itself, consequently implicating the spectator and making the viewer complicit in the work. Ideology and performance are an integral and inseparable whole. In this it is similar to "content" in abstract art, which, critic Clement Greenberg noted, "is to be dissolved so completely into form that the work of art or literature cannot be reduced in whole or in part to anything not itself."[17]

Avant-garde performance strives toward a radical restructuring of the way in which an audience views and experiences the very act of theatre, which in turn must transform the way in which the spectators view themselves and their world. Traditional ways of seeing are disrupted so that habitual patterns, which inevitably reinforce social norms, are broken. A change in an individual's attitudes, associations, or beliefs is effected not through a straightforward presentation of ideas but through a fundamental restructuring of perception and understanding. In other words, the very notion of what is theatre is brought into question. It requires, in the words of Lyotard, "letting go and disarming all grasping intelligence."[18]

On one level, the concept of the avant-garde is best explained through reference to semiotics. If we accept Jiri Veltrusky's statement that "all that is on the stage is a sign,"[19] then the understanding of these signs is fundamental to the theatre event. Performer and audience alike must be able to interpret the signs to achieve what Keir Elam calls "theatrical competence."[20] The most fundamental competence depends on the ability to recognize that one is watching a performance in the first place. As simple as this sounds, the recognition of the theatrical event is based upon a shared set of culturally learned rules and hinges upon the presence of a framing device (literal or metaphorical) that differentiates the theatrical activity from everyday life. Simply put, basic theatrical competence allows spectators to know that they are watching a performance and not some segment of daily existence. The illusionistic tradition of post-Renaissance theatre, however, has placed such a premium on representation that "good" theatre has often been synonymous with the suspension of disbelief – a willing inability to distinguish between illusion and reality. The Western tradition seems to thrive on reducing aesthetic distance to the barest minimum and flourishes on the resultant tension. While the avant-garde occasionally followed this tendency to extremes (historically, in fact, naturalism may be seen as an avant-garde movement; some three-quarters of a century later the Living Theatre's 1959 production of Jack Gelber's *The Connection* was a brilliant example of such a strategy), more often it sought to alter perceptions in other ways.

Much of the history of the avant-garde can be seen as an attempt to create strategies that will undermine theatrical competence. Normal systems of communication – the recognition and interpretation of signs – are thwarted or disrupted; signs become divorced from their culturally accepted signification, or the cumulative effect of the signs cannot be understood in any historically or culturally accepted way. Framing devices become vague or unfamiliar, so that the difference between life and art is brought into question. In some cases, the frame apparently disappears altogether. As a result, the emphasis shifts from the understanding of signs *per se* to the process of decoding signs. For much of the avant-garde, the emphasis shifted from questions of meaning to a focus on process. As new structures, strategies, and patterns were established, new understandings became possible and new forms emerged.

For the traditional spectator, the rules that govern how one views a musical, a comedy, or a drama have long been established. The customs of the playhouse, and the audience behavior therein – the sequence of events from the buying of tickets to rituals such as the dimming of the house lights as the orchestra begins the overture, to the behavior of the actors, and the cues for applause – are well known. Part of the delight of going to such theatre comes from the comforting and pleasurable repetition of these rituals. In many historical and classical forms of theatre, both East and West, actors were expected to replicate in detail certain gestures, actions, and speeches from performance to performance and from generation to generation – something still true to an extent in opera. The rituals link the cultural-aesthetic experience to the existing society while placing the experience in a historical tradition. Attending such a performance and participating in its rituals confirms the spectator's place in that society or initiates the viewer into the secrets and legacy of the culture. Because the traditional artwork appears to reinforce habitual ways of thinking and affirm accepted wisdom, ideology, and emotions, the spectator is comforted. But, as avant-garde playwright and director Richard Foreman has noted, such an approach may have a tendency to induce a somnambulistic response to the theatrical event, which in turn prevents any sort of active engagement with the work. "I don't want to reinforce what people already think," he declared. "I don't want to refrighten them, or reconvince them that they love what they already love. I don't want to deepen the roots of emotional habit."[21] Three centuries earlier, Blaise Pascal saw the same ironic contradiction: "How empty a thing is painting, which pleases us by its resemblances with objects that cannot please us!"[22] If the purpose of art is to create experiences one cannot have in everyday life – to create, in fact, a theatre that is not comforting – then a theatre that replicates the everyday world is meaningless and pointless. The aim should be, according to Lyotard, "no longer to please a public by bringing it into a process of identification and glorification, but to surprise it."[23]

In many forms of drama, especially in Western theatre, the predominant structural device has been the narrative. This was particularly true of the American theatre that emerged out of the nineteenth century. At a basic level, almost any play one can select from the repertoire – from *Oedipus Tyrannus* to *Miss Saigon* – are all *stories*. They may be told in varying degrees of complexity with a variety of performative components and strategies, but they are stories nonetheless. The old axiom that all drama is reducible to "boy meets girl, boy loses girl, boy gets girl," is not only a fairly reasonable synopsis of much of the world's drama, it also emphasizes the privileging of narrative in the dramatic form. In most performances that can be classified as avant-garde, however, narrative structure is eliminated. Narrative in the drama functions much as the objective image does in painting: it is an illusionistic replication of the external world framed and placed in a context so as to convince the observer of its reality, or at least of its clear connection to a recognizable and identifiable object, action, or emotion. Gertrude Stein was keenly aware of the prevalence of narrative in art and its function as a means of structuring and understanding everyday life. Because it was such a commonplace device it had limited power as an artistic tool, and she recognized the need to disrupt it in order to achieve the surprise that is essential to the avant-garde:

> Something is always happening, anybody knows a quantity of stories of people's lives that are always happening, there are always plenty for the newspapers and there are always plenty in private life. Everybody knows so many stories and what is the use of telling another story. What is the use of telling a story since there are so many and everybody knows so many and tells so many. In the country it is perfectly extraordinary how many complicated dramas go on all the time. And everybody knows them, so why tell another one. There is always a story going on.[24]

If theatre is to be a place for art, that is, for an experiential alternative to everyday life, then it must, according to the artists of the avant-garde, present a work or event not available through normal systems of behavior. Not only images and ideas, but whole patterns of reception and response to events must be challenged, disrupted, and reconfigured.

* * *

Why did it take sixty to seventy years from the beginnings of the historical avant-garde to the development of an American avant-garde theatre – from the symbolist productions of the Théâtre d'Art to the John Cage events at Black Mountain College, Happenings, and the work of the Living Theatre? Part of the answer lies in the necessity of the avant-garde's adversarial position within the traditional culture, the need for the avant-garde to emerge in opposition to an established, dominant culture – an ensconced and static culture. Lionel Trilling, for instance, discussing writing (although his observations apply equally well to theatre), stated that "any historian of the literature of the modern age will take virtually for granted the adversary intention, the actually subversive intention, that characterizes modern writing – he will perceive its clear purpose of detaching the reader from the habits of thought and feeling that the larger culture imposes."[25] Such a culture simply did not exist in the United States until the mid-twentieth century. Furthermore, as Andreas Huyssen has pointed out, this adversarial stance is generally taken against the dominant position of high art within the culture. "A European avantgardist revolt against tradition," Huyssen explained, could not make sense in the United States until "high art had become institutionalized in the burgeoning museum, concert, and paperback culture of the 1950s, when modernism itself had entered the mainstream via the culture industry, and later, during the Kennedy years, when high culture began to take on functions of political representation."[26]

While "high culture" may not have entered the mainstream of American society until the 1950s, it is questionable whether a theatrical high culture *ever* entered the mainstream. The dominant theatre of twentieth-century America was determinedly bourgeois and middle-brow, and though style and content may have become a bit more sophisticated, mid-twentieth-century American theatre was clearly descended from the melodrama and well-made plays of the nineteenth century. Certainly in the 1880s, the time of the first avant-garde in Europe, mainstream American culture was populist, not high, one reason being that there had already been a revolt against high culture – it had been a rebellion in the early part of the nineteenth century against the domination of English art and society, especially in theatre. The "official" culture, as it were, of the United States in the early nineteenth century, the culture adopted by the upper echelons of society, was resolutely English. Such events as the notorious Astor Place riots of 1849 were part of a populist attempt to overthrow imported elitist arts, manners, and customs while establishing an American identity. The American culture that triumphed over the English was popular in nature – an accessible art that reflected the spirit of the masses.

The new "official culture" that emerged with a self-consciously American identity was inevitably a product and reflection of the general perception of the country itself, which had become mythologized in a romantic aura. America was the land of the quest, the search for inno-cence and the ideal in opposition to the corruption and decay of the Old World; a land of perceived equality (no matter that the realities of the socio-economic structure may have suggested anything but such egalitarianism); and a land of endless bounty and ever-receding fron-tiers. In such a land, hope was eternally renewable by simply picking up and starting over, or, as Gertrude Stein would later say in a somewhat different context, "beginning again and again." Out of this European, Rousseau-inspired vision of the idyllic paradise came the frontier spirit, in which outcasts could be transformed into rugged and intrepid individuals – the explorer searching for new horizons, seeking and forging his own path. Wealth was boundless, potential unlimited. European societies were closed and finite, while the American was open and infinite. In a peculiar way, then, "Americanism" and "avant-gardism" were one and the same. Art, most definitely including theatre, in the nineteenth century became a primary tool for a century-long project to create the image of a nation. In a sense, the culture was not a *reflection* of society; it *created* the society and continued to do so into the twentieth century. If, then, the arts in the nineteenth century and beyond were playing out these themes and ideas, then there could be no established culture against which an avant-garde could rebel. While Stephen Mallarmé and Paul Fort were attempting to overthrow the stifling effects of a centuries-old cultural heritage in Paris, Clyde Fitch and David Belasco were trying to discover and define America. Avant-garde as metaphor was unnecessary in a land where the folk heroes were a true avant-garde in every sense of the word.

The idea of the individual quest and the boundless horizon were well established in American consciousness even before the Revolution. Implicit and embodied in this imagery was both the sense and structure of the narrative. We are told of the "story of America," the story of "how the West was won" – American history as a rich narrative tapestry. A 1929 multi-volume pictorial history of the United States, for instance, was entitled *The Pageant of America*, implying something grand, narrative, and theatrical.[27] If the romantic imagery and narrative structure of America needed a starting point or galvanizing event, it could be found in the Lewis and Clark expedition of 1804–06, which opened up the American west and established a kind of Ur-drama of America. Even literary critic Leslie Fiedler saw it in terms of a grand theatrical metaphor: "Jefferson and Napoleon [were] twin heirs to the Age of Reason, preparing the way for Lewis and Clark, that is to say, for the first actors in our own drama of a perpetually retreating west."[28] Embodied in the expedition were the crucial elements of American mythology: heroic individualists, exploration, a quest for a holy grail – in this case, a northwest passage – confrontations with forces of nature and the "noble savages" of the great western expanse, and an exploration of a strange new world, the purpose of which was to bring it into the American fold. All of this was shrouded in a virtually mystical-religious belief in the necessity and inevitability of the new nation. What possible function could an artistic avant-garde serve in such a context, where the creation of a nation and the ongoing discovery of a new world outstripped imagination? And of great significance from an artistic and literary standpoint was the primary means of exploration – great, rushing rivers. These mighty rivers served as paths into the exotic and primeval world that lay beyond, and they would ultimately be a tool for taming the land and creating industrial wealth. The river was at the heart of America. A river begins humbly and gathers strength, power, and majesty as it moves in an ineluctably singular direction toward an inevitable conclusion and is thus a perfect metaphor for a narrative structure. It is, therefore, the structure of America, and it is no coincidence that one of the most essential American novels is set on the Mississippi – the image of the river pervades the most significant American poetry from Walt Whitman onward. "Visions! omens! hallucinations! miracles! ecstasies! gone down the American river!" cried Allen Ginsberg.[29]

America saw itself as a grand narrative in which manifest destiny served as a thematic thread guiding the "story" to its denouement. All the components of the American mythos contributed to reinforcing the narrative structure. If the rejection of narrative is essential for the development of an avant-garde, then it was difficult for American artists to emulate their European cousins. The overpowering sense of narrative that pervaded the American psyche held sway until at least World War I and lingered until World War II. Artists and their audiences were swept up in the rushing current of narrative and popular culture, just as Lewis and Clark were carried by the Columbia River to the Pacific Ocean.

The most successful vehicle for establishing the characters of this narrative and disseminating the story to the greatest number of spectators was the melodrama. But the melodrama in Europe evolved as part of an ongoing theatrical tradition, whereas in the United States it was, to all intents and purposes, the first and only form of drama. What prior classical tradition existed in America consisted of no more than the received culture of Europe. Melodrama, by becoming the first mass cultural phenomenon of the United States, became the young nation's classicism – but it was, of course, simultaneously a popular art. Without the split between highbrow and lowbrow culture, a split that would not begin to emerge until the very end of the nineteenth century, there was no need, indeed no room, for an avant-garde.

The European revolutions had betokened a change in the structure and hierarchies of old civilizations. They signaled a break with the past and established a faith in the idea of the new. "Future" became the word of the day and was ensconced in the theatrical vocabulary from the moment Richard Wagner wrote his *Artwork of the Future* in 1849. Wagner laid the groundwork for the avant-garde, with its sense of forward-lookingness, rejection of tradition and the past, and an urgent need for change. "The avant-garde understands itself as invading unknown territory, exposing itself to the dangers of sudden, shocking encounters, conquering an as yet unoccupied future," wrote Jürgen Habermas. "The avant-garde must find a direction in a landscape into which no one seems to have yet ventured."[30]

Thus the avant-garde could be seen as the logical outgrowth of the romantic movement that had spawned the European revolutions of the mid-nineteenth century. But in America, ironically, the Revolution became transformed into a concretized event – it was, Thomas Jefferson notwithstanding, an end in itself, not an ongoing process. The Revolution became enshrined in marble like a classical sculpture. What Habermas describes as characteristic of the avant-garde, though, became the guiding spirit of the budding American culture. Lewis and Clark and their heirs *were* the American avant-garde, and the growth of the new nation became an ongoing narrative. This process was still in full swing in the last decades of the nineteenth century, the time of the birth of the European avant-garde.

For an avant-garde theatre to emerge in the United States of America it was necessary to disrupt the central position of narrative in the American mythos, and for artists to take an oppositional stance to established culture. As art critic Harold Rosenberg observed in his landmark essay "The American Action Painters," "The revolution against the given, in the self and in the world, which since Hegel has provided European vanguard art with theories of a New Reality, has re-entered America in the form of personal revolts. Art action rests on the enormous assumption that the artist accepts as real only that which he is in the process of creating."[31]

* * *

The process that led to the triumphant establishment of an American avant-garde took place largely in the world of the plastic arts. The famous Armory Show of 1913, which was the first major exhibition of "modern art" in the United States, functioned as a rupturing point in the development of American arts. It allowed the first tentative steps of

American modern artists to coalesce into a movement, and it thrust these new developments in art firmly into public consciousness. Modern art was no longer something confined to an elite world of aesthetes – it was hotly debated in the public forums of the media. In the words of organizer Walt Kuhn in planning the event, "It will be like a bomb shell ... it will show its effect even further and make the big wheel turn over both hemispheres."[32] The Armory Show did in fact set wheels turning in the visual art world, but not in the American theatre – theatre artists would have to follow the lead of their painterly cousins.

World War II effectively ended Parisian dominance of the art world, and American culture was able to rush in and fill the vacuum.[33] The United States, following the war, was a much-changed place. Echoing Henry Luce's proclamation of an "American Century," writer after writer declared America's triumphant position in the new world. Implicit in these proclamations was an understanding that the "story" of America had entered a new phase. The grand narrative, in fact, had apparently reached its inevitable conclusion, as writer Clifton Fadiman seemed to realize as early as 1940. "We have reached a critical point in the life of our nation," he stated in a radio discussion. "We are through as a pioneer nation; we are now ready to develop as a civilization."[34] And in a 1952 symposium conducted in the pages of *Partisan Review*, critic Alan Dowling could declare: "There is very little doubt left in liberal minds that the United States of America is the chief hope for the future of the world in this century."[35] It was Clement Greenberg, the primary articulator of the new formalist American aesthetic, who astutely perceived the inextricable connections between the development of avant-garde art and international supremacy. "The main premises of Western art," he wrote, "have at last migrated to the United States along with the center of gravity of production and political power."[36]

This supreme confidence, built upon clear and obvious military and economic superiority, combined with the return of many expatriate European artists to their homelands, allowed American artists to break free of their subservience to European (predominantly French) art and ideas and find a unique voice. The emergence of galleries devoted to new American art cemented this trend and provided a cocoon for developing artists. But, it should be noted, this voice of confidence was also tinged with doubt. American superiority, after all, was bought with nuclear technology. Moral questions about the necessity of the atomic bomb and a concomitant fear of Armageddon pervaded consciousness for the next several decades. Critic Dwight MacDonald, for instance, explaining the necessity of a new art, declared "Naturalism is no longer adequate, either aesthetically or morally, to cope with the modern horror."[37] Greenberg agreed that the horrors of the modern age could not be depicted and warned against the dangers of turning art to polemical ends. "In the face of current events painting feels, apparently, that it must be epic poetry, it must be theatre, it must be an atomic bomb, it must be the rights of man," but for modern art to be successful, he continued, it must emulate "the greatest painter of our time, Matisse," who "wanted his art to be an armchair for the tired businessman."[38] Art, in other words, could not successfully function as agitprop or as a bully pulpit; its political engagement would have to more subtle, even surreptitious. Unlike the modern American art of the 1920s and 1930s, which tended toward political engagement, the avant-garde of the 1940s was being steered toward a politically detached formalism, a tendency that would shape the emergent theatrical avant-garde as well.

So while the new art expressed fear and doubt over the instability and uncertainty of the world's future and the confusion over the contradictions of American society, with its mix of unprecedented wealth and abject poverty, democratic ideals and social injustice, it also embodied the energy and spirit of the confident, powerful, and exuberant new American society. Art historian William C. Seitz captured this spirit well; discussing the introduction of industrial elements and emblems into American art he noted:

> It is not hard to discern behind these vernacular subjects a striving, embittered by disenchantment, but mystical and moral as well as irascible and sexual. It is in part an outcome of insecurity that is more than economic, and of the aesthetic individualism that, following the failure of liberal politics during the thirties and forties, provided a motive force for abstract expressionism.
>
> The vernacular repertoire includes beat Zen and hot rods, mescalin experiences and faded flowers, photo-graphic bumps and grinds, the *poubelle* (i.e., trash can), juke boxes, and hydrogen explosions. Such objects are often approached in a mystical, aesthetic, or "arty" way, but just as often they are fearfully dark, evoking horror or nausea: the anguish of the scrap heap; the images of charred bodies that keep Hiroshima and Nagasaki before our eyes; the confrontation of democratic platitudes with the Negro's disenfranchisement.[39]

In this description, Seitz is echoing *Howl*, Allen Ginsberg's paean to the "best minds of my generation ... listening to the crack of doom on the hydrogen jukebox."[40] The first wave of the American avant-garde, primarily in the visual arts and embodied in abstract expressionism, moved toward an objective formalism with roots going back to Mondrian and Kandinsky, and even Monet and Cézanne, as well as the Bauhaus. The second wave, emerging in the 1950s, exploded across all the arts and, as *Howl* demonstrates, drew inspiration from the raw energy, form, and content of American pop culture and iconography, the wonder and fear of new technologies and media, and from the conflicting chaos of urban society. In this it owed something to the Italian futurists. But in painting at least, the urban art advocated by Greenberg was manifested in the work of Jackson Pollock. "For all its Gothic quality," he wrote in 1947, "Pollock's art is still an attempt to cope with urban life; it dwells entirely in the lonely jungle of immediate sensations, impulses and notions, therefore is positivist, concrete."[41]

The modern art movement in America captured the mantle of democratic righteousness after the war through a sort of chauvinistic assault – successfully elevating American artists to a level and prestige previously conferred only on European painters and sculptors – and then launching what today would be called a "buy American" campaign, suggesting that supporting American avant-garde artists was virtually a patriotic duty.[42] Briefly stated, both serious critics and pundits of the popular press began to pay attention to the new wave of artists and saw in them the new American spirit; they saw an art appropriate for the new postwar order. Spectators and buyers were urged to look and to buy. But just as non-objective art had been condemned in the Soviet Union as decadent, it was now attacked from the right in the United States for much the same reason. The perpetual problem faced by the avant-garde from Saint-Simon's time through the twentieth century was the apparent opposition between a revolutionary art (i.e., an avant-garde) and an art that would support the revolution – that is, one accessible to the masses that would clearly support the ideas and programs of those in power, in other words, an art that would reinforce the new status quo. In the realities of the political world, the avant-garde seldom won. In order to effect social change, it was believed, art had essentially to be realistic.

In the United States through the 1920s and 1930s, the avant-garde in art was associated with, even dominated by, left-wing political movements, and the product was a politically engaged and imagistically accessible art. But following World War II, the ideological battles between Trotskyites and Stalinists, and the revelation of the moral bankruptcy of Soviet communism, the arts strove to break away from political domination. Abstract expressionism became the form in which that artistic revolution found its voice, while divorcing itself from organized political operations. But the media – the voice of the middle class – viewed this emerging form of art with enormous suspicion and disdain, until its financial potential as a commodity became clear.[43] What abstract expressionist artists and their defenders succeeded in doing was reframing the discussion in terms of freedom, individual liberty, and classical American values. At a symposium at the Museum of Modern Art in 1948, Paul Burlin announced that "Modern painting is the bulwark of the individual creative expression, aloof from the political left and its blood brother, the right. Their common dictators, if effective, would destroy the artist."[44] Modern art was thus placed in an uplifting historical tradition and seen as an embodiment of all the mythological values of the United States. Supported by critics, notably Clement Greenberg, the American avant-garde was elevated to a position of power and centrality in the same league and importance as American social, political, and economic power. The practitioners of this new art became new American folk heroes in the tradition of the pioneers. Such influential media as *Life* magazine published articles on the artists and showcased their work, albeit with some skepticism; abstract art even began to appear in advertising. With abstract expressionism established as the voice of both rebellion and American individualism, modern art emerged as the true expression of the new American spirit. Painters such as Mark Rothko, Willem de Kooning, and Pollock could rise to the status of cultural icons. So-called modern art became a *de facto* official art in the United States. It was in this context that the avant-garde in American theatre emerged. But whereas abstract expressionism was embraced by official institutions and the culturally knowledgeable segment of society, quickly supplanting all other serious forms of art, avant-garde theatre, partly because it is not a commodity and cannot be bought and sold, never grew beyond a fringe movement and never attracted anything but an elite audience. The influence of avant-garde theatre, however, would be more widespread than its limited audience suggested.

In the artistic and intellectual cauldron that was New York city at the time, theatre artists, painters, writers, and musicians came together and shared ideas. The energy and innovations of one form flowed freely into others and back again. For theatre artists dismayed with the perceived banality of mainstream theatre, the raw energy and freedom embodied in avant-garde art pointed the way toward a dynamic renovation of the theatre. By the end of the 1950s, there was a veritable explosion of theatrical activity.

Chapter 2

Theories and foundations

> This obsession, in various forms, with the laws of chance ... made a
> place for itself, grew and grew, took hold of the world, gave it a
> new foundation and forced it to adopt a new consciousness.
>
> Georges Hugnet[1]

Throughout most of theatre history, theory almost always followed
practice; it was a means of explaining and codifying what already
existed. Neoclassicism was the notable exception, but even in the
Renaissance, the most vital forms of theatre – commedia dell'arte or
Elizabethan and Spanish drama, for example – emerged organically
from a variety of cultural forces. The avant-garde, however, reversed
this age-old process. In most if not all cases, intellectual idea preceded
practice, and the theatre was built upon a theoretical foundation. An
understanding of the avant-garde, therefore, requires a visit to its
ideational sources. For the postwar avant-garde, the wellspring was
Marcel Duchamp and its pillars were Gertrude Stein and John Cage.

Typifying the avant-garde were the dual impulses to eliminate
boundaries between genres or forms – blurring distinctions between
art, music, literature, and performance – and the related attempt to
eliminate boundaries between art and life, drawing on a wide range of
social, political, and scientific forces and inspirations for the creation of
avant-garde forms and their attendant methodologies. Beginning with
his cubist-inspired work in 1911, Duchamp quickly moved into new
realms and created art that did not depend upon traditional framing
and separation for its validity but virtually demanded that the viewer
see through the work to the surrounding world. With Duchamp, and
later with John Cage, art no longer depended upon its "difference" or
"otherness"; its essence derived from its connection and continuity
with the experiential world. In the early 1960s, Living Theatre co-

founder Julian Beck was asked to define the work of the company. His response was: "to increase conscious awareness, to stress the sacredness of life, to break down the walls."[2] The first and third of these aims, at least, could be applied to virtually all of the avant-garde, much of which was about the destruction of boundaries.

There is an obvious correspondence between this tendency and the Renaissance world view that conceived of all the arts, indeed all social interaction, in terms of a unified, fluid, and harmonious structure. In Renaissance culture, there was a continuity between what we tend to see as distinct art forms, and hence there was an inevitable interaction between these forms. While the twentieth-century avant-garde attempted to reintegrate forms that had separated into discrete genres, it did so while maintaining the distinct qualities and characteristics of each component and discipline rather than blending them or placing them within a hierarchical structure. When Richard Wagner introduced his idea of the *Gesamtkunstwerk*, or unified art work, in the mid-nineteenth century, it too was in response to the lack of communication between art forms, but his solution required each component to be totally subsumed under the absolute control and vision of a single artist. The twentieth-century avant-garde, especially the Duchamp–Cage school, moved in a somewhat different direction. The arts, asserted Cage, "are not isolated from one another but engage in a 'dialogue,'"[3] and a dialogue requires an equality between the "speakers" as it were. Each component element of the arts, and each art within multidisciplinary forms, would maintain its own identity and characteristics; nothing would be subsumed. This phenomenon – art composed of discrete elements in creative tension and dialogue – is an essential characteristic of avant-garde art and theatre, as it was central in Bertolt Brecht's concept of "epic theatre." "When the epic theatre's methods begin to penetrate the opera the first result is a radical *separation of the elements*," Brecht wrote in 1930. *Gesamtkunstwerk*, according to Brecht, produced a muddle in which each element was "equally degraded" and in which the spectator "becomes a passive (suffering) part of the total work of art." The solution was clear to Brecht: "Words, music and setting must become more independent of one another."[4]

The rejection of the *Gesamtkunstwerk* – fusion, unity, and harmony as guiding principles for multidisciplinary arts – led not only to the creation of new art but also to critical re-evaluations and new understandings of existing art, theatre, music, and literature. This process of re-evaluation and the influence of scientific thought emerged in the most surprising locations. Shakespearean scholar G. Wilson Knight, for example, in a remarkable 1930 study, proposed an approach to the understanding of not only Shakespeare's plays but also of drama in general that substituted spatiality for narrative sequence. "One must be prepared," he stated,

> to see the whole play in space as well as in time. It is natural in analysis to pursue the steps of the tale in sequence ... But by giving supreme attention to this temporal nature of drama we omit what, in Shakespeare, is at least of equivalent importance. A Shakespearean tragedy is set spatially as well as temporally in the mind ... There are throughout the play a set of correspondences which relate to each other independently of the time-sequence which is the story ... Now if we are prepared to see the whole play laid out, so to speak, as an area, being simultaneously aware of these thickly-scattered correspondences in a single view of the whole, we possess the unique quality of the play.[5]

If we did not know better, we might suspect Gertrude Stein of having proposed the above analysis. Knight was not an avant-gardist, and it seems highly unlikely that he would have been familiar with the theoretical writings of Gertrude Stein, but by the fourth decade of the twentieth century, the narrative organization of theatre and literature was under serious attack from all sides, largely the result of forty years of avant-garde activity. Knight, wittingly or not, was echoing Stein's theory of landscape drama, a theory that questioned the basic linear-narrative premise of Western theatrical practice and in so doing became a primary underpinning of avant-garde theatre. And, indirectly, Knight's proposal reflected the revolutionary influence of Marcel Duchamp.

In fact, Knight's astonishing new approach to Shakespeare – the conflation of time and space – reflects a fundamental reorganization of the perception and depiction of reality in the twentieth century, a reorganization that evolved largely as a result of the influences of science and technology on the one hand, and a discovery of Asian philosophy, religion, and art on the other. Reality, of course, is merely a way of organizing perceived phenomena, and Western reality had been shaped by neoclassical precepts since the Renaissance. The transformation brought about by Duchamp, Stein, *et al.* marked a major shift in modern Western cultural thinking. Seen in this light, the avant-garde may be defined in part as that which reorganizes the perception of reality. Although many of the manifestations of the avant-garde seemed, at first glance, antithetical to scientific rationality, the avant-garde is inextricably tied to the scientific revolution of the nineteenth and early twentieth centuries. In some cases, as with the Italian futurists, the very notion of technology itself inspired new forms of art and ideology, but more often it was a case of technology inducing new perceptions and modes of thinking. It is probably no accident that the first cauldron of avant-garde activity was Paris. For all the social, political, and cultural factors that contributed to the development of an avant-garde, it was the Eiffel Tower, built in 1889, that simply yet radically changed – quite literally – the world view of the average individual. For the first time in history, it was possible to look down upon a city, even upon the formerly dominant churches, and see it within a larger context; to see it not with the eyes of earth-bound humans but with the soaring vision of birds. The relation of these spectators to their world had changed; their mode of perception had changed. In an instant, the linear-temporal view of the world was transformed into a spatial one. As the airplane replaced the train as a mode of travel, this perceptual realignment was only magnified. Late nineteenth-century Parisians were surreptitiously transformed into a vanguard that would shape twentieth-century thinking.

Scientific theory could effect change in society without necessarily any direct understanding of the theories themselves. Freud's observations and writings on the subconscious mind crystallized a century of psychological explorations and shifted the focus of art from the depiction of observable phenomena to expressions of perceived inner truth. Much of the first wave of the historical avant-garde, from symbolism through surrealism, was a result of experimentation with Freud-influenced ideas. But the most pervasive shift in the Western world view may have resulted from one of the least understood ideas of the twentieth century: Einstein's theory of relativity. Though profoundly complex, even to specialists, simple conceptions (or misconceptions) of his ideas nonetheless entered popular consciousness. Slowly but ineluctably, the once fixed and reliable guideposts of life gave way to a landscape in which everything was relative, nothing concrete; the fixed points of reference of the physical world turned out to be mere chimeras. Rapidly, a Greco-Roman world view based on absolutes and logical analyses crumbled, giving way to a crazy-quilt of relational associations. In combination with Freudian explanations of the psyche, individual subjective reality replaced objective rationalism. Time and space were now understood to be interchangeable. Cubist experiments could be attributed in part to relativity; and, it turned out, so could the work of choreographer Merce Cunningham. "In classical ballet as I learned it," he explained,

> ... the space was observed in terms of a proscenium stage, it was frontal. What if, as in my pieces, you decide to make any point on the stage equally interesting? I used to be told that you see the center of the space as the most important: that was the center of interest. But in many modern paintings this was not the case and the sense of space was different. So I decided to open up the space to consider it equal, and any place, occupied or not, just as important as any other. In such a context you don't have to refer to a precise point in space. And when I happened to read that sentence of Albert Einstein's: "There are no fixed points in space," I thought, indeed, if there are no fixed points, then every point *is* equally interesting and equally changing.[6]

M. Cunningham talks about time and space

– in classical ballet, space is proscenium + center is important.

n Kaprow's description of the enter a painting of Pollock's in . Anywhere is everywhere and here you can. This has led to ession of going on forever – a

: seen not as an alternative or realization of a new scientific reflected the changing under-tury, it is not unreasonable to alien to the general populace.

Why did avant-garde art not become popular culture? Various explanations suggest themselves. First, Aristotle may very well have been correct when he stated: "the instinct of imitation is implanted in man from childhood ... and no less universal is the pleasure felt in things imitated."[8] This being the case, the desire for imitative, i.e. narrative, art might remain despite other changes. Second, the narrative did not disappear from the culture. Rather, it migrated to new forms, specifically movies and, later, television. These, the most pervasive and powerful forms of popular entertainment in the history of the world, exerted a phenomenal influence on mainstream culture. Ironically, then, film and television, two of the most significant products of the technical revolution – a revolution that reshaped modern thinking – served to reinforce post-Renaissance perceptual patterns, thereby creating a continuing tension with anti-narrative structures.

Although various "isms" emerged from this rapidly changing perception of reality, it was Marcel Duchamp who crystallized the inherent tensions and contradictions into a guiding aesthetic. Duchamp may have been the first artist of the twentieth century fully to grasp the implications of the shifting sense of reality and to understand that, accordingly, the reasons and methods for creating art had to change as well. Duchamp called into question the materials used for the creation of art, the nature of art objects, and the relationship of both the artist and the spectator to the work of art. In the words of art historian Michel Sanouillet, "Duchamp's attempt to rethink the world rests on two supports: the *machine*, the image and incarnation of our epoch, and *chance*, which for our contemporaries has de facto replaced divinity."[9]

One result of Duchamp's rethinking was the "ready-made." By taking everyday objects and transforming them by means of metaphorical framing devices into works of art, Duchamp challenged notions of art and creation while simultaneously calling into question the difference between art and life. For Duchamp, the act of creation was only partially the work of the artist. "All in all," he proclaimed, "the creative act is not performed by the artist alone; the spectator brings the work into contact with the external world by deciphering and interpreting its inner qualifications and thus adds his contribution to the creative act."[10] Thus began a key component of avant-garde art – the necessity and centrality of the spectator in the creation and completion of the work. For Duchamp, the artist was "mediumistic" – a person "from the labyrinth beyond time and space" through whom the work of art was expressed, thus implying that the artist is merely a connection between the idea and the spectator, who, in a sense, actually creates the work of art.[11] The incorporation of chance also served to deprive the artist of total control of the creative act. Nature and its operations entered into the process, thereby fusing art and nature in previously unimagined or unanticipated ways. Duchamp took the products of technology intended for utilitarian ends, such as a bicycle wheel or a coffee grinder, and transformed them into aesthetic objects, and similarly took processes of nature, sometimes mediated by man-made objects, and framed them so as to create art.[12] Many avant-garde artists saw the need to alter the means of art production, but only Duchamp fully understood that the very foundations of art had been altered.

Gertrude Stein

The person who was most acutely aware of the artistic tensions in contemporary culture was Gertrude Stein, who devoted much of her writing to finding an alternative foundation for twentieth-century theatre and literature, a structure that would accommodate twentieth-century sensibilities. Describing one path to this alternative approach, Stein recounted growing up in Oakland, California, and being taken repeatedly to see the popular touring productions of *Uncle Tom's Cabin*. As a young girl, her memories of the productions were of fragmentary and isolated events, often the most visually fascinating, such as the famous scene in which the slaves George and Eliza escape across the frozen Ohio River – a melodramatic *pièce de résistance*. The narrative did not exist for the young Stein. But as she approached adolescence and the narrative asserted itself in her evolving perceptions, she found the resultant experience increasingly unpleasant or disappointing. Part of the reason for her displeasure with the drama was a realization that within the temporal structure of drama there is always an emotional syncopation between the events on the stage and the response of the audience. The process of remembering information and anticipating action virtually precluded the possibility of experiencing the theatrical event in the present moment. What happens on the stage, she explained, is "a thing over which you have no real control."[13] This, she continued, "makes for nervousness ... and the cause of nervousness is the fact that the emotion of the one seeing the play is always ahead or behind the play."[14]

Stein was responding to the basic Aristotelian construction of drama, in which the plot was dominant. Plot, as a structural device, is such a strong and constraining factor in Western drama that it exerts an enormous control over the spectator, allowing, at best, a narrow range of response. One must follow a narrative slavishly wherever it may lead in order for it to make sense and to receive the promised emotional or intellectual payoff at the end. Of equal importance is the way in which plot is manifested spatially. The post-Renaissance approach to theatrical illusion is predicated upon a belief that if the audience accepts the physical environment of the stage (the visual-spatial presentation, or design) as emblematic of a real place, then it follows that they will accept the illusionistic temporal rhythms as well. Stein, however, realized that this was simply not the case. "In the first place," she explained,

at the theatre there is the curtain and the curtain already makes
one feel that one is not going to have the same tempo as the thing
that is there behind the curtain. The emotion of you on one side
of the curtain and what is on the other side of the curtain are not
going to be going on together. One will always be behind or in
front of the other.[15]

Space and time in Stein's epistemology are interdependent, but not in the
mutually causative manner of narrative drama. In fact, Stein seemed to
suggest that illusion was not possible in the twentieth century.

Searching for an alternative to narrative, Stein started to explore
theatre "from the standpoint of sight and sound and its relation to
emotion and time, rather than in relation to story and action."[16] As a
result, she concluded that "anything that was not a story could be a
play."[17] The focus on the unities in neoclassical dramatic theory had
been an attempt to control the relationships of time, space, and narrative within the dramatic structure. In neoclassical drama, time
determined space, which, in turn, limited physical action. Stein understood that the theatre is a temporal and spatial phenomenon, but she
set about to divorce the two structures. The audience brings to the
theatre other possible perceptual mechanisms and emotional needs that
do not require a narrative bound up in temporal and spatial considera-
tions. The result was the landscape drama:

> I felt that if a play was exactly like a landscape then there would be
> no difficulty about the emotion of the person looking on at the
> play being behind or ahead of the play because the landscape does
> not have to make acquaintance. You may have to make acquain-
> tance with it, but it does not with you, it is there and so the play
> being written the relation between you at any time is so exactly
> that that it is of no importance unless you look at it.[18]

Stein, not unlike Knight, explained that the basic structure of the landscape play was one of relations and juxtapositions rather than the linear
flow of conventional narrative.

> The landscape has its formation and as after all a play has to have
> formation and be in relation one thing to the other thing and as
> the story is not the thing as any one is always telling something
> then the landscape not moving but being always in relation, the

trees to the hills the hills to the fields the trees to each other any piece of it to any sky and then any detail to any other detail, the story is only of importance if you like to tell or like to hear a story but the relation is there anyway. And of that relation I wanted to make a play and I did, a great number of plays.[19]

She elucidated the landscape drama through the metaphor of train travel versus airplane travel. In the former, a rider looking out the window sees a series of images going by in sequence as the train moves through the landscape. As the images pass by, the rider is also remembering what has passed and is simultaneously anticipating what will come next. In contrast, a passenger on a plane looking out a window sees the entire landscape below in an instant. As in a landscape painting, the observer is then free to look at specific elements within the landscape at leisure and in any sequence. An entire image (complex of ideas) could be grasped immediately. Stein proposed a theatre with the structural equivalent of a landscape, where the parameters and content may be determined by the artist but the method and organization of viewing and processing information were largely controlled by the spectator. The experience for the spectator became more contemplative or meditative than the rushing experience of linear drama; relationships replaced sequentiality.

By eliminating the pressure of processing performance-generated material in a linear fashion at a predetermined pace, the spectator could remain, in Stein's phrase, in the *continuous present* – that is, in the moment-to-moment reality that makes up everyday existence. (In her writing, Stein used the technique of "beginning again and again" – disrupting the flow of a moment to return to the state of mind one has at the start of a work – to maintain the sense of continuous presence.) One result of this approach, as Stein-influenced director and playwright Richard Foreman has noted, is to focus on "the essence of the object, rather than its aura of cultural and emotional usage."[20] Ideally, then, the spectator is immersed in the direct experience of the images and ideas being presented. The mind is not encumbered with possibly irrelevant references or with memories and projections within the work that trigger a pattern of thought that leads away from what is happening on the stage. There is a freshness and immediacy not possible in more conventional forms of theatre.

Gertrude Stein's approach to drama and literature may be seen as a cultural equivalent to Einsteinian science. Her work shifted focus from a plodding time-bound narrative to a spatial construct in which all components are equally interesting and the contemplation of the work is controlled by the spectator.

Antonin Artaud

At first glance, Antonin Artaud appears an unlikely ideological partner for Stein. His association with the surrealists and his theories of "cruelty," which allied him spiritually with the expressionists, are far from Stein's intellectual and contemplative approach to the drama. But Artaud, with his shamanistic attempts to lead the spectators to a direct understanding of the work unmediated by language or thought – "I propose to treat the spectators like the snakecharmer's subjects and conduct them *by means of their organisms* to an apprehension of the subtlest notions"[21] – is attempting to return to the state that Stein experienced as a child watching *Uncle Tom's Cabin*. For Artaud, narrative became equated with the entire stultifying concept of Western literary theatre – "a theatre of idiots, madmen, inverts, grammarians, grocers, antipoets and positivists, i.e., Occidentals"[22] – and he demanded instead a theatre that elevated the *mise en scène* over the text.[23] Whereas Stein's theories and practice have no direct relation to Eastern thought or culture, Artaud's clearly do, and he thus represents another significant thread in the development of the avant-garde.

One of the characteristics that separates Artaud from Stein is his mysticism. His writings are suffused with concepts of magic and spiritual states in a way that Stein's never were; the trance-like state he desires of his spectators is different from the contemplative yet intellectually alert condition proposed by Stein. Yet on a certain level they sought the same thing. Artaud, as surely as Stein, rejected narrative and sought to divorce time from space in their traditional onstage relationships. He sought a direct apprehension of the images that would lead to an instinctive understanding of the art work. In short, he sought an alternative to the structures and perceptual mechanisms of post-Renaissance Western theatre, an alternative that he believed he had found in the Balinese theatre that he encountered at the Colonial Exhibition in Paris in 1931. Here Artaud saw the possibility for replacing the Western linear narrative structure with a relational model. "The [Balinese] drama does not develop as a conflict of feelings," he somewhat mistakenly observed, "but as a conflict of spiritual states, themselves ossified and transformed into gestures – diagrams. In a word, the Balinese have realized, with the utmost rigor, the idea of pure theatre."[24] Artaud, like Stein, saw theatre, at least in part, in spatial terms (which implies a theatre of relations rather than narrative). The new physical language that he proposed for the stage could not "be defined except by its possibilities for dynamic expression in space as opposed to the expressive possibilities of spoken dialogue."[25]

The amorphous ideas so ambiguously expressed in Artaud's essays ultimately gave rise to much of the avant-garde theatre from the late 1950s to the early 1970s, and his "Theatre of Cruelty" manifesto became a veritable bible for the avant-garde theatre artists of that time. In the manifesto and in other writings, Artaud called for a rejection of virtually all aspects of Western theatrical structure and content, including the reliance upon language ("giving words approximately the importance they have in dreams"), character, psychology, and literary texts. He further called for the elimination of the conventional stage and the auditorium, which would be replaced "by a single site, without partition or barrier of any kind," in which "a direct communication will be re-established between the spectator and spectacle, between the actor and the spectator, from the fact that the spectator, placed in the middle of the action, is engulfed and physically affected by it."[26] No one of these individual concepts was entirely new – in his essays, Artaud was manifesting many of the notions and approaches explored by the symbolists, expressionists, and surrealists, all of whom had tried in some way to bypass the rational mind and connect with the subconscious through art. But Artaud's focus on the spiritual and the utter fascination with speaking to the subconscious was at once more intense and more rigorous than any theory or practice that had preceded his writings. And unlike many who had forged new paths in the arts earlier in the century, Artaud focused almost exclusively on theatre.

He preached a sort of revolution in which the old forms, and anything apparently based on the old forms, would be destroyed, to be replaced by a fundamentally new type of theatre: new in ideology, new in form, new in its effect upon the audience. Artaud's writings were an immediate and direct progenitor of Happenings, much of the work of the Living Theatre, the physical-ensemble work of the Open Theatre, and the environmental theatre of the Performance Group, among others.

John Cage

In a sense, the link between Gertrude Stein and Antonin Artaud can be found in John Cage, who propagated their ideas and shaped them into a basis for postwar avant-garde theatre. It was Cage who, having discovered Artaud through composer Pierre Boulez, introduced the work to Mary Caroline Richards, who translated it into English. And when in 1960 Cage was asked to list the ten books that had influenced him most, he began the list with Gertrude Stein, "any title."[27] Along with Zen, Stein would have the most profound influence upon the man who in turn exerted the greatest influence on the development of the American avant-garde. Just as Stein sought an alternative means for understanding theatre and literature, so Cage looked for an alternative means for structuring music. But this very restructuring of music led to a radical reorganization and understanding of theatre and dance.

One of Stein's most revolutionary effects had been to shift part of the creative process from the artist to the spectator. Traditionally, the closure provided by the spectator occurs in completing a pattern set forth by the artist. But in the landscape drama, there is no one way, no "correct" way, to read the work. In this, Stein seems to have anticipated by thirty years the work of the French structuralists, who fought the idea of a closed text and definitive readings. "The goal of literary work [of literature as work]," proposed Roland Barthes, "is to make the reader no longer a consumer, but a producer of the text."[28] Much of the avant-garde, in fact, has been an attempt to replace consumerism with production, but in Cage the privileging of chance and indeterminacy raised this approach to centrality in the work. Cage eliminated virtually all artistic intention by creating structures that were filled by the performers and then completed by the spectators or listeners. Meaningful content was eliminated so as to refocus the spectators onto the environment in which the performance occurred and, significantly, the spectator's own process of consciousness. What "nonintentional music wants to do," explained Cage, "is to make it clear to the listener that the hearing of the piece is his own action."[29]

Essential to Cage's aesthetic was the concept of silence. It came to represent space, non-intentionality, freedom, and creativity. It derived from his realization – a profound and revolutionary realization, though one with roots in futurism and Dada – that it was impossible, from a definitional standpoint, to distinguish music from "noise." All sounds are equal, and the categorization of some of them as music was purely a value judgment. Of the traditional Western attributes of music – pitch, timbre, loudness, and duration – only duration was common to all sound, and implicit in a durational structure is the idea of silence. Stated simply, music, for Cage, thus consisted of all the sounds and silences within a given time structure. But, he discovered, there is no such thing as absolute silence. In 1951, as an experiment to experience total silence, he entered an anechoic chamber, only to realize that he could still hear two sounds: the hum of his nervous system and the circulation of his blood. From this came his definition of silence as "all of the sound we don't intend."[30] And, furthermore, if we choose not to "discriminate between intention and non-intention, the splits, subject–object, art–life, etc., disappear."[31]

Music thus becomes a means for structuring the environment so that the "music" of everyday life can be heard, so that life and art are blended. If, however, the boundaries between life and art disappear, the reason for art is called into question: "Why have the arts when we already have it in life?" Cage asked rhetorically. And he had a ready answer: "We thereby celebrate."[32] But, he continued, "The attitude I take is that everyday life is more interesting than forms of celebration, when we become aware of it. That *when* is when our intentions go down to zero. Then suddenly you notice that the world is magical."[33]

In his iconoclastic piece *4'33"* for example, which consisted of a pianist sitting at a piano for four minutes and thirty-three seconds, during which the piano lid was raised and lowered to designate the three "movements" but during which time no notes were played – in other words, four and a half minutes of "silence" – the "music" comprised the ambient sounds of the concert hall, which, at the premiere performance in an outdoor music shed, included leaves rustling in the wind and rain rattling on the roof, as well as the shuffling of the audience. Part of Cage's premise is that we are constantly surrounded by sound, some pleasing, some not, and by refocusing our attention it is possible to have a different experience of the world around us.

Almost inadvertently, a certain revelation came from this approach: if there is no such thing as silence, then any action may produce sound or may structure the hearing of sound; thus all action is, in a sense, music and, by reverse implication, all music is action. "Relevant action," he proclaimed, "is theatrical (music [imaginary separation of hearing from the other senses] does not exist), inclusive and intentionally purposeless. Theatre is continually becoming that it is becoming; each human being is at the best point for reception."[34] Given this aesthetic, the distinctions between previously discrete performance forms began to crumble. Just as there was no difference between music and noise, between sound and silence, so there could be no meaningful difference between music, theatre, and dance. All were visual and auditory forms of performance.

If, as Cage believed, all sounds were equal, the reasons for listening to one sound rather than another were purely a matter of personal taste. Building in part on the ideas of Gertrude Stein, Cage rebelled against the notion of being subjected to someone else's personal vision. Why, he asked, should anyone have to go to a concert to listen to what a particular composer feels is a pleasing or significant combination of sounds? So he began to devise schemes to eliminate artistic choice from composition, substituting instead chance and indeterminacy.

"Chance" described a method of composition. Using the *I Ching*, for example, or dice, or coin flips, Cage would determine through a painstaking series of operations the pitch, timbre, duration, etc. of each note, thus eliminating, as much as possible, the specific input of the composer. "Indeterminacy" described the accidental results found within given structures. In *4'33"* for instance, the structure of the piece – that is, the time frames – was given, but the particular sounds that would occur at any given performance were indeterminate since the sounds were completely dependent on the environment in which a particular performance of the work occurred. In other compositions, performers were given a structure such as a time limit, and a series of actions or sounds to create, but allowed total freedom as to how to perform the "music" within the given structure. For some pieces, tape loops that were created for the composition but randomly chosen and played in performance provided the indeterminate nature. Anticipating the pastiche of postmodernism and the "sampling" used in much pop music of the late 1980s, Cage quoted a snatch of Beethoven's Ninth Symphony in the *Williams Mix* and incorporated radios in *Imaginary Landscape No. 4.* By "catching sounds," as Cage called it, the radios could introduce apparently meaningful content into the piece, but the context negated any meaning and transformed language and conventional music into a tapestry of sound that was a new form of music.[35] Though his abandonment of choice and control struck some people as heretical, it was really no different in principle from the traditional practice of allowing a musician to create an improvised variation on a theme – a cadenza – within a musical composition, as is so typical of the classical concerto.

Silence functioned as an equivalent to visual space, and Cage has acknowledged that *4'33"* may have been influenced by Robert Rauschenberg's white paintings, shown at Black Mountain College in 1951. The paintings, in which paint was applied with a roller, had nothing to do with technique or even contrasts in tone. Rauschenberg

explained that he "always thought of the white paintings as being, not passive, but very ... hypersensitive. So that one could look at them and almost see how many people were in the room by the shadows cast, or what time of day it was."[36] Cage has described these paintings as "airports for the lights, shadows, and particles."[37]

Stein saw in spatial constructs an alternative organization for creating and receiving art; Artaud, in eliminating the physical and mental barriers between audience and performer space, that is between the work of art and the perception of it, sought a new way of apprehending art. But Cage incorporated space/silence into art as an "urgently necessary" component within the work, as something with equal weight and importance to the concrete elements that had been the focus of artistic analysis since the Greeks. For Cage, silence was like the stones arranged on the sand in a Japanese rock garden: "the emptiness of the sand which needs the stones anywhere in the space in order to be empty."[38]

By virtually stripping the creation and reception of theatre of value judgments, Cage developed a broad definition of theatre: "Anything that engages the eye and the ear."[39] In other words, theatre is created by the simple act of framing an action. Not only does such a definition eliminate questions of hierarchical quality – an Elizabethan tragedy, a juggler on a street corner, and activity seen through a window take on equal weight – but it places the question of intention upon the spectator. Thus, if a spectator places a mental frame around an activity it becomes theatre for that observer, whether the "performers" intend, or even realize, that they are participating in a performance. And, finally, it is important to note that Cage saw his work as naturalistic. What he was doing was not imitating external features of the observable world but creating by imitating nature "in her manner of operation."[40]

Bertolt Brecht

Although Bertolt Brecht was almost certainly unaware of Cage, and Cage makes no mention of Brecht, there is an uncanny echoing of certain ideas, especially in Brecht's essays on music and opera. While Brecht had no interest in chance or indeterminacy, he was very interested in the centrality of the spectator in the creative process. Brecht's ideas are now so pervasive and well explicated that there is no need to delve into them in detail here, other than to indicate points of reference for the avant-garde.

Like the other key figures of the avant-garde, Brecht's art was informed by the scientific revolution, and he demanded a theatre to match the new sensibility.[41] At the same time, much of the immediate foundation of his theatre came from Asian influences. It was seeing the Chinese actor Mei Lan-fang that helped to crystallize his idea of *Verfremdung*, or alienation. The concept of alienation and the "alienation effect" (*Verfremdungseffeckt*), can be seen, in part, as an effort to recapture the idea of aesthetic distance so crucial to most art, or, in Brecht's words, "the alienation that is necessary to all understanding."[42] Brecht rebelled against the sort of theatre that manipulated the spectator's emotions and swept the viewer into empathic identification. He proposed instead the epic theatre, which "must report. It must not believe that one can identify oneself with our world by empathy, nor must it want this."[43] And it must reject the illusionism that placed the audience "in a trance."[44]

Brecht achieved his goal through a series of strategies whose fundamental basis was, as he put it in one of his theatre poems, "Show that you are showing!" The spectators were always to be aware that they were observing and evaluating a theatrical event. The "oceanic" experience described by the romantics – that is, becoming completely lost within the world of the play – was anathema because an audience that abandoned itself to illusion would be incapable of thinking. The result of this process of alienation, according to Brecht's famous chart contrasting the dramatic and epic theatres, is that the epic theatre "forces [the spectator] to take decisions … he is made to face something … [is] brought to the point of recognition … he is alterable and able to alter."[45]

Part of Brecht's avant-gardism derived from his insistence on jarring the spectator into a conscious, decision-making state of mind. This state of mind was certainly not the trance-like condition proposed by Artaud, nor exactly like the contemplative frame of mind of Stein, although she too was constantly throwing the readers/spectators back on themselves. Brecht's alienation technique had aesthetic and affective affinities to Stein's continuous present, albeit with a political agenda. In his essay on *Mahagonny*, Brecht declared that "one of its functions is to change society."[46] Brecht's epic theatre was analytical and non-Aristotelian. His rejection of empathy and imitation was also crucial to the development of the avant-garde.

Black Mountain College

Most of these ideas began to coalesce not in New York but at Black Mountain College, an experimental school in North Carolina that had been established in 1933. Far from the cultural centers of the United States, it served as an oasis where artists, musicians, dancers, writers, and theatre practitioners could work untrammeled by the pressures and constant scrutiny of galleries, critics, and commercial demands. The precarious financial situation of the school continually forced the artists to re-examine their approach to art, always encouraging them to look for inexpensive and innovative forms of presentation. Many artists taught there in the summer in return for little more than room and board – it provided a place to research, experiment, and think. In the late 1930s it had become a refuge for many European artists fleeing Nazi terrors, especially several members of the Bauhaus. After the war, it provided a proving ground for many shapers of the nascent American avant-garde: Buckminster Fuller, Eric Bentley, Willem and Elaine de Kooning, Arthur Penn, John Cage, Robert Rauschenberg, Merce Cunningham, Franz Kline, Paul Goodman, and many others.

Early theatrical work there included Bauhaus émigré Xanti Schawinsky's *Spectodrama* (1937) and *Danse Macabre* (1938), both mixed-media, non-narrative, and largely non-verbal performances;[47] and an environmental staging of Irwin Shaw's *Bury the Dead* in 1939, directed by Robert Wunsch. Although these works seemed to presage many aspects of American avant-garde theatre, they had little immediate impact on performance outside Black Mountain. It was not until after the war that experiments at Black Mountain had a more wide-ranging effect.

Cage first taught there in 1948, spending the summer lecturing on composer Erik Satie. It was during this time that Satie's pre-World War I play, *The Ruse of the Medusa*, was produced for the first time in the United States, becoming, to all intents and purposes, the *ur* production of the American avant-garde theatre. The cast, directed by Arthur

Penn, who would become an influential television and film director, included Fuller, Cunningham, and Elaine de Kooning with designs by Willem de Kooning. Martin Duberman, in his landmark study on Black Mountain College, summarized the influence that this production had upon Penn: "the 'opening up of the space,' the disappearance of lines of demarcation, the play flowing out into the auditorium, temporarily catching up the audience, then flowing back onto the stage."[48] Penn believed it was this experience that led him away from naturalistic approaches to television in the 1950s, foreshadowing the "*nouvelle vague* techniques in film."[49]

Cage's iconoclasm, however, became too extreme, even for Black Mountain, when he declared that Satie's dependence on structure as a means of composition was correct, whereas Beethoven's use of harmony was wrong. "Beethoven was in error," proclaimed Cage, "and his influence, which has been as extensive as it is lamentable, has been deadening to the art of music ... Beethoven represents the most intense lurching of the boat away from its natural even keel. The derivation of musical thought from his procedures has served not only to put us at the mercy of the waves, but to practically shipwreck the art on an island of decadence."[50]

The revolution that Cage was preaching was so radical that it took this "heresy" to shock people into understanding. It also took four years and a change in administration before Cage was invited back to Black Mountain. During his residency in the summer of 1952, he created a gentle, almost whimsical theatre piece that subsequently became identified as the wellspring of Happenings and chance theatre.[51] This unnamed performance had a lasting impact far greater than any lecture. The impetus and theoretical foundations behind this performance came from Artaud, Duchamp, and the Huang Po doctrine of universal mind, which, according to Duberman, held that the "centricity within each event is not dependent on other events."[52] This idea is what Michael Kirby would later refer to as "compartmentalization." In a conventional piece of narrative drama, each segment or component of the work must follow in a particular order; the information presented at one moment is essential to an understanding of the information that is presented in the next. But in a compartmentalized structure – as in the acts of a vaudeville show or circus – each unit is discrete and complete, and while the ideas or images contained in one compartment may influence the response to a subsequent unit, it is not crucial to its understanding or reception. In a certain sense, the component elements of a work of art, each speaking in their own "language," as Brecht or perhaps Duchamp might have it, can also be seen as compartmentalization. According to Cage, the ideas of Huang Po, Artaud, and Duchamp "all fused together into the possibility of making a theatrical event in which the things that took place were not causally related to one another – but in which there is a penetration, anything happened after that happened in the observer himself."[53] For the Black Mountain piece, Cage arranged, through a process of chance operations, a series of time brackets totaling forty-five minutes, which were to be filled indeterminately by the participants, who included Robert Rauschenberg, Merce Cunningham (with whom Cage first worked in 1944), David Tudor, Charles Olson, and Mary Caroline Richards. Not surprisingly, each participant seems to have a different memory of the event.[54] As Cage recalled it:

> The seating arrangement ... was a square composed of four triangles with the apexes of the triangles merging towards the center, but not meeting. The center was a larger space that could take movement, and the aisles between these four triangles also admitted of movement. The audience could see itself, which is of course the advantage of any theatre in the round. The larger part of the action took place *outside* of that square. In each one of the seats was a cup, and it wasn't explained to the audience what to do with this cup – some used it as an ashtray – but the performance was concluded by a kind of ritual pouring coffee into each cup.
>
> At one end of a rectangular hall, the long end, was a movie and at the other end were slides. I was up on a ladder delivering a lecture which included silences and there was another ladder which M.C. Richards and Charles Olson went up at different times. During periods that I called time brackets, the performers were free within limitations ... compartments which they didn't have to fill, like a green light in traffic. Until this compartment began, they were not free to act, but once it had begun they could act as long as they wanted to during it. Robert Rauschenberg was playing an old-fashioned phonograph that had a horn and a dog on the side listening, and David Tudor was playing a piano, and Merce Cunningham and other dancers were moving through the audience and around the audience [eventually followed by a stray dog]. Rauschenberg's [white paintings] were suspended above the audience ... at various angles, a canopy of painting above the audience.[55]

The significance of this performance seems far greater in retrospect than it appeared at the time. At Black Mountain, where the unusual and iconoclastic were the norm, this was simply one more such event. But it quickly became apparent that with this performance the rules had changed. There was no narrative, no information structure, not even a hierarchy of seating. The structure, though determined by Cage in general outline, was created by chance operations, and the content was indeterminate (the original performance could never be recreated precisely). It was a time–space composition in which sound, movement, space, and performer carried equal weight. For Cage, it was a piece of music – after all, it created sound, or at least time structures in which chance sounds could be heard. It was also dance, and it was certainly theatre. But it was a theatre in which the conventions and traditions embodied in Western culture from Aeschylus through Arthur Miller ended. Every presupposition about the nature of theatre needed to be re-examined.

* * *

In a sense, the avant-garde can be seen in terms of a battle between nihilism and rationality – both exist within the movement – that reflected opposing forces in mid-century society. Certainly, much of the work of the Living Theatre, for instance, whose founders Judith Malina and Julian Beck were avowed anarchists, evinced this duality. And the works of Cage and Foreman, though seemingly nihilistic because of their failure to superficially reinforce outward perceptions of the objective world, were in fact based on an intense and rigorous rationality. Perhaps it was the peculiar pall that hung over the postwar era that created this conflict: the atomic bomb, the epitome of scientific progress, threatened the world with total annihilation. Sociologist Daniel Bell saw mid-century society on the point of cataclysmic change: "I believe we are coming to a watershed in Western society," he wrote.

> We are witnessing the end of the bourgeois idea – that view of human action and of social relations, particularly of economic exchange – that has molded the modern era for the last 200 years. And I believe we have reached the end of the creative impulse and ideological sway of modernism, which as a cultural movement has dominated all the arts and shaped our symbolic expressions for the past 125 years.[56]

The American avant-garde emerged at least in part as a response to the unanswerable questions posed by the nuclear age. The celerity of change since the end of the nineteenth century, largely the result of the rapid growth of technology, altered the world so completely that it was often unrecognizable from one moment to the next. The literary, narrative theatre that had dominated American cultural life for the first half of the twentieth century was no longer a satisfactory mirror of society rushing headlong into the future. Although the scientific revolution and the avant-garde may have begun in Europe, the twentieth century *was*, as Henry Luce claimed, the American century because of the peculiar American affinity for technology. America was the land of radio, television, movies, automobiles, airplanes, skyscrapers, super-highways, supermarkets, neon lights, planned obsolescence, atomic weapons, rockets, computers, and rock 'n' roll. It was a land where, at least through the 1960s, technology was promoted by government and commercial enterprise alike as a panacea, a means toward a better life, a virtual utopia. History had value only insofar as it created a mythology that reinforced the inevitable destiny of America as the technological champion of the world. To live in the USA was to be avant-garde. The avant-garde theatre that emerged did not always reflect the new tech-nology, but it often captured the rapidly shifting consciousness of the new age.

Chapter 3

Off Broadway, Happenings, and the Living Theatre

> I bought a ticket, walked in, and saw this marvelous curtain go up with the possibility of something happening behind it and then nothing happened of any interest whatsoever. The theatre was a great disappointment to anybody interested in the arts.
>
> John Cage[1]

In the decades following the end of World War II, there was an increasingly pervasive frustration with the existing theatre. Even Holden Caulfield, the protagonist of J.D. Salinger's novel *The Catcher in the Rye*, had something to say about it: "I mean I didn't care too much when anybody in the family [on the stage] died or anything. They were all just a bunch of actors ... They didn't act like people and they didn't act like actors. It's hard to explain."[2] A new spirit of iconoclasm and rapidly escalating costs combined to bring about substantial changes in the nature of theatre and the way in which it was produced. The result was the emergence of an alternative theatre, which came to be known as Off Broadway, a catch-all term that, in the popular imagination, suggested bohemianism and experimentation. Thus, a 1972 history of Off Broadway described the movement as "a state of mind, a set of production conditions, a way of looking at theater at every point at odds with Broadway's patterns,"[3] but it was really none of those things. Off Broadway was a contractual and economic institution. "The main difference between Broadway and Off-Broadway [was] economical," declared director Jose Quintero, a co-founder of Off Broadway's Circle in the Square.[4] In fact, there were two simultaneous developments in the theatre of the 1940s and 1950s: the creation of the Off Broadway movement as a response to the economic restrictions and increasingly narrow repertoire of Broadway; and the emergence of an avant-garde out of a confluence of trends in the visual and plastic arts, new music, Beat writing, and historical and contemporary European innovations in theatre. Aesthetically, the two had little in common, yet ultimately they were inextricably intertwined.

The term "Off Broadway" was coined by critic-editor Burns Mantle in *The Best Plays of 1934–1935* as a designation for revivals, classics, new plays, and even puppet and children's theatre performed in New York but outside the theatres of the Broadway district, although its spiritual roots can be traced to the late nineteenth-century art theatres of Europe such as Théâtre Libre, the Freie Bühne, and even the Moscow Art Theatre, and to the so-called little theatres in the United States from the teens and twenties, such as the Washington Square Players and Provincetown Players. In most cases, the founders of these latter companies were discontented with the repertoire of the mainstream and wished to explore and develop foreign plays, new approaches to American play writing, and even new styles of acting in the less restrictive contexts of smaller experimental theatres, which invariably had more intimate physical surroundings, fewer formal demands on production, and far less economic risk. Still, while the participants in these ventures challenged accepted practices and mainstream preconceptions, they rarely saw themselves as totally oppositional outsiders. The goal was to broaden or gradually transform the theatre, not to set up a permanent alternative. In most cases, the new work was eventually absorbed into the mainstream.

Inflation, recession, and a seismic shift in urban demographics following the war had a profound effect upon theatre production and the nature and composition of theatre audiences and, as in the 1920s and 1930s, there was a challenge to the established theatre. But this time, instead of being absorbed back into the mainstream after a decade or so, as its predecessor movements had been, Off Broadway became a shadow Broadway, as it were – a movement that ultimately replaced Broadway's function as a producer of serious drama. The result was therefore not so much an alteration of Broadway aesthetics as a permanent shift in the production landscape and geography of New York theatre.

Two small theatres that had been in fairly steady use since the 1920s, the Cherry Lane and the Provincetown, along with some recital halls and other non-traditional performance spaces, became home to the new Off Broadway movement. By 1949, seven groups were operating on a regular basis. Under the stipulations of a contract between the Actors' Equity Association and the newly formed Off-Broadway Theatre League, Off Broadway theatres were limited to fewer than 300 seats and to a geographic location outside the area bounded by Manhattan's Fifth and Ninth Avenues on the east and west, and 34th and 56th Streets to the south and north. Off Broadway's first truly successful theatre was the Circle in the Square, founded by Quintero and Theodore Mann in a defunct nightclub in Greenwich Village in 1951. Its long, narrow, thrust stage surrounded on three sides by the audience was emblematic of the innovations of Off Broadway, but the spatial configuration was not a factor of aesthetic choice but of necessity; the producers had to work with the existing space. They were not, however, producing avant-garde theatre. Typical was their 1952 revival of Tennessee Williams' *Summer and Smoke*, which had failed in its initial Broadway run in 1948. Off Broadway found its niche primarily as the rescuer of those shows overlooked or mishandled by Broadway or those to which Broadway closed its doors. These included plays of Williams and O'Neill, and also the more recent wave of European authors such as Genet, Sartre, and Beckett. Broadway, especially a Broadway now geared toward light entertainment and hit shows and the largest possible audience within a shrinking pool, was ill-equipped to tackle the darker, more intimate, structurally and stylistically more complex dramas emerging in the postwar era. Given the increasing cost of Broadway production, there was simply no longer a sufficient audience to make the production of such plays viable.

Because Off Broadway was filling the role that Broadway had filled in previous generations as a producer of serious drama, it quickly became economically and structurally like Broadway – a place for the production of individual shows that would run as long as there were ticket-buying patrons. The lower costs (in part because of a freedom from union crews and contracts as well as lower rents) and the more exotic surroundings (many, though by no means all, the Off Broadway theatres were located in Greenwich Village, still considered a bohemian enclave at the time) were all that separated it from Broadway. But the division of aesthetic properties between on and Off Broadway, exacerbated by television's expropriation of a significant portion of the drama together with its writers and audience, created a fragmented constituency and resulted in a ghettoization of the theatre. The perception was created that art and entertainment were completely separate entities when it came to the theatre, and those theatre artists who in earlier times might have contributed to the revitalization of the established theatre now rejected that venue for alternative theatres or for other media. The increasingly clear lines of demarcation led to outright hostility between the camps. "Who responds to Tennessee

Williams or Arthur Miller picking his liver apart?" asked Luis Valdez, founder of the agitprop Teatro Campesino in the 1960s. "You can't respond to that shit."[5] Mainstream theatre and its representatives were seen as irrelevant and possibly malevolent. A two-tiered system of art had emerged in which each contingent saw the other as a threat to societal sensibilities. By 1962, Julian Beck, co-founder of the Living Theatre, could lambast the commercial theatre as a dead world:

> I do not like the Broadway theatre because it does not know how to say hello. The tone of voice is false, the mannerisms are false, the sex is false, ideal, the Hollywood world of perfection, the clean image, the well pressed clothes, the well scrubbed anus, odorless, inhuman, of the Hollywood actor, the Broadway star. And the terrible false dirt of Broadway, the lower depths in which the dirt is imitated, inaccurate.[6]

But the response to mainstream theatre began to move beyond the simple rejection of content and sentiment. Just as avant-garde art, music, and poetry had overthrown the prevailing structures and sought new forms of expression, some theatre artists – notably Julian Beck and Judith Malina of the Living Theatre – began to search for new forms of theatre that would better express the ideas of a new world.

New forms meant the rejection of Western classical, neoclassical, and post-Renaissance theatre, which was dominated by Aristotelian precepts (or contemporary readings of those ideas) that generally manifested themselves in what Michael Kirby called an "information structure." In most traditional theatre, the play is understood through a cumulative "reading" and interpreting of information – dialogue, sets, costumes, action, and so on. Typically, an information structure meant narrative (Aristotle's privileging of plot), but the emerging avant-garde began to play with the idea of other kinds of structure.

Perhaps the greatest tool for effecting the desired change was, surprisingly, television. The profound effect of television upon culture and American society in general, and its staggering effect on the theatre after it became a viable mass medium around 1948 (to a degree that the movies never had), cannot be overstated. Throughout history, popular entertainment had always constituted a foundation for the theatre. Whatever was going on in mainstream or officially sanctioned performance, popular entertainment – singing, dancing, circus skills, comedy, and domestic skits, and the like – remained almost unaltered. And whenever the mainstream faltered or collapsed, a new theatre emerged from the steadfast popular forms. In theory, this should have happened again as the postwar American theatre seemingly lost its bearings. But television supplanted live popular performance. Everything that might have been found in vaudeville houses, and much of the drama and comedy that had been a staple of the popular Broadway stage for decades, could now be found on television, which viewers could see without ever venturing from their houses. In one sense, the transference of popular entertainment to television meant that almost everyone could now attend the "theatre"; mass entertainment had never been so "mass." But on the other hand, the possibility for variety and growth was being crushed beneath the homogenizing influence of the new medium. For example, the weekly *Ed Sullivan Show* – a television version of vaudeville – brought a wider melange of entertainment into homes than most people had ever encountered before, but now the entire American population was presented with a single bill of fare. As a result, the flow of ideas and the productive tensions between the popular, the mainstream, and the experimental was ruptured. The unorthodox and iconoclastic performances that had once survived and even thrived on the periphery of the great theatre machine was now banished to increasingly obscure venues. By the 1960s, television had usurped vast segments of the audience and absorbed the predominant theatrical genres. The live theatre, which had served as a mirror of national identity and a cauldron of cultural debate, had become an elitist entertainment aimed at a narrow segment of the population; at best, it was a tourist attraction.

Television would have another effect. Although its content seemed to recapitulate the major dramatic forms, its structure of short segments containing rapidly changing images, and especially its rupture of narrative flow by the repeated intervention of commercials and the resultant kaleidoscopic spectacle, would have a profound effect upon consciousness and the way in which an entire generation saw the world and perceived reality. Television – surreptitiously and inadvertently – did more to undermine the Aristotelian structure of theatre in a single generation than had a century of dramatic theory and practice.

Ironically, as the middle-class audience for theatre was diminishing, a new constituency of specialists was emerging out of college-based theatre training programs. Though still a limited factor in the 1940s, college and university theatre would swell in the next two decades – thanks in large part to the GI Bill, aimed at providing education for returning service men – to become a major force in American theatre. By the mid-1980s, there were 1,600 theatre departments around the country. These programs became training grounds for actors, designers, playwrights, and directors and fertile soil for the dissemination and exploration of new ideas – primarily twentieth-century European approaches to drama and acting (and through them, perhaps, at least a passing reference to classical Asian forms). The rising number of classes also created a demand for published scripts and created an audience for academic journals (not to mention a cadre of scholarly authors). Scholarly publishing became a major factor in the creation and growth of the avant-garde. From the 1920s through the 1940s, *Theatre Arts Monthly* had provided a source of information on the latest European developments. But it was translator and critic Eric Bentley who, from the late 1940s on, proved to be the single most influential source of information on the new European theatre and whose articles, translations of scripts and theoretical writings (particularly of Brecht), and anthologies of classical and modern European drama essentially invented the modern field of comparative drama in the United States. "Eric Bentley became my main source as I entered college," remembered Richard Foreman. "He spoke of a European art theatre of which I, and most Americans, had never heard, a non-naturalistic theatre that seemed informed by poetry and painting and music."[7] Foreman cited his preoccupation in those years with Brecht, Giradoux, Grabbe, Lorca, cummings, and Büchner, "all owing to the hypnotic fascination of a world made available to young would-be theatrical creators exclusively by Eric Bentley in those quite dark years of the late fifties."

In 1949, the American Educational Theatre Association (later the American Theatre Association; later still, the Association for Theatre in Higher Education) began to publish an academic journal, *Educational Theatre Journal* (later *Theatre Journal*). But it was the *Tulane Drama Review* (*TDR*) that would establish itself as the publication of record for the experimental and avant-garde theatre and have a significant international impact. Begun in 1955 by theatre professor Robert Corrigan as a journal of dramatic criticism at Carleton College in Minnesota, it soon moved to Tulane University in New Orleans. With strong input from Bentley, *TDR* developed into the major outlet for information on new European drama, in particular the rising tide of absurdism. In 1962, an iconoclastic and controversial young academic, Richard Schechner, became editor. He quickly moved the journal from a focus on drama to theatre – the performance – and from tradition to experimentation. He also added a section known as "*TDR* Comment" to provide a platform for editorializing and advocacy. The journal moved to New York University in the late 1960s (and became simply

The Drama Review), and in the 1970s Michael Kirby became editor. Through the late 1970s, *TDR* was not simply a place to document or comment upon theatre – it was an active and vital force in shaping the American avant-garde while remaining the primary conduit of new theatrical ideas between the United States and the rest of the world. The magazine devoted a whole issue to Happenings in 1963; it covered the Living Theatre, the Open Theatre, and the Bread and Puppet Theatre; it was responsible for introducing the work of Jerzy Grotowski to the USA; it virtually defined postmodern dance; and it played a significant role in the success of Robert Wilson, Richard Foreman, Meredith Monk, and the Wooster Group among many others. It was as much a player in the evolution of the American avant-garde as the artists and theatres themselves.

By the 1980s, changes in theatre and in society in general, combined with Kirby's almost fanatical disdain for value judgments and thus the sort of polemics with which Schechner often stirred up the readership, led to a significant decline in subscriptions and influence. Like the theatre itself, theatre journalism became ghettoized. Where *TDR* had once dominated world coverage of experimental theatre, by the 1980s there were over a dozen journals in the United States alone covering more or less the same field, yet the total readership for all these journals combined was not significantly more than the 12,000 that *TDR* had at its peak in the late 1960s and early 1970s. Such a fragmented field could no longer shape and define the theatre.

The Living Theatre

The Living Theatre emerged amid this general spirit of rebellion and iconoclasm. Beginning with its first productions in 1951, the work of the Living Theatre was a "reaction against naturalism, against the American version of Stanislavsky." Julian Beck and Judith Malina wanted nothing less than "a revolution ... one that had already transformed the other arts – music, painting, sculpture."[8] Though lumped together with Off Broadway – how else to categorize it at the time? – the Living Theatre had little in common with Circle in the Square, the Phoenix, and other similar companies. It became, to all intents and purposes, America's first avant-garde theatre company. Moreover, with its unyielding and passionate commitment to both political and aesthetic ideals, it prevailed as a ground-breaking troupe for the first twenty years of its existence and remains an inspirational, if anachronistic, influence to the present day.

Judith Malina's family – her father was a rabbi – emigrated to New York from Germany when she was two. She met Julian Beck, a Yale drop-out and the son of a fairly well-to-do Upper West Side Manhattan Jewish family, in the early 1940s. They were both passionate about the theatre and began attending performances together as often as four times a week. While theatre was certainly more affordable then than now, Beck's relative affluence was significant. Though not wealthy, he did not have the burden of having to work at regular jobs to support himself during this time. It allowed him and Malina the luxury of attending theatres, museums, galleries, and cafes. And while Beck and Malina took on jobs in the 1950s to support themselves and the theatre, his family was also able to help to prop up the cash-strapped Living Theatre from time to time. Beck was not alone in this regard in the postwar avant-garde – many of the leading artists in all fields had at least a degree of financial independence that freed them from the constraints upon time and energy faced by most working-class individuals.

The primary influences on the developing theatre aesthetic of Beck and Malina were not the ones shared by most of their Off Broadway colleagues. In 1943, Malina worked at the Beggar's Bar in Greenwich Village, run by German cabaret performer and actor Valeska Gert, and she later studied at the New School with German director Erwin Piscator, the founder of Epic Theatre and one-time colleague of Brecht. Beck studied art and moved in the circle of American abstract expressionists. From Gert came an appreciation of the exaggerated and distorted anti-naturalistic acting of expressionism; from Piscator came the notion of theatre as a force for social and political change effected through non-Aristotelian means but with "reason, clarity, and communication."[9] From the art world, which for Beck included acquaintanceships with Jackson Pollock, Mark Rothko, and Robert Motherwell among others, came a rejection of narrative space in painting and consequently a rejection of conventional narrative in drama, and an emphasis on process over content and product. Although the elimination of the objective image in favor of formal elements seemed to ally these artists to the formalist movements of the first decades of the century, they were actually closer in spirit to the symbolists and surrealists in their glorification of the inner life of the artist. What the public perceived as abstraction the artists saw as a liberation of truth and a rejection of "the lie, the cliché, the standardized."[10] Motherwell, who in the late 1940s considered designing sets for Beck and Malina, described what he called the School of New York in terms of what it was not:

Its painting is not interested in giving information, propaganda, description, or anything that might be called (to use words loosely) of practical use ... The School of New York is not intellectual, but intensely emotional ... Its extreme tendency might be described, in the words of a critic summarizing the notion of Paul Valéry's, as an "activity of bodily gesture serving to sharpen consciousness." ... it is ... a sustained, systematic, stubborn, sensitive, and sensible effort to find an exact formulation of attitude toward the world as concretely experienced. The interest in the language of art is quite simply an interest in the tool that can lead one to being honest.[11]

This description of abstract expressionism could just as easily apply to the work of the Living Theatre. In a 1948 diary entry, for instance, Malina quoted André Gide: "Dramatic art must no more seek to create the illusion of reality than does painting; it should work through its own special means and aim towards effects that belong to it alone. Just as a painting is a space to set in motion, a play is a space of time to animate."[12]

This idea of honesty in art was a pervasive theme among artists in all disciplines in the postwar years. There was an overwhelming sense, reflected in the mainstream culture, that the institutions of society were false, dishonest, and corrupting. This belief was especially profound among the Beat writers and poets centered around Allen Ginsberg, Jack Kerouac, Neal Cassady, Herbert Huncke, and William Burroughs in New York, a group whose influence would also be felt by Malina and Beck, in part through the gatherings, poetry readings, and jazz performances at bars and coffee houses such as the San Remo, the Cedar Tavern, Café Bizarre, and the Five Spot. Beat writer John Clellon Holmes expressed the sense of alienation felt by much of this generation:

Conventional notions of private and public morality have been steadily atrophied in the last ten or fifteen years by the exposure of treason in government, corruption in labor and business and scandal among the mighty of Broadway and Hollywood ... Orthodox religious conceptions of good and evil seem increasingly inadequate to explain a world of science-fiction turned fact, past-enemies turned bosom-friends, and honorable-diplomacy turned brink-of-war. Older generations may be distressed or cynical or apathetic about this world ... But the Beat Generation is specifically the product of this world, and it is the only world its members have ever known.[13]

For Malina and Beck, this sensibility meant that their art, their personal beliefs, and their politics were inextricably entwined. The most immediate influences on Malina and Beck, however, were the European symbolist and surrealist poets and writers and those who followed in their footsteps, a canon that included Ezra Pound, James Joyce, Gertrude Stein, e.e. cummings, André Breton, W.H. Auden, and Rilke. It is perhaps because of that influence that the Living Theatre began with an attempt to revive or recreate poetic drama for the contemporary world. This was not to be an imitation of Elizabethan verse. "The plays of Shakespeare," declared Beck, "do not impart to us the significance and wisdom that Elizabethan audiences were able to obtain from them. We simply cannot hear a distant language with the sense of immediacy the words once carried. Our audience must listen to its own poets speaking about the life of our times in a language significant to us."[14]

The idea of forming a company had developed over Beck's and Malina's years together, and in 1947 they came up with the name, had stationery printed, and wrote for advice to a variety of artists, including Jean Cocteau (with whose *Infernal Machine* they planned to launch their theatre), e.e. cummings, Alfred Kreymborg, Frederick Kiesler, and the designer Robert Edmond Jones. Jones had been one of the proponents of the New Stagecraft movement in the teens and a producer of the Provincetown Playhouse, which staged the early work of Eugene O'Neill. In November 1947, Beck and Malina brought him their sketches and models for the proposed Cocteau play and for some one-acts. Jones admired much about the settings and costumes but felt that these young artists were trapped in conventional ways of thinking. "I wish you had no money, no money at all," he said. "Perhaps then you would create the new theatre, make your theatre out of string and sofa cushions, make it in studios and living rooms. Forget the big theatres ... Here, if you want, take this room ... if you want to begin here you can have it."[15] Not fully understanding what he meant, Malina and Beck turned down Jones' generous offer. "He had expected us to go further," remembered Malina. "He wanted us to build sets out of sound, out of dreams, out of who knows what. He wanted something 'totally new'."[16] It would take the Living Theatre another decade to realize the significance of Jones' exhortations and to begin to achieve them.

Beck and Malina were married in 1948, and in the fall of that year they attempted their first production in a basement on Wooster Street in what is now the Soho district of New York. After considering a range of options, they settled on three medieval mystery plays. But the cramped basement space did not meet fire codes, they had trouble finding and retaining actors, and when they attempted to place an ad for performers in the *Daily News* they were rejected and told it sounded like a solicitation for prostitutes and would result in police action. The project collapsed. They wrote to Ezra Pound, whose plays they hoped to produce in the future, to tell him that they were closed for suspicion of running a brothel; Pound scrawled a famous postcard reply: "How *else* cd a seeryus tee-ater support itself in N.Y.?"[17] Finally, in August 1951, the Living Theatre premiered by presenting four plays in the couple's living room in their West End Avenue apartment. The plays – all of which emphasized one kind of poetic diction or another – were *Childish Jokes* by Paul Goodman, *Ladies' Voices* by Gertrude Stein, *He Who Says Yes and He Who Says No* by Bertolt Brecht, and *The Dialogue of the Mannequin and the Young Man* by Federico Garcia Lorca. In December, they opened at the venerable Cherry Lane Theatre in Greenwich Village with Gertrude Stein's *Doctor Faustus Lights the Lights*, and over the following year they produced more Stein and Goodman and plays by Beat poets Kenneth Rexroth and John Ashberry, and works by Picasso, T.S. Eliot, and Alfred Jarry.[18] Although there would be exceptions, the division of labor between Malina and Beck was established at this time: she directed and he designed.

The theatre at the Cherry Lane was eventually shut down by the fire marshal for violations of the fire code – the Living Theatre did not have the funds to make the necessary corrections. There was a hiatus of more than a year and a half before productions resumed in March 1954, this time in a loft at the corner of Broadway and 100th Street – near the Beck's home but far from even the newly developing Off Broadway. The Studio, as it became known, was actually a model for the Off Off Broadway theatres that would emerge a decade later. It was a third-floor walk-up above a grocery. The rent was $90 a month (five months due in advance). The sixty-five seats were chairs scrounged from the streets and abandoned lots and buildings, repaired and painted by Beck. The old wallpaper was covered with brown wrapping paper, and curtains were created out of *Ubu Roi* costumes from the Cherry Lane production. The entire cost of "renovating" the space and preparing the first production, other than rent, was $136. The

Studio opened with W.H. Auden's *The Age of Anxiety*. No admission was charged, but a bread basket or tambourine was placed at a table by the door for voluntary contributions; the actors shared the receipts. Through October 1955 the Living Theatre produced six more plays, including works by Strindberg, Cocteau, Pirandello, Racine, and Paul Goodman, but at the end of the year the theatre was closed down by the City Buildings Department because it violated occupancy laws.

In the 1960s, as the burgeoning Off Off Broadway movement followed in the footsteps of the Living Theatre and transformed lofts, storefronts, and garages into theatres, companies were often hassled and closed by the Building or Fire Departments. There is no question that many of these theatres violated city ordinances and, at times, may have posed legitimate safety threats, but many believed at the time that the investigations were often politically instigated. Beck and Malina, as avowed anarchists active in the Ban-the-Bomb movement and the War Resisters League – activities that could get one labeled as "communist" at the time – certainly drew attention to themselves (by 1963 they had been arrested six times for participating in pacifist demonstrations). Furthermore, the plays sometimes violated acceptable or even legal codes of decency. Goodman's *The Young Disciple*, for instance, the last play produced at the Studio, employed the word "fuck" repeatedly. Though almost banal today, such language was unheard-of on a public stage in the mid-1950s.

The emphasis upon Goodman's plays (rarely if ever produced by anyone but the Living Theatre and virtually unknown today) reflected a personal friendship as well as an almost disciple-like belief in his utopian, pacifist anarchism. Goodman, a leading social critic of the 1940s and 1950s, had a significant impact on much of the leftist activism of the 1960s. In particular, his emphasis upon creating cities made up of communities based upon "political, cultural, and moral reintegration"[19] led Beck and Malina toward two goals – creating a theatrical art that reflected their own political beliefs, and making the Living Theatre itself a community. The theatre, in other words, would not merely produce plays *about* utopian and anarchist ideas, it would be a model for such a society. This latter aspect was ultimately the most significant difference between the Living Theatre and other Off Broadway companies. The Circle in the Square or the Phoenix, for example, may have been run by passionate and idealistic individuals, but ultimately they were business organizations devoted to the productions of certain types of drama. The Living Theatre, by contrast, was first and foremost a community of artists whose approach to art and

Plate 2 *The Young Disciple* by Paul Goodman, produced by the Living
Theatre at the Studio at 100th Street and Broadway, New
York, 1955. Directed and designed by Julian Beck. Actors (l. to
r.): Hooper Dunbar, Judith Malina, Shirley Stoler, William Vines,
Walter Mullen.

Photo: courtesy the Living Theatre.

even to life was a reflection of socio-political ideals and was intended to
serve as a model for utopian communities within the larger society.

In an attempt to achieve this model, two significant motifs ran
through the majority of work that the Living Theatre produced in
these first few seasons: an emphasis on poetic language and a meta-
theatrical structure of a play within a play or a play commenting upon
its own theatricality. Looking back from a vantage point of nearly fifty
years, the connection between these aesthetic devices and the avowed
goals seems tenuous at best, but at the time it was part of an effort to
break free from the constraints of conventional drama, which, the
Becks believed, trapped the artists and audiences in habitual patterns of
perception and behavior. The poetic diction could be seen as part of
the same impulse that drove the Beat writers to explore the rhythms

and sound of language as a method of getting beyond the superficial meanings of words. "How can you have a lively civilization," Beck asked, "if the language is outmoded and no longer says what anyone can possibly want to mean? How can you enlarge the limits of consciousness if language atrophies?"[20] Thus, for the Living Theatre, poetry was not merely beautiful language, it was a revolutionary method for the restructuring of theatre and a utopian tool that provided a direct connection to the subconscious. Poetic language, the Becks believed, would allow them to achieve their goal of a theatre "as a place of intense experience, half dream, half ritual, in which the spectator approaches something of a vision of self-understanding, going past the conscious to the unconscious, to an understanding of the nature of all things ... Only poetry or a language laden with symbols and far removed from our daily speech can take us beyond the ignorant present toward those realms."[21]

The meta-theatrical element of the drama arose out of an attempt to break through the fourth wall, to reach the audience. Looking back on some of the productions that utilized this device – Pirandello's *Tonight We Improvise*, William Carlos Williams' *Many Loves*, and Jack Gelber's *The Connection* – Beck believed that "these play-within-the-play devices arose out of a crying need on the part of the authors, and of us, to reach the audience, to awaken them from their passive slumber, to provoke them into attention, shock them if necessary, and, this is also important, to involve the actors with what was happening in the audience."[22] Beck saw this approach as a return to the religious, mystical, ritualistic roots and purpose of theatre: "The intention was to equalize, unify, and bring everyone closed to life. Joining as opposed to separation."[23]

Jack Gelber's *The Connection* embodied all these impulses and marked a culmination of the first phase of the Living Theatre's development. *The Connection* opened on July 15, 1959 and was the third production at the Living Theatre's new space, the former Hecht's department store on Sixth Avenue and 14th Street. Beck designed the space with architect Paul Williams. The first floor of the four-storey building remained occupied by shops; the second storey contained the lobby and theatre; the third was for a lecture hall, a rehearsal room, and dressing rooms for up to thirty actors; and the fourth was used partly for scenery and costume storage and partly as a dance studio for Merce Cunningham – often filled with noise rising from the street. ("I ... liked greatly being in the same building with the theatre," he recalled. "After classes, I used to go and watch at the back of the house when they played."[24]) To save money, no contractors were hired – all the work was done by volunteers drawn from actors, writers, artists, and musicians who supported the Living Theatre. The whole decor became a statement. The lobby walls were exposed brick "like the walls of a courtyard,"[25] the ceiling was painted sky blue, and there was a running fountain "as in a public square." There were kiosks for selling books and coffee. The theatre itself was half circus, half Bayreuth. The 162 seats – donated from the old Orpheum movie theatre on Second Avenue and Saint Marks Place – were painted in "hazy gray, lavender, and sand, with oversize circus numbers on them in bright orange, lemon and magenta," while the walls were painted in black stripes, which became narrower as they converged "toward the stage, concentrating the focus, as if one were inside an old-fashioned Kodak, looking out through the lens, the eye of the dream in the dark room." *Village Voice* critic Jerry Tallmer rapturously saw the space itself as a beacon, "blazing in the night through all its windows like a glorious Mondrian cathedral," from which "the joy of theatre gets pumped back into a desiccating off-Broadway season."[26]

The theatre functioned as a focal point for the artistic community. In addition to the performances, there were theatre classes taught by Beck, Malina, and others, including "Artaudian acting" taught by Geraldine Lust. There were lectures by Goodman, architect Frederick Kiesler, filmmaker Maya Deren, anthropologist Joseph Campbell, critic Eric Bentley, choreographer Erick Hawkins, and M.C. Richards on her translation of Artaud's *The Theatre and Its Double*. There were concerts of new music by John Cage, Christian Wolff, Alan Hovhaness (who held the title of music director for the theatre), and Henry Cowell; poetry readings by Goodman, Dylan Thomas, Allen Ginsberg, Gregory Corso, Frank O'Hara, Lawrence Ferlinghetti, and Anaïs Nin; avant-garde film showings by Deren, Stan Brakhage and other New American filmmakers; concerts of Renaissance and Baroque music; dance concerts; children's theatre; and play readings and stagings of one-act plays outside the repertory. The Living Theatre had become the physical and spiritual heart of the full range of avant-garde arts in New York.

Twenty-seven-year-old playwright Jack Gelber brought his script of *The Connection* directly to the Becks in 1958 because he could not afford the postage to send it. The play revolved around a group of drug addicts, including four jazz musicians, who are waiting in an apartment for their "connection," Cowboy, to arrive with heroin. Act One was about the waiting; in Act Two, Cowboy arrives and the addicts "shoot up" and get high. Critics noted the inevitable similarities to *Waiting for Godot*, *The Iceman Cometh*, and *The Lower Depths*, but Gelber had added a Pirandellian framework. The play was presented as if it were an improvisation by real drug addicts who have gathered at the theatre to make a documentary film on drug addiction. The cast of characters included a producer, a playwright, and two cameramen with lights and cameras. Gelber's script indicated that the actual names of the director (in this case Judith Malina) and the theatre be used. While all the characters in the play had fictional names, the musicians used their own. As the play began, characters were sprawled on the set, "a room full of home-made furniture" with a visible toilet at the rear.[27] A bare green light bulb hung over the stage, and Beck had painted a mural of two pyramids, palm trees, and a winged surrealist eye. To the perceptive spectator, waiting for the play to begin, there was already something different in the feel of this scenario. "The imaginary fourth wall has not been constructed," noted Robert Brustein in his review in *The New Republic*. "The actors are aware of the audience, and even somewhat distressed at the presence. It is making them nervous, disturbing their peace."[28] As the house lights dimmed, the "producer" and the "playwright" entered through the auditorium onto the stage. The first lines, spoken by the producer character, were: "Hello there! I'm Jim Dunn and I'm producing *The Connection*. This is Jaybird, the author." Invariably, the audience would applaud at that point. Over the next few minutes, the two characters attempted to set the scene, during which there were exchanges with some of the other characters and musicians. Part way through Jim's first speech, the 4th musician asked, "Hey, Jim, is Cowboy back?" to which Jim replied, "No, man, Cowboy is not back." The theme of waiting was established, and a touch of Clifford Odets' *Waiting for Lefty* was even evoked. Jaybird and Jim seemed to lose their train of thought and stumbled over seemingly prepared statements to the audience; there were apparent problems with the house lights. From the beginning, the characters seemed truculent, unable or unwilling to function as "agreed" and therefore threatening the collapse of what was being presented as a tenuously constructed evening to begin with.

Throughout the first act, the "structure" broke down as actors went off on tangents, fights broke out, and Jaybird left in disgust. The whole play seemingly ground to a halt when the character Harry entered with a portable phonograph and played a Charlie Parker record. For two minutes – an inordinately long time on stage – nothing else happened; the characters (and audience) just listened. Afterwards, the musicians played for another minute. There were several similar moments throughout the play when the action, such as it was, stopped, and the musicians played. Malina saw the structure of the play moving between the two liberating forces of drugs and jazz. Thus the music was neither background nor mood nor transition, but an essential and independent element of the text equal to the dialogue and action.

During the intermission, some of the actors – as characters – mingled with the audience in the lobby, asking for handouts. In the second act, Cowboy arrived and took the characters one by one into the bathroom for their fix. Jaybird, who had returned, and one of the cameramen also got high. A Salvation Army sister joined the group and preached to the addicts, blissfully unaware of what was going on around her. The character of Leach, in whose "pad" the action was supposedly occurring, shot up in full view of the audience and over-dosed – although he ultimately revived. Over the run of the show, in Europe as well as in New York, according to Beck, fifty spectators – interestingly, all men – fainted at this point or left the theatre; the realism of the needle was apparently too much to watch.[29] At the beginning of the play, Jim assured the audience that no real heroin would be used; at the end of the first act, he explained that the actors "will be turned on by a scientifically accurate amount of heroin in the next act."[30] Some observers claimed that real heroin was used at times.[31]

Thematically, *The Connection* was in the tradition of the thesis or social-problem plays of the nineteenth century and occasionally wore its politics on its sleeve. In its attempts to confound the real and fictional world – to create the ultimate illusion – the play can be seen as the logical end of the naturalistic movement. In critic Kenneth Tynan's introduction to the published version of the script, he compared the production to the Moscow Art Theatre production of Chekhov's *The Three Sisters*: "The stage exuded a sense of life, pre-existent and continuing," he noted; "it was not like going to the theatre, it was like paying a call on old acquaintances."[32]

But in its structure *The Connection* did indeed break new ground, though with obvious precedents in Chekhov and symbolist drama. It had the structure of jazz. The individual sequences were like themes and variations on a melody, with long speeches equivalent to jazz riffs. The play was held together not by logical sequences of action but by an almost musical affinity of sounds. Some critics took the apparent

Plate 3 The Connection by Jack Gelber, produced by the Living Theatre
at the Loft at 14th Street and Sixth Avenue, New York, 1959.
With (l. to r.) Garry Goodrow, Warren Finnerty, Jerome
Raphel.

Photo: John E. Wulp. Courtesy the Living Theatre.

alogicality as a form of absurdism. But Gelber's methodology was not the
purposeful disruption of cause and effect or the verbal *non sequiturs* of
Ionesco; the structure was the replication of the stream-of-conscious
naturalism of real – albeit drug-altered – life. The essentially passive,
contemplative, and non-verbal quality of most of the characters militated against the usual theatrical conventions of action and dialogue.

Malina further blurred the boundaries between life and theatre with a
directorial approach that encouraged improvisation within the performance. (Since we are told that the characters are improvising, Malina's
approach created a situation of actors improvising characters who were
improvising.) The improvisatory strategy marked the beginning, in
Beck's view, of the director relinquishing her "authoritarian" position,
the position that directors had held at least since the Duke of Saxe-
Meiningen created the modern director in the nineteenth century. The
actor now became a partner in the creation of the piece of theatre. Beck
also saw in their production of *The Connection* the beginnings of a new
kind of naturalism that he felt would move the theatre forward and create
a new style of acting. "A resurgence of realism was needed," he believed.

There had to be pauses. Directors had to learn to let actors sit still for a long time in one place as in life, and actors had to learn to adapt to this new idea. There had to be an end to sets with angled walls, the whole false perspective bit. There had to be real dirt, not simulations. There had to be slovenly speech. If there was to be jazz, then it had to be real jazz and not show-tune jazz. If there was to be real speech, then there had to be real profanity; the word "shit" would have to be said, not once but again and again and again until audience ears got used to it.[33]

There was a "roughness" to the acting of the Living Theatre that had been present almost from the beginning but that with *The Connection* began to coalesce into a signature style. The actors were, by Beck's own admission, "awkward, untutored, unconsciously defiant of the conventions which portray the people who live in democracies, who are rational, good, well-balanced, and who speak museum verse."[34] While this willful disregard of actor training reached a point by the 1970s in which an actor's political beliefs and position within the Living Theatre community outweighed any regard for talent, it was, in the late 1950s and early 1960s, an invigorating and inspiring liberation from the conventions and restrictions of both classical and "method" acting, which then dominated. Just as the Living Theatre rejected the Aristotelian concepts of form, it similarly rejected Aristotle's directive concerning appropriate language and diction. Thanks in part to the Beat poets, the "vernacular, idiomatic, rhythmic … cadences of actual talk … the actual spontaneous mind of the moment,"[35] as Allen Ginsberg described it, began to replace the carefully crafted dialogue of stage speech. This technique borrowed from jazz and opened the door for non-speech sounds and music-like speech within stage performance. But whereas the slurred speech and casual mannerisms of Marlon Brando and the Actors Studio actors, by the late 1950s, had gone from shocking technique to easily parodied stylistic conceit, the Living Theatre actors seemed at the time to embody an acting indistinguishable from life. The actors in this production were praised for their intensity, discipline, and believability.

But the realism in the production of *The Connection* began to raise questions for the Becks. The musicians were real musicians, some of whom *did* get stoned during the performance. Was this acting? Which was better? And what of the improvisatory aspects? An improvising actor, even within the constraints of character and plot matrices, is still responding spontaneously in real time and space. For the Becks, this was often more interesting – and more true – than even the best traditional acting. Ultimately, though, they felt that *The Connection* was deceptive. "Here we were, night after night, lying to the audience," confessed Beck. "We were lying to the audience that this was a bunch of junkies who were haphazardly collected on stage to make a movie ... And in fact many members of the audience were taken in; that was the worst of it!"[36]

Thus the irony of *The Connection* was that while it was one of the most illusionistic pieces of American theatre ever produced, it launched the Living Theatre on its journey toward the elimination of fictional characters and space on the stage. It was the first step toward a theatre in which the actors presented themselves as themselves on a stage that represented a stage. Obviously, neither improvisation during a performance nor actors as themselves was new in the theatre. But such devices had almost always been framed within a strong fictional or dramatic matrix or else removed from conventional drama, as in a cabaret performance. In a 1972 essay entitled "On Acting and Not-Acting," Michael Kirby argued that acting was not an absolute category but an activity that could be measured along a continuum; that audiences perceived certain behavior as acting because it was contained within a theatrical context or matrix.[37] The Living Theatre actors began to explore acting on different points of the continuum, an exploration both provoked and enhanced by the advent of Happenings.

While some people focused on the thematic importance of *The Connection* – Tallmer, for instance, saw it as an exposure of the world of heroin with its "tired knowing endless deep-freeze of detumescence and utter hopelessness" – and while *The Connection* was still illusionistic, it was a watershed event that launched American theatre in a new direction. Brustein, looking back, remembered that it "changed my mind about the theatre – what it was and could be. Not simply because of the text ... but what this meant as a theatrical event, produced by people who had somehow managed in this one play to break down barriers between what was going on onstage and what was going on in life."[38] In its slow pace, its lack of action, its jazz structure, and its chipping away at centuries of fourth-wall illusionism, the play was laying the groundwork for a new era in theatre.

Happenings

The Becks' association with John Cage and several of the artists who would create Happenings led them deeper and more resolutely into what might be called non-objective theatre. In 1960, almost a year after *The Connection*, and after a production of Pirandello's *Tonight We Improvise*, the Living Theatre presented a Cage-inspired evening called *The Theatre of Chance*, which included *The Marrying Maiden* by Jackson MacLow and *The Women of Trachis*, adapted by Ezra Pound from Sophocles. The catch-all title was really a bit of a stretch, since the latter play fell into the category of chance only because Heracles' death is a result of fate. But the six-scene MacLow play was a pure chance-theatre composition derived from the methodologies proposed by Cage. As MacLow explained in his introduction:

> The action of the play and its total performance time are completely indeterminate, but the order of the scenes, of the speeches within the scene, and the delivery of the speeches (in regard to speed, loudness, manner, and pauses) are relatively determined by explicit notations.
>
> All determined aspects of the play – including the names and number of the characters, the amount each character speaks in a line, their actual speeches and the regulations of the delivery, the titles and number of the scenes, the particular characters and the types of words used in each scene, the lengths of scenes and the order of speeches within them – are the results of chance operations rather than of choices (whether conscious, preconscious, or unconscious) of the author.[39]

Using the *I Ching*, as well as a book of a million random digits, a dictionary of folklore, and a standard dictionary, MacLow came up with the nine characters and the text. Although the play bore a structural resemblance to a conventional play – there were named characters, dialogue, and a scene structure – it proved baffling for anyone looking for narrative, theme, or just traditional dramatic coherence. Rather, it might be termed a concrete poem for the stage. A few lines from the opening of Scene 1 give some sense of the play. Words in parentheses indicate tone, words above the line indicate speed, and the musical notations below the line indicate volume.

moderate

A MERCHANT AND STRANGER: (*obviously*) Gathering (*calculatingly*)

f

moderate
together would not helpers influence wooing furthers furthers

pp   *pp*

slow
THE RULER: (*reminiscently*) Return (*gigglingly*) The It furthers not

pp   *f*

coming

The play continued in this vein for forty typed pages. Because there were no directions for action, Malina created the character of a dice thrower and an "action pack" of cards with instructions for physical activities. Based on the roll, the dice thrower would hand an actor a card before he or she spoke. The actors would never know in advance what their action might be. In addition, a roll of five would result in "music" being played. The music, created by Cage, consisted of a recording of the dialogue, sometimes distorted, sometimes not. The result was that recorded and spoken text sometimes overlapped and sometimes existed in counterpoint. "Things were beginning to happen on our stage which had never happened before," explained Malina a few years later. "Each performance was different from the next, and the production was a notorious failure. We insisted on keeping the play in repertory for almost a year, usually playing it only once a week, usually to no more than ten or twenty persons. Not arrogance, but a stubborn belief that we needed the play, we the company, that it had something to teach us if only we could stick with it."[40]

Clearly, the play broke loose of narrative, character, psychological motivation, literary style, intentional mood, theme, message – in other words, almost everything we associate with theatre. Form and object, cause and effect were sundered; Aristotelian structure was abandoned. And yet it was, by Cage's broad definition, theatre. Here were actors, on a stage, in front of an audience, speaking a written text whose order remained unchanged from performance to performance. The piece was so radically different from anything that had ever been put on the stage that it forced the members of the Living Theatre, and the few brave audience members, to re-examine the whole concept of acting, directing, and playwriting. In fact, for spectators willing to enter into the spirit of the play, there were often moments of startling effect – as when a clear and coherent sentence emerged from the bewildering text – and great pleasure in the sound and rhythms as the lines between theatre, music, and dance blurred.

While many of their Off Broadway colleagues were experimenting with neo-symbolist explorations of the subconscious or with absurdism, the Living Theatre was following the lead of contemporary visual art in rejecting conventional form and structure. In part through the influence of Happenings, in part through the influence of John Cage (and through him Gertrude Stein and Antonin Artaud), this rejection of narrative structure and psychologically based characters that had dominated virtually all Western theatre would be abandoned. If theatre had traditionally functioned as a mirror of society, the new theatre structured around sound, movement, form, and object – would function as an extension of the everyday world. It would create a situation analogous to the paintings of Jackson Pollock, in which, according to Allan Kaprow, "the artist, the spectator and the outer world are ... interchangeably involved."[41]

The piece generally acknowledged as the first Happening was Kaprow's *18 Happenings in 6 Parts* in 1959. The immediate impetus for the creation of Happenings was a 1956 class on experimental composition taught by Cage at the New School for Social Research in New York. The class attracted more poets and artists than composers and included Jackson MacLow, Dick Higgins, George Brecht, Al Hansen, and Kaprow, all of whom would go on to create Happenings or related events (see Chapter 6). Cage taught them about the ideas of chance and indeterminacy as well as introducing them to Artaud's conceptions of a unique theatrical language of sounds and objects and Gertrude Stein's conception of landscape drama. For Kaprow, Cage's ideas and inspiration combined his own work on environmental sculpture and his fascination with Pollock and Duchamp, as well as with Dutch painter Piet Mondrian, on whom he had written his master's thesis. Looking back on the origins of Happenings, Kaprow outlined their line of descent from cubist collage:

> With the breakdown of the classical harmonies following the introduction of "irrational" or nonharmonic juxtapositions, the Cubists tacitly opened up a path to infinity. Once foreign matter was introduced into the picture in the form of paper, it was only a matter of time before everything else foreign to paint and canvas would be allowed to get into the creative act, including real space. Simplifying the history of the ensuing evolution into a flashback, this is what happened: the pieces of paper curled up off the canvas, were removed from the surface to exist on their own, became more solid as they grew into other materials and, reaching out further into the room, finally filled it entirely. Suddenly there were

jungles, crowded streets, littered alleys, dream spaces of science fiction, rooms of madness, and junk-filled attics of the mind.[42]

The term "Happening" was first used by Kaprow almost offhandedly in his article on Pollock. In attempting to answer the implicit question of what path art should follow in the wake of Pollock's near total break with Western artistic traditions, Kaprow suggested the abandonment of traditional painting altogether. Artists must turn to "space and objects of our everyday life," he declared.

> either our bodies, clothes, rooms, or, if need be, the vastness of Forty-Second Street. Not satisfied with the *suggestion* through paint of our other senses, we shall utilize the specific substances of sight, sound, movements, people odors, touch. Objects of every sort are materials for the new art: paint, chairs, food, electric and neon lights, smoke, water, old socks, a dog, movies, a thousand other things which will be discovered by the present generation of artists. Not only will these bold creators show us, as if for the first time, the world we have always had about us, but ignored, but they will disclose entirely unheard of *happenings and events* [italics mine], found in garbage cans, police files, hotel lobbies, seen in store windows, and on the streets, and sensed in dreams and horrible accidents.[43]

He proposed, in other words, using the materials of life to create the sensations of life – no illusions, no substitutions, no simulacra. Theatre, in a sense, had an advantage over the plastic arts in that it already used bodies, space, and time to create its art. The new artistic sensibility fused with the vocabulary of theatre to create a new form.

A 1959 issue of the *Anthologist*, a literary review published at Rutgers University, where Kaprow taught art history at the time, contained a scenario for an event entitled "Something to take place: a happening."[44] Kaprow proposed a massive environment – a space 500 by 350 feet and 20 feet high. There would be colored bands on the floor and colored chairs, a "cubic framework covered with transparent plastic film," changing lights, a projection screen, and loudspeakers for recorded sounds. Fourteen groups of silver and yellow chairs were to be arranged randomly so that spectators would face in a variety of directions. At various times during the performance, the spectators were to change seats according to numbers on their entry tickets. Some of the directions read: "a young boy goes to a striped pole of

black and white hung with red lights and grasping it SHAKES for a
while like a victim of palsy returning to his seat when he wishes"; "an
artist dressed in white duck sneakers and dress shirt sits on a red stool
in the center of the enclosure and lights NINETEEN WOODEN
MATCHES blowing them out in turn slowly without great movement"; "a nude girl painted all white emerges from some doorway and
walks to a long white and red bench ... She lies down on it as an odal-
isque raises her eyebrows shoulders drawn up mouth slightly set but
apart (very stiffly and blankly) breath indrawn gets up after a few
moments and walks back to the doorway and out."

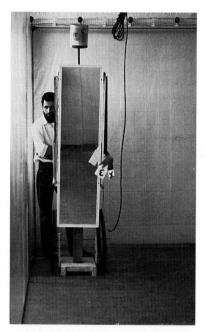

Plate 4 Allan Kaprow with the "sandwich man" from his 1959
Happening, *18 Happenings in 6 Parts*, at the Reuben Gallery, 61
Fourth Avenue, New York. The construction had mirrors front
and back with a paint can for a head and wooden arms, one
with a hand that held cards. There was a phonograph inside
the "body" on which a polka was played. The object moved on
bicycle wheels without tires and was pushed by a performer
from one "room" to another during the performance; the
phonograph was plugged in once the construction was rolled
into a room.

Photo: © Fred W. McDarrah.

In October 1959, an adaptation of this script, now entitled *18 Happenings in 6 Parts*, was presented at the Reuben Gallery in Manhattan. The gallery was divided into three rooms by partitions of translucent plastic on wooden frames; a collage covered one wall. Chairs were arranged in each room – the first room had a series of red and white lights, the second a single blue light globe, and the third a series of white and blue lights. The audience members were handed cards upon their arrival that indicated the "cast of participants" and had instructions noting that the performance would be divided into six parts, with each part containing "three happenings which occur at once."[45] These "happenings" consisted of disparate, seemingly random, activities as well as slide projections and electronic sounds broadcast from speakers.[46] The beginning and end of each part was signaled by a bell. The cards contained careful instructions for changing seats, which ensured that the audience composition in each room would be different for each part. When Kaprow began creating environments in the mid-1950s, he had realized that the viewers moving through the spaces were moving, colored shapes, qualitatively no different from the other materials in the sculpture. They also added unplanned elements of speech and sound. Thus, Kaprow believed, the spectators were as much a part of the art work as the creator and the inanimate objects, and at the Reuben Gallery the "cast of participants" included "The visitors – who sit in various chairs." The performers, who were artists, not trained actors, had been painstakingly rehearsed; they moved simply and directly, their faces remained neutral and unin-flected. (The popular notion that Happenings consisted of spontaneous and unplanned activity was never true. Although some Happenings allowed for indeterminate action – improvisation of a sort – they were carefully scripted and detailed and generally well rehearsed.)

The Happenings that were created by a dozen artists over the next few years varied in their use of space and the degree of incorporation of the spectators, the specific methods of composition and the degree of aesthetic control exercised by the artists, and what they were called (Kaprow regretted that his use of the term became a catch-all for this type of art), but they were similar enough that they could be identified as a genre. Michael Kirby, in his book *Happenings*, arrived at a succinct definition of the form: "a purposefully composed form of theatre in which diverse alogical elements, including nonmatrixed performing, are organized in a compartmented structure."[47] The action, speech, images, and sounds contained within the performance were independent of logical analysis; the performers, except in rare instances, wore street clothes, did not create characters or any psychological or motivational basis for their behavior – they carried out tasks as determined by the script in as neutral a way as possible; and the performance, though broken into sections analogous to scenes in a play, was more like a series of sealed compartments – no information was passed from one scene to the next.

If Happenings had remained within the world of art galleries and had been seen as mere extensions of environmental sculpture and action painting, then their importance for theatre might be negligible. But such events were seen as theatre by both creators and viewers and they thus called into question the basis of Western drama. Just as plastic artists had for a half century been calling into question the nature of the space of the canvas and the frame and challenging the supremacy of the objective image, and just as writers were challenging the dominance of meaning over form and even the relationship of the text to the page, now the theatre was questioning dramatic structure and theatrical meaning. Unlike the absurdist dramas, which remained within the framework of Western drama and thus pushed gradually at its confines, Happenings, at one stroke, shattered all rules and expectations. Happenings framed the materials of the everyday world and emphasized their "everydayness." The Living Theatre would put these ideas into practice in *Mysteries and Smaller Pieces*, the first original production of their European "exile."

Mysteries and Smaller Pieces

After the *Theatre of Chance*, the Living Theatre produced another Gelber play and two by Brecht. Then in 1963 the company produced Kenneth H. Brown's *The Brig*, its biggest critical success. The play depicted the brutalizing and dehumanizing regime of a Marine prison. Malina's production was seen as an example of Artaud's Theatre of Cruelty, and she also allowed for a degree of improvisation in the creation and performance of the piece. But while the theatre's reputation for theatrical innovation was growing, it was falling deeper and deeper into debt, including owing many thousands of dollars of back taxes to the Internal Revenue Service and months of back rent to a remarkably lenient landlord. None of the productions was extravagant by any stretch of the imagination: the actors received a mere $45 a week, and the theatre's policy of repertory – it was virtually the only true repertory theatre in the country – allowed it to keep "hit" shows like *The Connection* in performance. Nonetheless, a combination of fiscal naivete and paranoia about the capitalist system and government policies meant that the company was in constant financial straits. Finally, in 1964, the theatre was padlocked by IRS representatives. There was a famous sit-in – the actors refused to leave the theatre, and audiences climbed in over the rooftop and through a window to see performances. Standing in the midst of protesters with a megaphone, Richard Schechner interviewed Judith Malina for the *Tulane Drama Review* from the street.[48] The Becks' mastery of civil disobedience allowed them to turn the government action into a rallying cause for freedom of the arts. Interestingly, though, while most of the theatrical community admired the work of the group and many sympathized with their leftist politics, and all bemoaned the closing of a unique company, the general response was that the Living Theatre had brought this catastrophe upon itself through fiscal ineptitude and foolish decisions.

The Spring 1964 issue of *TDR*, which was to have contained simply the text of *The Brig*, grew to include a section on the demise of the Living Theatre. Schechner wrote to a wide range of theatre companies and organizations asking for their response to the closing of the theatre; several of the responses were published. It is important to understand that during the 1950s – the same period in which the Living Theatre was evolving – the regional theatre movement, or the Resident Professional Theatre movement as it called itself, was also developing, largely with grants from the Ford and Rockefeller foundations, grants that were, for various reasons, withheld from the Living Theatre. These theatres had carefully nurtured audiences and supporters, put a great deal of time and energy into fundraising, and were generally proud of the way in which they balanced their artistic and financial needs. Needless to say, all of them were more traditional than the Living Theatre and more driven by audience and box office demands. The most detailed response to the closing that *TDR* received from these theatres came from Herbert Blau and Jules Irving, producing directors of the Actor's Workshop of San Francisco, which at the time was probably the most innovative theatre group outside New York city. (Blau and Irving would go on to become directors of the Repertory Theatre of the Lincoln Center in 1965.) "We have no brief for the bureaucrats, and we are often enough depressed by the conspiracy of mediocrity in American culture," they began. "But the closing of the Living Theatre seems to us an open-and-shut legal case, however regrettable ... Free expression does not depend only on the number of soapboxes around, but on the scrupulosity with which we use the ones we have." They went on to note the Catch-22 of foundation (or government) funding, that even as they themselves were faced with bankruptcy, they continued to pay taxes. "We were bailed out of *our* predicament by that most cunning of bureaucratic maneuvers – subsidy by the Ford Foundation," they admitted. "We should have known the ruse for what it was, for we nearly went bankrupt on a larger scale. Even now we are demoralized – looking every gift horse in the mouth."[49]

Julian Beck spent some time in prison for tax evasion, then joined the company in its self-imposed exile in London, where it performed *The Brig* before going to Paris, where the American Center for Students and Artists offered the group space in return for a free performance. Preferring not to present scenes from works in progress, or to recreate *The Brig*, the group prepared a new piece entitled *Mysteries and Smaller Pieces* – the title was invented by Malina as a reference to the Eleusian mysteries of ancient Greece – presented on October 26, 1964.[50] Nothing quite like it had ever been seen. The piece – it cannot be called a play – consisted of nine scenes of five to fifteen minutes duration. It was created collectively by the company; there were no costumes other than the actors' street clothes; there was no set other than four boxes at the start of Part Two. Although the company believed that the piece made a political statement through its references to militarism and capitalism, *Mysteries* was, to all intents and purposes, a Happening.

Part One began with an actor revealed onstage in rigid military posture. Critic Gordon Rogoff, writing about the first American production of the piece at Yale University in 1968, remarked, "There is every reason to suspect that he will stay in this posture indefinitely, all night, perhaps forever. Impossible, of course, but maybe they are just sane enough to try."[51] After several minutes in which nothing happened, the audience invariably began to react – growing restless, shouting at the immobile figure, even throwing things. A lone, motionless actor did not, for most spectators, constitute theatre. At an appropriate moment, determined by the actors who had been waiting behind the audience, the performers began to jog down the aisle onto the stage and launch into a mime sequence based on the bed-making and floor-cleaning routines from *The Brig*. This was carried out both on the stage and in the audience. As an imaginary bucket of water was thrown, six to twelve actors scattered throughout the theatre begin to recite the "Dollar Poem," an abstract poem derived from all the words and numbers printed on a dollar bill. The scene ended with more rigid military movements. As all the actors fell into rank, the one portraying the corporal barked an unintelligible sound, to which all answered, as in *The Brig*, "Yes, Sir!" Out of the ensuing blackout, a woman accompanied by guitar began to chant a Hindu *raga*. The chant went on for about ten minutes, improvised at each performance. The Living Theatre saw the *raga* as something pleasurable for the eyes and ears as well as an attempt to create an integrated community of actors and audience through the peaceful and meditative sounds.

The next section, "The Odiferie," was dedicated to the sense of smell. The actors lined up on stage with sticks of glowing incense, seen at first in the darkness. The house lights were brought up and the performers moved slowly through the auditorium, becoming part of the audience. This was followed by "Street Songs," an incantatory poem by Jackson MacLow based on the chants of the anti-war and civil rights movements ("Stop the war," "Freedom now," "Free the blacks," etc.). There was no fixed order to the text, which was decided by the performers at each performance. The intention was to get the audience to respond and participate so as to merge with the performance. The fifth section was "The Chord," derived from an exercise developed by the Open Theatre, an offshoot of the Living Theatre (see Chapter 4). For the chord, all the actors formed a circle with their arms around each other. Out of the breathing a hum emerged, which led to responsive sounds from all the actors. "Out of this humming and listening comes an open-throated sound," explained the text. "It grows. It rises. The sound gets high and carries everyone up with it. Unification of the community." After ten minutes or so, the "chord" faded and "audience and performers drift into audience space." The Open Theatre used this exercise as a tool for unification within the ensemble, but the Living Theatre transformed the exercise into a performance piece. For the final section of Part One, the performers sat cross-legged in a line across the stage facing the audience. Passing a roll of toilet paper among themselves (often seen as scandalous in parts of Europe), they blew their noses to clear the breathing passages and began a yoga chant.

Part Two began with the "*Tableaux vivants*," in which performers assumed a series of different postures inside four wooden compartments, while their faces expressed a range of emotions. The positions and expressions were created spontaneously for a total of seventy-two *tableaux*. The next section was derived from another Open Theatre exercise, a sound-and-movement exercise. The ninth and final section

Plate 5 Mysteries and Smaller Pieces in a 1995 revival in Bologna, Italy. With (l. to r.) Gene Ardor, Judith Malina, Judi Rymer, Johnson Anthony.

Photo: Nancy Motta. Courtesy the Living Theatre.

was derived from Artaud's essay on the plague. In dim light, the actors groaned and writhed as if in the grips of the plague. Slowly they "died." Six actors, as doctors or survivors, removed the shoes of the actors and lined them up at the front of the stage (an image that evoked the Nazi death camps) and piled the stiff "corpses" into a pyramid as the lights faded. However, this section was a later addition. At this first performance, "Sound and Movement" was followed by a nearly three-hour "free theatre." The actors began to play an organ that was in the theatre and to create sounds with every element and part of the theatre they could. The audience joined in, so that totally unstructured and chaotic activity consumed the stage, auditorium, lobby, and surrounding street. Beck later explained that the group was trying to move away from conscious interpretation on the part of the actor to arrive at a "state of inspiration" and to bring the audience into the creative act.[52] The "free theatre" ending was never used again, but "The Plague" often inspired audience participation, and some spectators would "die" in the aisles. If they remained rigid when picked up, the actors would add them to the body pile. At a performance in Amsterdam, some audience members grew hostile and attempted to get the "corpses" to respond by burning them with cigarettes and even throwing an actor into a canal adjacent to the theatre.

Although *Mysteries and Smaller Pieces* included fragments of characterization in the *Brig* section, some "acting" – the "Dollar Poem" was to be spoken in a "loud clear bored voice" – and some generalized social and political commentary, the piece was closer to ritual and participatory communal activity than to traditional theatre. Because it was done inside a theatre and proclaimed itself to be theatre, it was a provocative act on a par with Duchamp's "ready-mades." This production suggested that all that separated theatre from life was the frame or matrix in which the event occurred. In mingling the performers and spectators and their respective spaces, even the frame was called into question. Those intellectuals and artists who had formerly supported the Living Theatre in its experiments, and who reveled in the challenge to accepted notions of theatre, were suddenly challenged themselves to accept something that seemed to defy the very *raison d'être* of theatre. Jackson Pollock's action paintings were ultimately acceptable because at the end there was a finished product that could be hung on a wall like any other painting. A play like *The Connection* ultimately left a script, memorable characters, some wrenching emotion, and socially relevant themes to discuss. *Mysteries*, however, was like an action painting with no canvas; it seemed to leave the component elements of the theatre in their raw form, forcing the audience to create its own framework and its own meanings. The spectators could no longer rely on their habitual responses to conventional theatre. Gordon Rogoff, writing about the Yale presentations, opined:

> The Living Theatre is now the most beautiful acting company in the world. Their bodies are supple and totally available to them, clean, sculptured, at ease, without the steel-spring hardness of dancers. Their presentational energy is boundless, their engagement in the smallest action total and large (with exceptions, of course). Their voices can be hoarse, but their breathing is open, expansive, loaded with reserves. They are more comfortable now in scenes with the audience than in scenes with themselves. They are radical, but they feel like a family. They play menace all the time, but their aggressions are deeply gentle, They keep reminding me of my vulnerabilities: the lassitude of my body, the protective clutter in my mind. They are beautiful, I suppose, because they don't look like actors.[53]

Although the Living Theatre returned to at least partially narrative texts in the following years, it never again returned to illusion, the fourth wall, or actors fully subsumed within characters. The influence of the pre-European Living Theatre was already making a mark on American theatre, as was the ensemble work of the developing Open Theatre. But when the Living Theatre returned to the USA with thirty-two European and American actors in the fall of 1968 with productions of *Mysteries*, *Antigone*, the ensemble-created *Frankenstein*, and *Paradise Now* – a piece structured somewhat like *Mysteries* – the company changed the face of American experimental theatre permanently. The productions, particularly *Mysteries* and *Paradise Now*, provoked responses not unlike those for Jarry's *Ubu Roi* at the Théâtre d'Art in 1896. As W.B. Yeats said in response to that production, "after us, the savage god."

The Living Theatre continued a nomadic existence after the 1968 American tour. It went to Brazil in 1970, back to the USA in 1971, and to Europe in the mid-1970s. The company returned to New York in 1984, and Julian Beck died the following year. The Living Theatre has continued to produce in New York and elsewhere to the present day. Although admired for its tenacity and its political commitment, and revered for its historical importance, it has had no real impact on avant-garde or experimental theatre in the United States since the early 1970s. But its legacy of communal creation, formal experiment, integration of performance and audience, and its revising of the art of acting has resonated throughout virtually all postwar alternative theatre in both the United States and Europe.

Chapter 4

The 1960s: collectives and rituals

> As I look back, what stands out for me ... is the spirit of that time: a
> dare-devil willingness to 'try anything', the arrogance of our
> certainty that we were breaking new ground.
>
> Yvonne Rainer[1]

The motionless actor who began the Living Theatre's *Mysteries and
Smaller Pieces*, who stood defiantly silent, staring at the audience, for
over six minutes, signaled a departure. Much postwar theatre had grap-
pled with the disintegration of language as a means of communication,
but now words were being emphatically renounced in favor of the
eloquence of silence and the expressiveness of the body. "I use the
words you taught me. If they don't mean anything anymore, teach me
others. Or let me be silent," says Clov in Samuel Beckett's *Endgame*.[2]
In the midst of the increasingly ineffective onslaught of language, the
Living Theatre actor's wordless defiance – an Artaudian confrontation
of the physical performer and the spectator – was intended to jolt the
audience into a new awareness. As Susan Sontag has observed, "Silence
administered by the artist is part of a program of perceptual and
cultural therapy, often on the model of shock therapy rather than of
persuasion."[3]

In the 1960s, the festering dark underside of the American century
– racial inequality, poverty in the midst of plenty, the threat of nuclear
holocaust, and ultimately political assassinations and the disastrous
involvement in Vietnam – bubbled to the surface as the nation faced
civil rights demonstrations, race riots, anti-war marches, acts of anti-
establishment violence, and the emergence of a so-called
"counterculture," which was the product of the youthful rebelliousness
and idealism of the demographically explosive "baby-boom" generation. At least some of the seeds of discontent that led to the massive

rejection of the status quo – not just in theatre but also in society at large – were sown by the French existentialists, notably Albert Camus, whose novel *The Stranger* was published in English in 1946. More so than the straightforward philosophical works of his contemporary Sartre, Camus' novels and essays appealed to American readers and created a sense of the absurdity of human existence in an alogical universe, and laid out the need for engagement in the issues of society in order to combat the alienation of daily life. These works became touchstones for a generation coming of age and seeking direction in the postwar years. However, while Europe and Asia had to confront the severe physical destruction, economic upheaval, and moral implications of World War II, the United States, despite its own significant losses, was relatively distanced from the most immediate effects and ravages of war. In the midst of unprecedented postwar prosperity, in fact, the sense of meaninglessness and alienation for Americans came not from the devastation of war and genocide but from rampant materialism. Existential philosophy may have informed the development of absurdist drama in France and elsewhere, but absurdism had little currency in the USA, at least until the early 1960s. Americans grasped the superficial form and style of this movement, and "absurd" became a popular noun and adjective applied to everything from politics and the human condition to commercial products. If the existential hero existed in the United States he was to be found in Hollywood, first with Marlon Brando in *The Wild One* (1954) and then James Dean in *Rebel without a Cause* (1955) – a title with echoes of Camus. Both films embodied a spirit of nihilism but, particularly in *Rebel without a Cause*, it was placed firmly within the confines of the "affluent society." The development of the avant-garde in the 1960s became inextricably bound up in the political and social sensibilities and upheavals of the decade, while a general spirit of iconoclasm, mixed with a gentle spirituality and a romantic longing for rituals that might re-instill a sense of meaning in an apparently disintegrating society.

The new theatre movement was also fueled by an influx of young theatre artists. Members of the very same baby-boom generation that was altering the economic, political, and social fabric of the country were beginning to flood into a theatre that did not have the capacity to accommodate them. While much of the new theatre of the 1960s was generated by strong artistic goals and a real desire for new forms of expression, much was also the result of what might be termed an excess labor pool seeking to create its own artistic outlets. By the time the Living Theatre left for Europe in 1964, there was a thriving alternative and experimental performance movement in New York and a few other outposts, notably San Francisco, where Jules Irving and Herbert Blau founded the Actor's Workshop as early as 1952 to explore the new European repertoire with innovative productions, and where a young actor named R.G. Davis created the San Francisco Mime Troupe (initially the R.G. Davis Mime Troupe) in 1959. As early as 1960, *Village Voice* critic Jerry Tallmer coined the term "Off Off Broadway" to describe the loose conglomeration of theatres springing up in coffee houses, storefronts, lofts, and churches, mostly in the Greenwich Village and East Village sections of New York city. But it came to stand for any theatre outside the mainstream doing the unusual, the daring, or the provocative – usually on a shoestring budget. The spirit was precisely captured in a 1967 *New York Herald–Tribune* obituary for Joe Cino, founder of Caffe Cino, which is generally considered the first Off Off Broadway theatre: "Twice each night, and sometimes three times, the Caffe Cino presented the outrageous, the blasphemous, the zany, the wildly poetic, the embarrassingly trite, the childish and frequently, the moving and the beautiful."[4]

Caffe Cino opened in December 1958 in a coffee house at 31 Cornelia Street in Greenwich Village. Its minuscule stage was initially used for readings of classic and modern plays, but by 1962 original works were being produced, its most famous alumnus being playwright Lanford Wilson. The Off Off Broadway theatre scene soon migrated from Greenwich Village to what became known as the East Village – the upper portion of Manhattan's Lower East Side immediately to the east of Greenwich Village. It was bounded roughly by 14th Street to the north, Broadway to the west, Houston Street to the south, and the East River. Unlike Greenwich Village, with its town houses, quaint shops, and winding tree-lined streets, the East Village was made up largely of tenements populated mostly by Eastern European immigrants. The low rents and inexpensive coffee shops and ethnic restaurants made it attractive for the new wave of "immigrants" – artists looking for affordable space and, by the mid-sixties, the hippies, who replaced the Beats as the new anti-establishment generation. Second Avenue, which was a major thoroughfare through the neighborhood, had also been the home of the so-called "Yiddish Broadway" in the earlier part of the century, and a few of the Yiddish theatre buildings still provided functional theatre space, although most of the Off Off Broadway theatres were created in lofts and storefronts. Other Off Off Broadway theatres included Take 3, Café Manzini, Phase 2, the Old Reliable, Café LaMaMa, Judson Poets Theatre, and

Theatre Genesis. The latter three in particular became the most significant, and LaMaMa still thrives, known today as LaMaMa Experimental Theatre Club. Playwright Sam Shepard remembered a sensibility that separated Off Off Broadway not merely from Broadway but from the bourgeois society that Broadway represented.

> On the Lower East Side there was a special sort of culture developing. You were so close to the people who were going to the plays, there was really no difference between you and them – your own experience was their experience, so that you began to develop that consciousness of what was happening … People were arriving from Texas and Arkansas in the middle of New York City, and a community was being established. It was a very exciting time.[5]

The schism between the establishment and the counterculture became embodied in the geography of Manhattan: mainstream was "uptown," alternative was "downtown." The dividing line was 14th Street, the cross-town street that marked the northern border of both Greenwich and East Villages, and to go north of 14th Street was to enter the enemy territory of shallow materialism. (A mile to the south of the villages lay Wall Street – the anti-establishment culture thus saw itself as an island surrounded by hostile territory.)

The Off Off Broadway theatres had to contend with restrictive city licensing and occupancy laws, so some of them styled themselves as private clubs. Café LaMaMa in particular followed this route. The weekly ads in the *Village Voice* were labeled "Club News" and gave no address. Patrons had to fill out membership cards and when calling for reservations identified themselves as club members. This approach not only circumvented certain restrictions but also created an atmosphere of belonging to a secret society – going to these theatres carried a sense of participating in surreptitious activity. The venues were unusual enough that even the locals were not always aware there was theatre in their midst. Ellen Stewart, for instance, began LaMaMa in her semi-basement storefront on East 9th Street, where she also sold her own fashion designs. Neighbors, seeing customers going into a black woman's establishment at night, called the police assuming it was a brothel.

Actors Equity Association, believing that the Off Off Broadway movement was a repetition of the Off Broadway phenomenon, thought it was protecting its members by trying to impose the Off Broadway contract on the Off Off Broadway theatres. The costs and restrictions would have killed the movement instantly. Ultimately, Equity relented and created the Showcase Code, which to this day allows Equity actors to rehearse for two weeks and appear for up to sixteen performances in approved productions in return for carfare.

There was a democratic, communal spirit to this new movement that distinguished it from its Off Broadway predecessor. Although many of the theatres were dominated by the personality of their founders – Cino, Stewart, Al Carmines at Judson Poets Theatre, Ralph Cook at Theatre Genesis – there was an amazing lack of artistic shaping or control. The producers chose playwrights or directors mostly on the basis of instinct and let them produce their works – hundreds a year – without interference. The free-for-all spirit of Off Off Broadway also meant that most of the rules of structure and the conventions of content were treated with abandon or simply ignored. The dizzying montage of action comics, the bizarre and rapid juxtapositions of television, and the repetitive and driving rhythms of rock 'n' roll (most often heard in the context of the manic monologues of radio disk jockeys, whose patter overlapped the songs), all provided new paradigms of structure, rhythm, and content for the new drama.

Because a considerable portion of the Off Off Broadway repertoire and style seemed to flout mainstream practices and aesthetics, it became synonymous for many with the term "avant-garde." But much of the alternative fare was not avant-garde at all. In retrospect, in fact, much of it reads as rather conventional and even sentimental, its initial shock value having derived from then scandalous subject matter or a structure that owed more to television than to the nineteenth-century well-made play. But the capaciousness of the Off Off Broadway world was capable of containing a true avant-garde theatre as well. In general terms, the avant-garde theatre of the 1960s could be divided into two broad categories. One branch was the formalist work to be found in performance art and the creations of Jack Smith, Richard Foreman, Robert Wilson, and others that was informed by Happenings, Cagean aesthetics, and influences from other arts (see Chapter 5). But another branch – the one most popularly associated with the 1960s – was founded on an Artaudian search for a non-literary theatre and a non-verbal means of communication.

This latter avant-garde was most often identified with theatrical collectives – sometimes referred to as ensemble theatres – consisting of associations of actors, playwrights, and directors dedicated to the creation of new work and innovative approaches to the production of existing work. Although sharing some traits with the older models of collective theatre, such as the Provincetown Players or the Group Theatre, there were significant differences. While the earlier groups had allowed for deeper and richer explorations of texts than were possible in commercial theatre, and for the development of a coherent acting style, the structure of these companies had tended to remain that of any conventional producing organization: actors performed playwrights' scripts under the guidance of a director for a producer. What made the new ensembles different from their predecessors was the ostensible elimination of this organizational structure, the self-consciously non-hierarchical creative process, and often a belief in the collective as a model for their social and political philosophies. An ensemble theatre was, at least in the ideal, a communal enterprise with no absolute leader. This arrangement meant the lack of not only an autocratic director but also the hegemony of the playwright, whereas the older groups were always identified with the work of one or more playwrights: O'Neill or Odets, for example. The ensembles of the 1960s, however, such as the San Francisco Mime Troupe, the Bread and Puppet Theatre, the Performance Group, the Manhattan Project, the Teatro Campesino, and the Open Theatre were identified with energetic acting styles and collectively created works exploring contemporary mythology and politics. In rejecting the primacy of the playwright's text, these companies tended to diminish the role of language – at least language as a primary means of expressive communication – replacing it with an Artaudian vocabulary of physicality, sound, and imagery. The ideal collective theatre production was created not from a pre-existing script but from thematic explorations of an idea by a closely knit ensemble of actors through improvisations and theatrical exercises. (The reality rarely lived up to the ideal. Most groups functioned more on the model of the totalitarian phase of communism: there was a collective of actors, but the groups tended to have autocratic, even dictatorial, leaders in the form of visionary directors, who, in essence, replaced the playwright as the creative fount for texts.)

Language

The ability of words to communicate and to convey ideas was compromised in the post-Holocaust, post-atomic age. Language had become "worn, threadbare, filed down," wrote Arthur Adamov. "Words have become the carcass of words, phantom words; everyone drearily chews and regurgitates the sound of them between their jaws."[6] If the language of the theatre was no longer viable, then a new language had to be found, a situation already anticipated by Artaud, who had forecast the semiotic meltdown. "If confusion is the sign of the times," he declared, "I see at the root of this confusion a rupture between things and words, between things and the ideas and signs that are their representation."[7] *The Theatre and Its Double* was, in essence, a call for the replacement of spoken/written language with a new language and a new vocabulary, a "concrete language, intended for the senses and independent of speech" in which "the thoughts it expresses are beyond the reach of the spoken language."[8] Artaud went on to declare that "in this theatre all creation comes from the stage, finds its expression and its origins alike in a secret psychic impulse which is Speech before words."[9] Artaud's strategy was to create a theatre that would speak directly to the spectator on a physical, vibratory level.

Spoken, literary language was not abandoned in the collective theatre of the 1960s, but words became simply one tool among many in an expanded theatrical vocabulary. As playwright Jean-Claude van Itallie observed about the Open Theatre's *The Serpent*, "Words are part of this ceremony, but not necessarily the dominant part, as they are not the dominant part either in a formal religious ceremony. The important thing is what is happening between the audience and the action."[10] The rejection of conventional language, in fact, seemed more in keeping with the romantic or symbolist attempt to express the inner truth hidden by the manifestations of outer reality. Just as certain forms of modern art shifted the focus of painting from the narrative content of objective images to the fundamental vocabulary of form, line, and color, so the Open Theatre and others shifted from conventional verbal story-telling to the actors' vocabulary of the body, movement, and sound to express emotion and convey content. It is important to note that the shift toward non-verbal communication was not a move toward non-semiotic performance – that is, an elimination of recognizable code systems. Non-verbal or non-text-based theatre was an attempt to replace conventional language with equivalent forms that, it was believed, would create a more direct and honest form of communication. "We work on exercises using sounds and movement in 'give-and-take' rather than in words," explained Open Theatre director Joseph Chaikin.

When we do use words we try to understand the unexpressed in the situation – not in a logical way, but rather through behavior's irrational and more fragile qualities. Inner truth is not a fixed thing. The word "reality" comes from the Latin *res*, which means "that which one can fathom." This challenge of the unspeakable in a natural situation may be that when a character is drinking water he is wondering if there is a God. When we locate the inside of a situation in its abstract and elusive texture we then try to make this thing *visible*.[11]

The erosion of language as a means of communication can be traced to the avant-garde movements in Europe at the turn of the century: the poetry of the symbolists, the distorted sounds of the expressionists, the "transrational" language of the Russian futurists, the "Merz" poems of Kurt Schwitters, and the work of the dadaists, who divorced words from their referents and objects from meaning. In postwar America, the subversion of language began, ironically, with the Actors Studio, whose emphasis on emotional truthfulness in acting led to a slurred and mumbling style of speech first popularized by Marlon Brando in *A Streetcar Named Desire* and reinforced in the popular culture a few years later in the movie *The Wild One*. It stood not only in stark opposition to proper stage diction but also in opposition to the proscriptions of proper societal behavior. To speak badly was to defy authority, and it was a rebuff to the sometimes duplicitous eloquence of political leaders. Anti-language was a response not only to the irrationality of war but also to a materialist society run amok, where culture was being shaped by television advertisements and situation comedies. As philosopher George Steiner suggested, "The English spoken by Mr. Eisenhower during his press conferences, like that used to sell a new detergent, was intended neither to communicate the critical truths of national life nor to quicken the mind of the hearer. It was designed to evade or gloss over the demands of meaning."[12]

But for the postwar generation, the disintegration and transformation of language also owed much to the development of rock 'n' roll. With roots in African-American rhythm and blues, rock 'n' roll exploded on the scene in the mid-1950s with Bill Haley's *Rock Around the Clock*, popularized by the movie *The Blackboard Jungle* (1955), and the appearance of Elvis Presley on the *Ed Sullivan Show* in the fall of 1956, which transformed American popular culture in one evening. Almost overnight, the arbiters of popular taste had shifted from the middle-aged middle class to rebellious white youth drawing on black-inspired music that was raucous, raw, and pulsating with a barely concealed sexual energy. The language of rock 'n' roll was usually simplistic and, even with the three-minute format of most songs, repetitive. It often relied on nonsensical syllables, grunts, half-articulated and distorted words, and sounds that functioned more as percussion and rhythm than as communicative vocabulary. While historically, nonsensical choruses could be traced back to Aristophanes' *The Frogs* and was common in popular song from medieval madrigals to modern times, the use of rhythmic choruses in rock music was foregrounded and became the essence of the song. The message seemed to be that proper language was insufficient and it was incapable of communicating the pain, anger, heartbreak, or simple confusion of teenage angst.

However, a more quantifiable influence in the theatre could be found in the work of Jerzy Grotowski's Polish Laboratory Theatre. For instance, they adapted Wyspianski's *Akropolis* to express the horrors of the Nazi death camps. "All means of vocal expression [were] used," literary adviser Ludwig Flaszen explained:

> starting from the confused babbling of the very small child and including the most sophisticated oratorical recitation. Inarticulate groans, animal roars, tender folksongs, liturgical chants, dialects, declamation of poetry ... The sounds are interwoven in a complex score which brings back fleetingly the memory of all the forms of language. They are mixed in this new Tower of Babel, in the clash of foreign people and foreign languages meeting just before their extermination.[13]

And a decade later, British director Peter Brook would take an international company of actors through parts of West Africa searching, among other things, for a common language of the theatre, one that could communicate without dependence on a shared spoken language – "without the help and hindrance of the shared cultural signs and tokens"[14]

The search for new forms of language in the avant-garde theatre of the 1960s inevitably led to a concurrent attempt to create new myths and rituals in the belief (naïve as it turned out) that these ceremonial-like activities and quasi-religious enactments would create new communities that would serve as an antidote to the perceived failures of modern society. This impulse can be traced back at least to Richard Wagner, whose ideas served as the romantic basis for much of the avant-garde. Wagner believed in the ideal of Greek art, which served to unite the society into a single community. Wagner's goal was to recreate the Athenian sense of community in the modern world: "The individual man … can experience no higher need than that which is common to all his kind; for, to be a *true* Need, it can only be such an one as he can satisfy in Community alone."[15] The ideal of community was to be achieved at least in part through a rejection of the strictures of modern civilization and by finding a means of reunification with nature, a theme that would be echoed throughout the avant-garde for the next century. "The theater must make itself the equal of life," proclaimed Artaud,

> not an individual life, that individual aspect of life in which CHARACTERS triumph, but the sort of liberated life which sweeps away human individuality and in which man is only a reflection. The true purpose of the theater is to create Myths, to express life in its immense, universal aspect, and from that life to extract images in which we find pleasure in discovering ourselves.[16]

In both Wagner and Artaud there resides a fundamentally sentimental and nostalgic desire for a return to a presumably more innocent time of undifferentiated humanity living in a harmonious state. By recreating (mostly non-verbal) rituals and by tapping into images from – to borrow Jung's phrase – the collective unconscious, performance could function almost as a religion to lead the community of spectators back to this paradisiacal state. Clearly, this is what John Lahr believed the Open Theatre had achieved with its production of *The Serpent*, which he described as "primitive' ritual":

> *The Serpent* aspires to the most holy (and fundamental) theatrical impulse – to return the actors and the audience to an intuition of the primordial state and a fuller comprehension of the immediate moment, retracing (to understand) the myths which shape Western consciousness.[17]

While the degree and explicitness of political engagement varied from group to group and production to production, all of them had a fundamentally socio-political aim of altering spectator consciousness through an essentially Artaudian strategy of theatre that "provokes the most mysterious alterations in the mind of not only an individual but an entire populace."[18] Most of the actors and directors of these ensemble theatres would have agreed further with Artaud that "the true theatre … disturbs the senses' repose, frees the repressed unconscious, incites a kind of virtual revolt ... and imposes on the assembled collectivity an attitude that is both difficult and heroic."[19] Implicit in such a strategy is the sense of community – a community of spectators and performers acting upon each other. If in fact some transformation of the spectators' consciousness were to occur, then it was essential that the audience become part of the performance, if not on a physical level then at least on a spiritual. In one of his earliest interviews about the Open Theatre, director Joseph Chaikin set forth a manifesto that was clearly influenced by the aims and goals of the Living Theatre, but which emphasized the new communal direction:

> [The goals are] to redefine the limits of the stage experience, or unfix them. To find ways of reaching each other and the audience. To encourage and inspire the playwrights who work with us. To find ways of presenting plays and improvisational programs without the pressures of money, real estate, other commercial considerations which usurp creative energy. *To develop the ensemble.*[20]

The Open Theatre

The Open Theatre was born, Athena-like, from the Living Theatre. In its relatively short life, it had the greatest effect upon acting training in the United States since the Stanislavsky-inspired innovations of the Group Theatre of the 1930s. In addition, the group's artistic leader, Joseph Chaikin, could be seen as part of an international triumvirate of innovative theatre artists that included Polish director Jerzy Grotowski and British director Peter Brook. While much of the early work of these three developed independently along similar tracks, there was ultimately communication between them and a sharing of techniques and ideas, which led to a change in approaches to acting, directing, and production in both Europe and the United States, thereby creating something of an international avant-garde style.

Chaikin joined the Living Theatre in 1959 and after several small roles took over the part of Leach in *The Connection.*[21] He achieved real recognition, however, in 1962 as Galy Gay in the Living Theatre's production of Brecht's *Man Is Man.* His initial attraction to the Living Theatre had nothing to do with its aesthetic; rather, as a young actor, he would take any job that might bring him visibility, and the Living Theatre was a "hot" company in the late 1950s. He was amused and baffled by the Becks' political passions, but the environment of an ensemble company and its political engagement slowly penetrated, and he admits to an epiphany during *Man Is Man* as he spoke his lines at each performance:

> There I was, night after night, giving all my attention to pleasing, seducing, and getting applause from the audience, which is the very process wherein Galy Gay allows himself to be transformed from an innocent and good man into a thing, a machine ... I'd go every night in front of the audience, and I'd give Brecht's speeches. I would stand next to the coffin which my old self was supposed to be buried in, and I'd talk about life and death ... I'd do Brecht's lines again and again, and it made me *earnest* in a certain sense ... All the while the Becks were doing the protest demonstrations, and I started to go along ... I started getting busted at peace things and sit-ins, and I felt a profound link with Brecht. And I felt enormously fulfilled in the performance night after night; no part has ever meant so much to me ... I got to the point where I was really talking to the audience, as Brecht would have it.[22]

His earlier goal of commercial stardom seemed hollow, and he became devoted to an art theatre as epitomized by the Living Theatre. At the same time, he was frustrated with the Becks' lack of concern and attention to acting training and, more important, the inability of many of the actors to enter into roles that required anything but a method or Stanislavksy-based naturalism. Here was a theatre devoted to exploring and creating new forms, but the actors possessed few tools to achieve this end. In a sense, Chaikin's realization of the inadequacies of contemporary acting training and styles in the face of new forms of drama was not unlike Stanislavsky's sixty years earlier. Only now, Chaikin was rebelling against a system dominated by interpretations (and misinterpretations) of Stanislavksy. The Off Off Broadway movement had been fairly successful at nurturing new playwrights, but it had done little to develop new styles of presentation.

Chaikin began to lead workshops at the Living Theatre as early as 1962, but the chaotic atmosphere of the theatre militated against any coherent process. In 1963, however, he was approached by a group of actors who had been working with acting teacher Nola Chilton, whose Stanislavsky-inspired approach was tempered by theatre games and improvisations that, she believed, would make the training more useful for the new absurdist drama and other non-American – i.e., non-realistic – forms. When Chilton left for Israel, the actors from her workshop wanted to continue their training and asked Chaikin to join. This group of seventeen actors and four writers, some from the Living Theatre, would become the nucleus of the Open Theatre.

Chaikin had in fact taken a class with Chilton when he first came to New York, and he had also spent one summer in Chicago taking a class with Viola Spolin, whose work with theatre games was instrumental in the creation of improvisatory comedy groups such as Second City and The Compass Players. The group went through some inevitable upheavals and transformations as it tried to discover its identity. Chaikin said that the name "Open Theatre" was ultimately chosen because "it was an unconfining name, it implied a susceptibility to continue to change … to stay in process."[23] As Chaikin and his explorations came to dominate the group, some of the original members left; others joined. Informed from the beginning by the Living Theatre, Brecht, and Artaud, the members of this new group were as much concerned with socio-political questions as with acting training. The fundamental explorations concerned the relation of the individual to society and Chaikin's sense of the alienation of the individual in the modern world – but also his sense of the inadequacy of language to deal with these questions.

Psychologically based acting training – the foundation of American naturalism – proceeds from an exploration and understanding of the emotions and motivations of the character with the belief that appropriate physical responses and gestures will follow. However, the Chilton- and Spolin-inspired exercises developed by Chaikin were based on physical interactions between performers, with an emphasis on physical transformation. From such exercises, Chaikin evolved what amounted to the fundamental vocabulary of the Open Theatre – the sound-and-movement exercises. In its basic form, sound and movement were done by pairs of actors. One actor would begin a movement, accompanied by a sound that emanated directly from the movement. Both movement and sound had to be clear, precise, and focused. These gestures were not meant to mimic a particular behavior or action or to express identifiable emotions; they were pure actions and sounds. The second actor would recreate the sound and movement. Once the action was absorbed, the first actor would drop out and the second actor would transform the sound and movement, preserving the underlying form and dynamics, into his or her own. This sound and movement could be passed on and transformed through the whole company. Many variations of this basic exercise were developed, including the "machine," in which actors joined the group one by one, each remaining instead of withdrawing, adding complementary sounds and movements to create a kind of abstract machine. These exercises required acute concentration as well, since the act of transformation worked only if the initial action was fully understood and kinesthetically absorbed.

It is the idea of transformation that may have been the Open Theatre's most significant contribution to the American theatre and that took both acting and playwriting into new territory. The Living Theatre had succeeded in eliminating conventional notions of character on the stage, instead allowing the actors to perform as themselves. The Open Theatre reverted to a concept of character, but a character that was infinitely transformable. The actor was always present within the context of the script and could transform from character to character, even character to object, *ad infinitum*. This meant that the actor was not concerned with "becoming" a character in a psychological or emotional sense, but in embodying physical and vocal characteristics appropriate to the demands of the moment. Truth and consistency were thus a result of what Chaikin called "the presence of the actor." By presence he meant that quality that emphasizes the liveness of the actor and the sense of shared experience between audience and performer. "It's a quality that makes you feel as though you're standing right next to the actor, no matter where you're sitting in the theatre ... It's a kind of deep libidinal surrender which the performer reserves of his anonymous audience."[24]

Ironically, however, Chaikin was ambivalent about public performance within the Open Theatre, which he saw as an acting laboratory, not a performance group. For all his own former interest in performing, for all his belief in the power of theatre as a transmitter of ideas, he believed that the success of the Open Theatre as a training ground for actors was dependent on the almost monastic quality of the group. The moment an actor began to create and perform with an audience in mind, Chaikin felt, the honesty and freedom disappeared; the actor's goal became to please the spectator.

(In the early days, their "monastery" was a loft on 24th Street that provided a retreat from the stresses of the city. The actors supported their endeavors with monthly dues of $5 each. By the late 1960s, the group was increasingly supported by grants and by 1970 was operating on an annual budget of $100,000, part of which went to paying actors between $20 and $75 a week and providing health insurance.)

The exercises developed over the first few years were focused on trust and the development of an ensemble. One of these, the Chord (described in the previous chapter) became the company's signature piece in the early days. As Robert Pasolli explained in his book on the group, "The chord affirms the Open Theatre as a collective. In it, the actor perceives the group as an entity of which he is a part. He experiences 'I' in 'it,' rather than 'you' or 'them.' The actor is in the group, but alone in it; the chord does not submerge his ego but subsumes it."[25] Just as many of these exercises aimed to create an ensemble without a clearly defined leader, so the Open Theatre itself strove for leaderless direction. While Chaikin was, from the very start, the acknowledged leader and the guiding force behind all that was done, he refused to accept any formal acknowledgment of that position. (Peter Feldman, an early member of the company who ran many of the workshops, was often listed as co-director.) Similarly, though the company had playwrights from the very beginning – Maria Irene Fornes, Megan Terry, Michael Smith, and Jean-Claude van Itallie were among the early members – this was not a playwright- or script-driven theatre. Ideas emerged through the improvisations and explorations of the actors and were later molded and shaped into performances by the playwrights.

Many of the exercises had an innate theatricality, and the desire of the actors to perform was strong. From time to time they invited friends to the loft to watch presentations of the exercises, and in December 1963 and April 1964 they presented public performances at various Off Broadway theatres. The program note for one performance summarized the general social and artistic discontents of the period:

> This group of actors, musicians, playwrights and directors has come together out of a dissatisfaction with the established trend of the contemporary theatre. It is seeking a theatre for today. It is now exploring certain specific aspects of the stage, not as a production group, but as a group trying to find its own voice. Statable tenets of this workshop: (1) to create a situation in which the actors can play together with a sensitivity to one another required of an ensemble, (2) to explore the specific powers that only the live theatre possesses, (3) to concentrate on a theatre of abstraction and illusion (as opposed to a theatre of behavioral or psychological motivation), (4) to discover ways in which the artist can find his expression without money as the determining factor.[26]

Typical of the presentations at the time was "An Airplane: Its

Passengers and Its Portent," structured by van Itallie out of group exercises. It began with the performers embodying parts of an airplane. They then transformed into passengers, a stewardess, and pilots – each a comic stereotype. As mechanical problems developed with the plane the pilot parachuted out, leaving it to crash; the play turned serious as the characters confronted mortality. The pilot returned in a death mask, and the actors transformed into parts of the plane disintegrating as it fell to earth. The piece ended with the actors lining up at the front of the stage as the dead staring at the audience. In retrospect, the piece seems melodramatic and facile, but the juxtaposition of the satiric-comic with the serious and tragic, and the implication of the spectators in the indictment of the superficiality of daily life, would become trade-marks of much of the group's work.

Despite Chaikin's reluctance to expose the group to public scrutiny, the performances were extremely well received, leading to increasing pressure to create and perform more. This inevitably increased the tensions between those who wished to remain an acting workshop and those who believed in using the acting exercises and explorations as a means for developing and presenting scripted public performances.

Plate 6 A scene from "Motel," part of Jean-Claude van Itallie's *America Hurrah*, in the original 1965 production directed by Michael Kahn at Café LaMaMa. The large "doll" costumes and masks were created by Robert Wilson.

Photo: Phill Niblock. Courtesy of the LaMaMa Archive.

Despite these struggles, or perhaps because of them, some notable productions emerged at this time. *America Hurrah*, three thematically related pieces by van Itallie ("Interview," directed by Chaikin, and "TV" and "Motel," directed by Jacques Levy), was presented at the Pocket Theatre in November 1966 and was even selected for the *Best Plays of 1966–67*. The pieces examined the perceived emptiness and underlying hostility and violence of American society. At the same time, Megan Terry was conducting workshops with Open Theatre actors based on improvisations around media accounts of the Vietnam War. The resultant production, a collection of vignettes entitled *Viet Rock*, culminated with actors moving into the auditorium and touching the spectators, this being based on philosopher Herbert Marcuse's idea that increased social interaction was a viable means of addressing social problems. After workshop productions at Yale and LaMaMa, the play opened at the Off Broadway Martinique Theatre to generally poor reviews complaining that the play was preachy and strident. Although Chaikin had been involved during the development, he withdrew his support for the production prior to opening, and there was no mention of the Open Theatre in the program. Like a rock group in which the musicians go their separate ways, the rift caused several members to leave and led to a restructuring of the theatre.

Vowing never to work commercially again, Chaikin reorganized the ensemble. He selected a company of actors from Open Theatre veterans and members of a workshop run by member Lee Worley, eventually coming up with eighteen. Working in a 14th Street loft reached by long, dingy stairs, the reconstituted company began a workshop exploration of the Bible in October 1967 with the original goal of exploring the life of Jesus. Out of this came the production of *The Serpent*, which, in its content, theme, method of creation, and style of performance, was one of the most significant productions of the era and a paradigmatic ensemble creation.

The actors had to commit to a schedule of four hours a day, four days a week. Their outside commitments, including jobs, could not take them away from the workshop for more than two weeks during the year.[27] With a $5,000 grant from the National Endowment for the Arts, Chaikin was able to hire specialists to work on physical training, particularly voice (with Kristin Linklater), dance and movement (with Joseph Schlichter), and singing (with Richard Peaslee). Grotowski came to speak to the group in November, and his leading actor Ryszard Cieslak demonstrated some of the exercises that the Polish Laboratory Theatre had developed.

The company began its work by reading the book of Genesis, whose stories, myths, and questions became so fascinating that the original plan was shelved and the group focused on Genesis alone. They researched mythology, anthropology, and the work of biblical historians. They invited scholars, including Joseph Campbell, Susan Sontag, and Paul Goodman, to address the workshops. Knowingly or not, they were moving toward the mythological and non-literary theatre proposed by Artaud. In the published text, *The Serpent* was subtitled a "ceremony" and Robert Pasolli, describing the performance in a *Village Voice* article, noted that "a ceremony is a way of expressing things held to be true by all those present, but not accessible through discourse or rational disclosure."[28] Or, as the Chorus of the play says, "Whatever I know, I know it without words."

For an audience to participate in a ceremony or mythological creation, there must be a common experience shared between all the spectators and between spectators and performers. In 1968, the book of Genesis could still safely be assumed to be shared knowledge – if not necessarily shared belief – among the spectators. But the most common shared experience for American audiences, perhaps for world audiences, was the 1963 assassination of President John F. Kennedy, which was fresh and vivid in the minds of most in the audience. Since much of Genesis, the group felt, had to do with violence and its effects, the immediacy of *The Serpent* was found in connecting Biblical events with current events. In 1966–67, an Open Theatre workshop led by Jacques Levy had developed a scene based on the Zapruder film – the amateur movie that is the only visual documentation of the Kennedy assassination and which has been repeated frame by frame on television, searing it into the public consciousness. A version of this improvisation would find its way into *The Serpent*.

The evolution of the production embodied the contradictions and problems of ensemble creation. The emphasis in the workshops was on the process of discovery – much as Adam and Eve must have experienced – and the realization that everything was a "first." The company worked on creating the animals in the Garden of Eden, ultimately coming up with half a dozen mythological creatures. An inevitable problem arose, however. Improvising animals was one thing, but once humans were introduced into the garden, dialogue had to follow. The actors had attempted to write some scenes themselves, but these were not working well. Finally, Megan Terry, Patricia Cooper, and van Itallie were brought into the process and by January, van Itallie alone was writing, aided by Roberta Sklar, who had joined as assistant director and dramaturg. There is virtually no dialogue in any conventional sense in *The Serpent*; there is what van Itallie called "incantation." "The problem with Adam and Eve was how do you get them to speak," explained van Itallie, "The moment you have actors and actresses open their mouths in a naturalistic fashion, you've lost their mythic potential. How do godlike figures speak? How do images which are larger than life speak? The sound has to carry a lot of grandeur or extend a stage image."[29] Wanting to avoid the pressures of opening the new work in New York, the group agreed to a European tour from May to July 1968, performing in Italy, Germany, Switzerland, and Denmark. But once a commitment had been made to do the tour, the workshop process of gradual development was overshadowed by the need to develop a finished product. The play evolved in Europe and then back in the United States, in part in response to current events (the assassinations of Martin Luther King, who was killed a month before they sailed, and Robert Kennedy, who was shot while they were touring), in part in response to the audience reaction to the performances. Although there is a published version of the script, the production was never frozen.

The play began with the actors warming up on the stage and amidst the audience. They were generally wearing jeans and tee-shirts and were barefoot. The warm-up provided a Brechtian affirmation of the presence of the actor and lack of illusion and was intended to connect the life of the actor to the life of the audience by showing the performance as a continuous aspect of the actor's life. In the opening, at the end, and at least once during the performance there was movement by the actors into audience space and an attempt to engage the spectators spiritually, if not physically, in the performance. But the Open Theatre never seemed fully comfortable engaging the audience on this level. It did not possess the spirituality of the Bread and Puppet Theatre, which began each performance with a ceremonial sharing of bread with the audience, nor were they as aggressive as the Performance Group, which actively engaged the audience through a destruction of the boundaries of spectator space.

The warm-ups evolved into a procession, which slowly transformed into an autopsy scene and then into a sequence of assassination scenes. The Kennedy assassination was broken into a sequence of twelve movements, all painfully well known to everyone of the era from the Zapruder film and re-enacted in various orders as if in a non-sequential stop-action film. Fragments of King's "I have a dream" speech were interpolated into the scene, as was the repeated action of Robert

Kennedy smiling, brushing his hair back, and then holding out his hand to shake hands. Slowly the crowd began to chant, "I was not involved, I am a small person, I hold no opinion, I stay alive." The scene built to a crescendo, then subsided into rhythmic breathing.

As a chorus of four women came downstage, the other actors were forming the creatures of the Garden of Eden. Five of the male actors formed a combined tree and serpent made of writhing arms and legs, apples in each hand, accompanied by darting tongues and hisses. Eve, who had been lying on top of Adam, sat up and opened her mouth in amazement, but the scream she emitted came from the Chorus, who "are also Eve." Gradually, the entire company became the serpent, and dozens of apples were rolled across the stage and offered to the audience. This was followed by a scene of God's delivery of curses destroying the paradisiacal state. Contrasting Biblical imagery with the present, this scene was followed by a choral "confessional." Each Chorus member in turn spoke a few lines, such as, "I hugged my

Plate 7 The Serpent. The actors representing a combined Tree of Knowledge and the Snake offer apples to Eve (Tina Shepard).

Photo: Courtesy the Open Theatre Archives, Department of Special Collections and Archives, Kent State University.

child/And sent him off to school/With his lunch in a paper bag/And I wished he would never come home," followed by a sudden bright smile. Many of these "confessions" were taken from statements made by the performers themselves in meetings with van Itallie. According to van Itallie, "the guilt of the apple is something every one of us carries around. The speeches of the women in the Chorus are intended to indicate what it is like to be alive now. It's very hard."[30]

The story of Cain and Abel followed. The Chorus narrated the story as two actors mimed the events (while other actors mimed Abel's sheep). The scene proceeded from the idea that Cain did not know how to kill and tried various methods before he succeeded. But once he has achieved his goal he wants Abel to live again, for Cain in his anger wanted to kill Abel, but, as the Chorus says, "it did not occur to Cain/That killing his brother/Would cause his brother's death." Critic Ross Wetzsteon described Cain's desperation as "the most profound and terrifying image of murder I've ever seen in the theatre, and one in which, in their desperate unity, murderer and murdered become a kind of black and violent pieta."[31]

The penultimate scene was the "Begatting." As the actors began slowly to explore each other's bodies, the Chorus began to recite the "begat" sequence from the Bible, which traces the descendants of Adam and Eve through Joseph. The physical explorations became increasingly energetic as the actors mimed various copulations – it was funny, ecstatic, and joyous. Following a "climax," there were mimed births and a mimed sequence of the growth of children into old age, until there was a line of "old people" facing the audience. The play ended as the actors moved around the stage. "Each is overtaken by a slow kind of dying, not so much a physical one as a kind of "emptying out." They stopped, experienced a final tremor, and then rose to sing "a sentimental song" – "Moonlight Bay" was selected – as they left the stage walking through the audience. The original ending was more open and attempted a greater involvement of the audience but created uncertainty instead – audiences did not respond, or if they did the actors would not always know what to do. Chaikin summed up the intent: "The ultimate value of even a temporary community of people – that of the audience and actors – is to confront our own mortality."[32]

Following the group's return to the USA there was a single public performance of *The Serpent* in December, which disappointed the company. The script was reworked, and the official US premiere was at Harvard University in January 1969. Through the year they performed it at various colleges, at their loft, on a second European tour, and in

May 1970 at Washington Square Methodist Church, which had provided a home for several avant-garde productions, including Grotowski's American performances. The play received laudatory reviews from both the mainstream and alternative press, and it received an Obie Award.

The Open Theatre created three more pieces – *Terminal* (1969), *Mutation Show* (1971), and *Nightwalk* (1973) – before disbanding in December 1973, a little more than ten years after its founding. Despite the acclaim that its work gathered, the Open Theatre, or at least Chaikin, had never overcome the discomfort with the idea of public performance. Furthermore, public performance meant that the laboratory or workshop process that was the Open Theatre's *raison d'être* had to grind to a halt while the company went into production mode. Following the formal dissolution of the group, Chaikin resumed workshops with some Open Theatre actors and became involved in several other projects. Some of his most notable collaborations over the next two decades were with playwright Sam Shepard.

While the work of the Open Theatre, especially prior to 1969, was better known within the theatre community than by the theatre-going public at large, some Artaud-inspired ensemble work achieved more popular notice. This awareness came first through the Royal Shakespeare Company's 1966 Broadway production of *Marat/Sade* directed by Peter Brook, and then through the work of director Tom O'Horgan with the LaMaMa company. Although O'Horgan's productions of Rochelle Owens' *Futz* (1967), Paul Foster's *Tom Paine* (1968), and the highly commercialized *Hair* may have lacked some of the rigor and theoretical foundation of the Open Theatre work, they proceeded from similar sources. Nonetheless, O'Horgan's work gained notoriety because of the somewhat scandalous nature of the sexual-erotic content, the seemingly orgiastic physicality, and the occasional near or full nudity. Clearly, it was not simply the thematic content that disturbed audiences; after all, many plays had questioned contemporary mores, social structures, and political systems. Traditional political drama that attacked the status quo through dialogue and rhetoric could be easily applauded without upsetting the complacency of a spectator sitting comfortably in the dark. But in the new productions, audiences were confused over the relationship of the performers to the content – were these actors or were these people on the stage part of some cult, religion, or belief system that, if allowed outside the walls of the theatre, would be a dangerous influence? Furthermore, the literary aspects were subsumed under an intense and provocative physicality. The actors were not "acting" nudity, they were naked; they were not acting orgiastic rituals, they were, or so it appeared, participating in them right in front of the audience; and at times these seemingly dangerous individuals broke through the fourth wall and entered audience space. The revolutionary possibilities of theatre – its liveness – created either acute discomfort among the spectators or cult-like worship. Whether supportive of the new productions or disdainful, the audiences seemed to have difficulty in distinguishing performance from life, which was often the desired effect.

The Performance Group

The most notorious and far-reaching of these efforts came from the Performance Group, which grew out of a New York University workshop led by Richard Schechner in 1967. Borrowing performance techniques from the Open Theatre and Grotowski and drawing on Schechner's anthropological research into the nature of performance, the group developed a highly disciplined physical style as it explored Euripides' *The Bacchae*. Under the title *Dionysus in 69*, with the sexual connotation of the title fully intended, the group opened a ritualistic adaptation of the play in June 1968, which played until July 1969. As editor of the *Tulane Drama Review*, Schechner had been the harbinger, conduit, and sometimes origin of much of the theoretical foundation of the avant-garde, and the primary source of information on new performance for most American and even world theatre practitioners. While at Tulane in the early 1960s, Schechner had begun to experiment in his own productions and theoretical writings with what he would call "environmental theatre." On its most basic level, environmental theatre describes a production in which the setting actually or implicitly surrounds the spectators, thereby incorporating them into the same physical space as the performers.[33] The environment could remain essentially visual or architectural, in which case the spectators' involvement was primarily psychological; but more often, especially in Schechner's conception, the actors shared the same space as the spectators, and there was physical and verbal contact between the two.

In 1968, Schechner published "6 Axioms for Environmental Theatre," which combined elements of transactional analysis, Brecht, and Meyerhold as it explored the nature of the theatrical event both as a self-contained work of art and as an interaction with an audience:

> The theatrical event is a set of related transactions ... All the space is used for performance; all the space is used for audience ... The

> theatrical event can take place either in a totally transformed space
> or in 'found space' ... Focus is flexible and variable ... All produc-
> tion elements speak in their own language ... The text need be
> neither the starting point nor the goal of the production. There
> may be no text at all.[34]

Schechner was setting out not merely to disrupt traditional understandings of the nature of theatre but to explore and re-situate the role
of the spectator in relation to the performance. He saw traditional
theatre as a "closed system" because it was not possible for the audience to enter into the performance – to engage the performers –
without destroying the art work in the process. This is the problem
that the Open Theatre had encountered in its experiments with audience participation. Other groups allowed limited participation, often at
the start of a performance, through some ceremony meant to convince
the audience that they were participants – the Bread and Puppet
Theatre's sharing of bread, or the Manhattan Project's production of
Alice in Wonderland (1970), in which the audience entered the seating
area by ducking through a small entrance analogous to the rabbit hole
– but quickly re-established conventional boundaries once the performance proper was underway. The Performance Group was attempting
to alter the very nature of performance. "Participation," explained
Schechner, "is not about 'doing a play' but *undoing* it, transforming an
aesthetic event into a social event – or shifting the focus from art-and-
illusion to the potential or actual solidarity among everyone in the
theater, performers and spectators alike."[35] As he noted about *Dionysus
in 69*, "participation occurred at those points where the play stopped
being a play and became a social event – when the spectators felt that
they were free to enter the performance as equals."[36] For Schechner,
environmental theatre was democratic theatre, and one of his goals was
to destroy theatrical illusion by making the spectators believe they were
equal to the performers.

Environmental theatre not only transformed the entire theatre into
a potential performance space, it also destroyed the unified focus of the
audience. Drawing upon the Cagean notion of art imitating life in its
method of operation, Schechner sought to create multiple points of
focus by presenting competing actions simultaneously so that no one
spectator could observe everything going on at any one time; each
member of the audience would have a slightly different experience of
the performance.

Dionysus in 69 was presented in the Performing Garage, a converted commercial space on Wooster Street in an industrial area of Manhattan that would soon become the chic neighborhood known as Soho (for *South* of *Hou*ston Street) as artists and then galleries took over vacant lofts left by departing industry. The space was cleaned, repainted, and rewired over a two-month period. Most of the actors had to work at various jobs to survive, and like their counterparts in the Open Theatre they paid dues to be part of the group. Schechner, who was the undisputed leader of the group, had a steady income from teaching at NYU and secured a $5,000 loan for the renovation. For the production, an environment of wooden platforms and towers was designed by Jerry Rojo. Spectators were encouraged to sit anywhere within the theatre, although they were sometimes asked to move if a space was needed for a scene. The performance was structured so that there were narrative scenes that told the story derived from the Euripidean text, and ritual-like scenes – such as the birth of Dionysus, the ecstasy dance following the birth, and the killing of Pentheus – derived from the myth or from descriptive speeches within Euripides' text but not found as action in the original play.

Upon entering the theatre, spectators were greeted by casually dressed actors, who spoke to them informally and helped to guide them to seats. Once the play began, dialogue and speeches mixed classical diction with the contemporary. Parts of the text were designed to incorporate improvised speeches by the actors in which they would talk about personal events that had happened to them that day. This latter component had a very disconcerting effect. Brecht had shown the actor behind the character, and the Living Theatre had eliminated the character, but the Performance Group actors were moving fluidly back and forth between character, themselves as actors, and – seemingly – their very real and informal selves confessing personal moments to strangers. At any given moment, spectators could be confronting the character Pentheus or an actor about whose life intimate details had just been disclosed. Separation of actor and character became impossible.

The lack of any traditional stage or seating area and the lack of clear spatial demarcations within the Performing Garage, the melding of actor and character, the nudity[37] and ritual activities, the encouragement to participate, the final procession into the street, even the location in a then desolate part of the city, all contributed to an experience new for most spectators. (The Living Theatre's post-exile American tour would not start until September 1968, more than three months after the opening of *Dionysus in 69.*) Some spectators assumed

Plate 8 The Performance Group's *Dionysus in 69*.

Photo: From the Richard Schechner Papers, Theatre Collection, Department of Rare Books and Special Collections. Courtesy Princeton University Library.

that the Performance Group was a kind of cult and wanted to join. Occasionally, the audience participation crossed acceptable boundaries as some male spectators took advantage of ritual-like scenes to join the action and fondle the female performers. The performers demanded that Schechner restructure these scenes more rigidly so that clear-cut and appropriate boundaries would be established. In other words, it became clear that if the audience was to participate in the performance, they too needed some sort of script. The loss of traditional boundaries and rules for audience behavior could also lead to near comic situations. At one performance, a group of college students kidnapped the actor playing Pentheus. The crisis resulting from the sudden loss of a central actor led to tense discussions and arguments among spectators and performers alike, and the show finally resumed after a teenager who had seen the performance several times volunteered to play the role. While Schechner admitted his exhilaration at the time that something "real" had occurred within the performance, the actors were far less sanguine. They were not prepared to deal with such massive and disruptive intervention by spectators. In *Commune*, a piece created by the group in 1970, audience participation was specifically built into the script and carefully structured. But even so, dependence on the acquiescence of the audience had its dangers, as demonstrated one night when the chosen spectators refused to participate and the performance ground to a halt.

These glitches in performance caused by the failure of the audience to participate according to the "script" points up a fundamental problem with audience participation and ritual-style (or, more accurately, faux-ritual) theatre. Theatre, by definition, is a presentation by actors to an audience. Even if the performance is largely improvised and malleable, the performers still approach the text with different knowledge, training, beliefs, and understandings than those of the spectators. They have a text of some sort (or "score" as Schechner and Grotowski referred to it), they have a shared experience, and they have – at least in a general sense – articulated goals and needs. The moment the audience enters in an uncontrolled, unscripted, and unguided fashion the performance must, perforce, collapse.

In para-theatrical performance, or performative activities, such as those found in certain religious rituals, weddings, funerals, civic festivals, and the like, there may be, properly speaking, no separation of performer and spectator, or else the spectators may have "roles" or clearly delimited participatory behavior. In true religious, communal, or ritualistic performance there is a shared experience in which everyone participates according to the historical customs and practices of the community – in other words, everyone, performer and spectator alike, knows the "script." But the spirit of rebellion of the late 1960s, and the emphasis on individual freedom – fostered particularly by the writings of R.D. Laing and Norman O. Brown – suggested the need to break down the supposedly restrictive elements of society, including all established conventions of performer–spectator interaction. The new theatre was specifically designed to allow the spectator to partake in some sort of spiritual experience. But the belief that such theatre was creating new communities or creating modern rituals was soon proved wrong. In the American society of the late 1960s (indeed, of the twentieth century), there was no common community with shared beliefs, shared experiences, or, most important, shared rituals. As Schechner himself admitted, the performance of *Dionysus in 69* "was often trans-theatrical in a way that could not last, because American society in 1969 was not actually communal."[38]

Schechner saw environmental theatre as political in the sense that encouraging participation "is to demand changes in the social order."[39] Had such theatre replaced the practices of mainstream theatre, it might ultimately have revolutionized aspects of society, but in retrospect it is clear that aesthetic and social conceptions would have had to alter before the theatre could change so fundamentally. Nonetheless, there was a brief period in which it seemed that a change in the theatrical order might be occurring. *Dionysus in 69* received surprisingly positive reviews from the *New York Times*, the heart of the establishment. More and more Off and Off Off Broadway productions began to experiment with environmental scenography, notably a production of Amiri Baraka's *Slaveship* at the Brooklyn Academy of Music (1970) and the imported *Orlando Furioso*, directed by Luca Ronconi in a huge inflated tent in New York's Bryant Park behind the New York Public Library. Environmental theatre even reached Broadway with the revival of *Candide* in 1974, in which designer Eugene Lee gutted a Broadway theatre and built the setting throughout parts of the auditorium. *Candide* succeeded not just because of the novel use of space but also because of the excellent Leonard Bernstein score and the high-quality production directed by Harold Prince. The few subsequent attempts at environmental theatre on Broadway fizzled due to poor scripts or productions. Once the initial novelty had faded, and without something of certified quality as a draw, audiences were, by and large, unwilling to forgo the security of assured seating and the safety of a darkened auditorium. The prohibitive costs of renovating Broadway theatres for environmental production quickly brought an end to the experiment.

Andrei Serban and LaMaMa

The ensemble theatre movement had essentially disappeared by the mid-1970s, but in a sense it went out with a bang. The work of Chaikin, Grotowski, Brook, and Schechner was brought together in what most agreed was a stunningly powerful production of three Greek tragedies under the title *Fragments of a Greek Trilogy*, directed at LaMaMa by a young Romanian director named Andrei Serban.

Described as an *enfant terrible* of the Romanian theatre, he was seen in Bucharest by Ellen Stewart, who brought him to LaMaMa on a Ford Foundation grant in 1969 at the age of 25.[40] Serban arrived in New York at the height of the counterculture "revolution," with the streets of the East Village filled with hippies, anti-war protests in full force, and the Off Off Broadway movement at its peak. Serban had been artistically radical in his homeland, but he was appalled at what passed for avant-garde in the United States (other than the Open Theatre, which he admired). "Coming here in the '60s and seeing the whole looseness of the avant-garde, where the idea was to be free in this very sentimental way, smoke drugs, let the hair grow – it seemed cheap to me," he recalled. "There's something in me more connected to discipline and intensity than to this freedom and looseness."[41] Serban was, in essence, paraphrasing Artaud, who defined his famous "Theatre of Cruelty" as "lucid, a kind of rigid control and submission to necessity."[42] The term "rigor" appears again and again throughout Artaud's "Letters on Cruelty," and it was this sense of rigor that Serban brought to the American experiment in the Artaudian avant-garde.

Serban's first LaMaMa creation was in fact an Artaud-inspired adaptation of the Elizabethan tragedy *Arden of Faversham*, which received glowing reviews and, just as important, the notice of director Peter Brook, who invited Serban to the International Centre of Theatre Research in Paris. Working with Brook here and on the production of *Orghast* at Persepolis in Iran in 1970–71, Serban was able to delve deeper into the ideas of Artaud and Grotowski as well as Brook's own work, some of which had traces of Chaikin's exercises. But the primary focus of Brook's work, the investigation that would have a significant effect on Serban's future work, was, Brook wrote, "a study of the structures of sounds. Our aim was to discover more fully what constitutes living expression ... We needed to work outside the basic system of communication of theatres."[43]

When Serban returned to LaMaMa in the fall of 1971, he began to work on Euripides' *Medea*. Over the next three years, he also developed productions of *Electra* and *The Trojan Women*, which would eventually be combined as *Fragments of a Greek Trilogy*. His guiding aesthetic was taken directly from Brook's *Orghast*, whose program contained the following questions:

> What is the relation between verbal and non-verbal theatre? What happens when gesture and sound turn into word? What is the exact place of the word in theatrical expression? As vibration? Concept? Music? Is any evidence buried in the sound structure of certain ancient languages?[44]

Serban included the same program note in the *Trilogy*.[45]

His four-month development of *Medea* was an exploration of how to communicate the power and passion of the play without the mediating influence of modern language. The production was done with not a word of English; it was performed using only the ancient Greek and Seneca's Latin version of the text, with an elaborate sound score created by a young composer, Elizabeth Swados, using, among other things, African drums, Filipino percussion instruments, and various metallic objects. Serban's rejection of recognizable language came from a desire to find the emotional core of the drama – something that was not merely hidden under inadequate translations but, he felt, impossible in a modern language whose relation to the emotions and to the very structure of society had become dulled. English was simply inadequate to convey the essence of Euripides. Serban explained his approach to language in an essay entitled "The Life of a Sound":

> The ancient Greek language is perhaps the most generous material for actors that has ever been written. At that time, poets felt the need to invent a poetic language to try to accomplish an enormous task: to send messages through words over great distances in a space open not only to the assembly of Athenian citizens but also to the sea, the air, and the stars. We can imagine, therefore, that these words must have carried within them a certain force and energy to make possible and sustain this contact. When we speak ancient verse, it is not only the rhythm which comes alive but the entire imagination which begins to stir in many directions. We try to see the images in the sound. We believe that we become those who first pronounced the words. Hidden vibrations start to appear, and we begin to understand the text in a way truer than any "analysis" would have afforded. It is not only the imagination but our entire being which lives through the words. It is a matter of discovering the paradox that the head, the heart, and the voice are not separate but connected with each other. The entire body is a complex, sensitive instrument which must be tuned if we wish to use it. For the sound to emerge properly, it is necessary to search for and become aware of a source, to find within oneself a support which allows the sound to grow. To develop the potential for a complete affirmation. Movement and voice rediscover one another in a common effort. Gesture and breathing exist mutually indispensable as the expression of a whole. This potential cannot be realized by means of any technique, but rather through the opening of a particular sensibility.[46]

Here was an attempt to achieve Artaud's "speech before language."

The subsequent parts of the trilogy included fragments of English, but also, in *The Trojan Women*, fragments of pre-Columbian languages.[47] The language became an aural score – the text was not fully comprehensible even to Greek and Latin scholars – with actors, particularly Priscilla Smith (who had also been in *Dionysus in 69*), generating non-verbal sounds that evoked the primitive and passionate aspect of the text. None of the pieces was intended as a literary narrative. Instead, as the critic for the *Soho Weekly News* commented, "You *feel* the meaning of the Greek text; you don't *hear* lines."[48] Swados' musical score was crucial in shaping the experience for the spectators. In both the *Medea* and *Electra* fragments, those in the audience could feel as if they were present at some kind of ancient ritual – not as participants *per se* but as privileged observers.

Serban also employed a form of environmental theatre. The original production of *Medea* was performed in LaMaMa's long, narrow base-ment rehearsal space. The audience entered through a candle-lit corridor, where the prologue was delivered; once inside the room, also lit primarily by candles, the audience was seated on benches along each long wall. The full trilogy was presented as the inaugural production of LaMaMa's new annex, a vast, converted television studio approxi-mately 100 by 40 feet and 30 feet high, with a proscenium at one end. In a setting designed by Jun Maeda, wooden scaffolds were erected along the side walls, somewhat like those at the Performing Garage. In *Medea* and *Electra*, the audience remained seated once they had entered the space, though the process of entering from the lobby and the staging and the environment implicitly incorporated them into the action. In *The Trojan Women*, the audience was encouraged to move with the action as it was performed throughout the space through the first half of the performance. As Helen, in a caged wooden cart, was dragged through the theatre, the audience had to scramble to get out of the way. After Helen's brutal and graphic humiliation and rape, the audience was asked to move to seats along the sides and on the scaf-folds for the remainder of the production.

Despite the proximity of actors and spectators, and despite the ritual-like aspects of parts of the production, and even despite the direct physical involvement of the audience in *The Trojan Women*, there was never any question of the audience joining in the action as they had with the Living Theatre and the Performance Group. (And even though the actress playing Helen was naked as she was pulled through the audience, there was never any question of audience members touching her.) Nor was there the sense of uncertainty that sometimes accompanied the Open Theatre's attempts at audience involvement. Serban's productions created a vibrant emotional connec-tion and intimacy through the staging, but it never violated the

Plate 9 *The Trojan Women*, from Andrei Serban's *Fragments of a Greek Trilogy* in a 1986 revival at LaMaMa E.T.C.

Photo: Gerard J. Vezzuso. Courtesy of the LaMaMa Archive.

implicit boundary between performer and spectator. It was an attempt, in modern times, to recreate the sense of connection with a powerful aesthetic, religious, and civic event that the Greeks might have experienced. The audience implicitly understood its role and responded accordingly.

The critics attested to the success. "The immediacy of Mr. Serban's theater," wrote *The New York Times* critic Clive Barnes, "far transcends the narrative notion of knowing what happens in any literary sense. Mr. Serban makes you feel such basic emotions as love, suffering, anguish, disgust, and fear, at a level not so far removed from reality."[49] Harold Clurman, writing in *The Nation*, declared that this was "the only effective and nearly complete application of Artaud's inspiration I have thus far seen."[50]

But following these productions there seemed to be no place further to go. Interestingly, Serban's next projects were with Brecht's *The Good Woman of Setzuan*, Shakespeare's *As You Like It*, and a controversial but landmark production of Chekhov's *The Cherry Orchard*, all of which required a concentration on text and language and a certain, more traditional, aesthetic distance for the audience. When Serban returned to the Greeks in his 1977 Lincoln Center production of *Agamemnon*, it was a more straightforward rendering of the text, and the actors were no longer part of an ongoing ensemble. And while some of the spectators were placed on the stage, they remained passive – it was the bleachers on which they sat that were moved about on air casters. The spectators were not observers or participants at a ceremony; they were on a carnival ride. Ensemble theatre had truly played itself out.

Conclusion

By-passing language or creating non-verbal means of communication had a cleansing effect in the theatre and served to revitalize the power of words. But, ultimately, language and clearly demarcated boundaries between performer and spectator re-emerged as necessary elements for those artists who wished to use the theatre to tell stories or convey specific ideas. Furthermore, collective theatre required the maintenance of a close-knit group of actors, and this was no longer economically viable. The cost of living in New York was escalating, actors needed steadier incomes, and theatres needed regular box office revenue. But more important, the tenor of the times had changed. The idea of community had been shattered by the Vietnam War and by racial tensions, which led some in the black community to call for racial separatism rather than integration. The rise of gay rights and the women's movement led to a further splintering of society and to what would come to be known as the politics of identity. There was no longer a single community but a collection of communities, often with competing and antithetical needs and goals. At the same time, the scandal of Watergate was contributing even further to a national mood of cynicism. Many of the pop philosophers of previous decades, who valorized emotions and the body, were now being derisively dismissed. Although the work of the Open Theatre and Serban's company at LaMaMa, through their deep commitment to ideals and through the rigor and professionalism of their work, managed to surmount much of the changing ideology, the general atmosphere was no longer ripe for continued exploration along these avenues. A formalist avant-garde, highly intellectualized and structured, and embodying the vision of individual artists, would emerge to take its place.

Chapter 5

Smith, Wilson, and Foreman

In 1968, the theater became hopeless.

Richard Foreman[1]

In the minds of many people, the Artaud-inspired physical and ritual-istic performances of the collective theatres became synonymous with the theatre of the 1960s. Even Robert Wilson, looking back from the 1990s, saw himself as a reaction against the dominant theatre of the time:

> I hated the theatre in the 60's ... What I was doing did not resemble the Living Theatre, The Open Theatre, or the Performance Group. I went against everything they were doing. I loathed the way their theatre looked. I had more in common with nineteenth-century theatre and vaudeville than with those groups. I was formalistic. I used the proscenium arch. My theatre was inte-rior, and I treated the audience with courtesy.[2]

Yet the formalistic theatre of chance and Happenings never really disappeared, and even before the ensemble theatre movement reached its peak in 1968 with the productions of *The Serpent* and *Dionysus in 69* and the Living Theatre's return from exile, a very different form of avant-garde theatre was emerging in the lofts of Soho. In November 1967, Robert Wilson performed a solo piece, *Baby Blood*, in his loft at 147 Spring Street, the former home of the Open Theatre – the group for which he had created the doll costumes for the "Motel" sequence of *America Hurrah* a year earlier. The performance, seen by only a handful of spectators, went undocumented save for the recollection – several years later – of a participant in the event. Spectators climbed to the loft up a staircase littered with "dismembered dolls' bodies." At the top a red-hooded figure, Andy de Groat, collected a $2 admission as people entered the dark room.

There was a wire with rings on it stretched in front and above the spectators' heads. The piece started when the hooded figure came inside and moved these rings. Bob Dylan's record *Bringing it all [back] home* went on, the red figure moved some lighted candelabras, 1 candle in each, the only light in the room. Eventually the music became [Dylan's] *Maggie's Farm* and Bob [Wilson] came out, walking like an equilibrist on a narrow wooden plank using a giant lollipop as equilibrating stick. He was dressed only in a T-shirt. He crossed the plank which was about 2.5 meters long and bending under the weight during the whole duration of *Maggie's Farm*. Then he went away and the hooded figure moved more rings and candles. The hooded figure stood against the righthand wall all the time Bob was on stage … A toy train was being set up above the ground, about 1.5 meters, just the rails, without other support. Bob eventually lay under the rails dressed as before, making movements like a baby in a crib. The sound of a locomotive came full blast over the amplifier while he was writhing on the floor as if in extreme pain and the toy train was passing above him. Then darkness for a while, rings being moved, candles put away and a block was placed in the farthest part of the loft. A Texas revivalist preacher's voice came over the amplifier very dramatic, as well as his audience's response. During this time Bob whose face was painted white was … draping himself in, long strips of colored plastic that made him progressively grow in size, till he seemed very tall. The effect was that of a shaman performing a ritual. This lasted for about 15 minutes.[3]

The performance ended with Wilson leaving and a light shining on the piano with a photo of a baby.

Although the Dylan music – the iconic soundtrack of the counterculture – seemed to place *Baby Blood* squarely within the sociopolitical milieu of the 1960s, the performance was apolitical, nonconfrontational, and emotionally distanced, and it clearly was not an ensemble creation. A spectator might try to find thematic connections among the disparate images and actions of *Baby Blood*, but there was no readily apparent meaning, no political message, and certainly no discernible narrative. In its use of objects and temporal structure it bore some relation to the Happenings of a few years earlier, a connection reinforced by a 1965 Wilson statement: "What I am doing – in painting, design, dance, electronic music – are happenings. Very few are predetermined. They have an order and a time limit, yes, perhaps even a rough outline, but what happens just happens."[4] But the centrality of the figure of Wilson himself, together with the "amount" and intensity of the acting in this piece, placed it outside the framework of Happenings.

A few months later, in April 1968, Richard Foreman presented *Angelface* at the Cinematheque on Wooster Street – the then new home of the New American Cinema movement and literally around the corner from Wilson's loft. As with *Baby Blood*, it was seen by only a handful of people. The script[5] designates seven characters, but as with most of Foreman's subsequent work, these were not the psychologically based characters of modern drama or even theatrical or symbolic representations of real-world characters. They are best seen as manifestations of aspects of Foreman's consciousness, and the plays exist as a kind of monodrama. "The scripts themselves read like notations of my own process of imagining a theatre piece," explained Foreman.[6] Like Gertrude Stein, Foreman was creating a continuous present by isolating, as Kate Davy explained, "his own present, internal time so that the words he writes exist in suspended time, moving as they move in each moment of his consciousness as he focuses on his own internal process or state."[7] Foreman's highly self-referential, contemplative text proceeds somewhat like the frames of a film, only a film in which each frame is complete in and of itself, achieving its result through the accumulation of images and actions that do not necessarily flow from one to the next. *Angelface*, like many of Foreman's productions through the early 1970s, employed *tableaux*, glacial pacing, and a performing style devoid of the usual conventions of acting – performances that were at once uninflected, almost somnambulistic, yet taut with tension and energy. This production also introduced the use of recorded dialogue, which typified much of his subsequent work (though as Foreman later explained, this device was devised originally as a means of relieving the non-professional actors from the task of memorizing a long script of fragmentary lines that did not flow like conventional conversation). Foreman's explanation of the use of tape for *Angelface* is the only real description of the event:

> The actors recorded, monotonously and at a fairly quick speed, all of the lines. They read through the play with the pauses. In performance the tape was played and the actor, as soon as he

heard one of his own lines coming over the tape, would start to repeat that line as soon as it began. But where the recorded line was spoken at normal speed, he would, in repeating it, delay after each word, so that he never got to finish the line. If on the tape, he started another line in that same unit, he could either continue his original line or pick up the new line. Another rule was that when they got to a pause, wherever they were on stage, when the tape stopped, all of the actors stopped.[8]

The few spectators who saw the four performances of *Angelface* would have seen Foreman himself at a control panel in the audience space operating the sound and lights like a kind of conductor, a position he continued to occupy through most of his productions, further emphasizing the highly personal nature of the performance and his absolute control over all elements.

Both these directors began to turn out a prodigious amount of work and garner increasing attention. Wilson's projects, often referred to as operas, quickly grew in scale. *The King of Spain* (1969) was presented in the large, decaying, proscenium-style Anderson Theatre, a former Yiddish theatre on lower Second Avenue, and *The Life and Times of Sigmund Freud* (1969) was presented in the cavernous Opera House of the Brooklyn Academy of Music. While Foreman's work continued to be presented in lofts or other small venues that rarely seated more than 100 spectators, by the mid-1970s his productions ran for several months to usually sold-out houses.

These productions were noteworthy not simply because they marked the start of the careers of two of the most significant figures of the theatrical avant-garde but also because they stood in direct opposition to the creative methodology, form, and content of the physically energetic, ensemble-based theatre of the 1960s. Somewhat like modern-day Wagners, Foreman and Wilson each created a *Gesamtkunstwerk* that was the product of a unique and very personal vision. Although complex spiritual, social, and political ideas entered into their works to varying degrees at different points throughout their careers, ideology was neither the starting point of the creative endeavor nor the goal of the performance, as it tended to be for the majority of 1960s experimental groups. There was no theme or message in any traditional Aristotelian sense, nor was there an attempt to create an emotional identification with the audience. These performances were private visions – cool, distant, and often hypnotic – that rejected strategies of confrontation and manipulation in favor of an art that engaged the spectator in an aesthetic dialectic. "Only one theatrical problem exists now," declared Foreman in his "Ontological-Hysteric Manifesto I" of 1972:

> How to create a stage performance in which the spectator experiences the danger of art not as involvement or risk or excitement, not as something that reaches out to vulnerable areas of his person, but rather the danger as a possible *decision* he (spectator) may make upon the occasion of confronting the work of art. The work of art as a *contest* between object (or process) and viewer. Old notions of drama (up thru [*sic*] Grotowski–Brook–Chaikin) = the danger of circumstance turning in such a way that we are "trapped" in an emotional commitment of one sort or another.[9]

The theatre of Foreman and Wilson was in fact about a post-Einsteinian way of apprehending the universe, a universe of uncertainty principles and chaos theory. (In fact, one of Foreman's plays is called *Particle Theory*, and Wilson's most famous opera is *Einstein on the Beach*.) It challenged post-Renaissance (i.e. modern) understandings of time and space within theatre; it disrupted the act of viewing by slowing down action to almost imperceptible movement, extending the length of performances beyond normal limits of concentration, and fragmenting both the viewing frame and the arc of the production, thereby forcing the spectators to re-examine their own notions of performance and their own perceptual processes.

Because the work of Wilson and Foreman was so stunningly different from any other theatre being produced at the time, and because of superficial similarities in their earliest works, critics often discussed them as almost identical; their names were linked as if a single word: "Foremanandwilson." Critic Bonnie Marranca joined their work with the eclectic productions of Mabou Mines – a collective of theatre artists including Lee Breuer, JoAnne Akalaitis, Ruth Maleczech, David Warrilow, and Philip Glass – and coined the term "Theatre of Images." For audiences who sensed the significance of the work of these artists but were often baffled by it, the term seemed to provide a much-needed handle. By reducing the pieces to an easily identifiable element – their striking visual imagery – they seemed accessible, and it relieved spectators of the need to indulge in the often complex work of interpretation. It also echoed the term "Theatre of the Absurd" of two decades earlier. The American theatre could now lay claim to a major home-grown avant-garde movement. But just as the earlier term had massed together disparate styles that in retrospect had little in common, so had this new label. But also like the earlier term, it stuck.

The work of Foreman and Wilson did derive from some shared impulses, influences, and theories. It drew upon the ideas and aesthetics of Gertrude Stein, abstract expressionist painting and Russian suprematism, Happenings and chance theatre, pop art, minimalism, and to some extent the philosophical ideas of Ludwig Wittgenstein and Martin Heidegger. It also reflected the powerful influence of avant-garde film, and in particular the influence of filmmaker and performance artist Jack Smith. But whereas Wilson's work can now be seen as a culmination of a branch of modernism best embodied by the surrealists, Foreman, despite some affinities with expressionism and a stated indebtedness to Brecht, was beginning to move past the aesthetics of modernism.

Minimalism

In his manifesto, Foreman rejected what he deemed the "absurdity ... [of] the orchestrated speech and activity" of productions like Peter Brook's *A Midsummer Night's Dream* (1971).[10] In its place, he called for the repudiation of "composition in favor of shape (or something else)," as in the work of artists Frank Stella and Donald Judd. Judd and Stella emerged in the mid-1960s as leaders in the reaction against abstract expressionism. In a well-known 1964 interview on WBAI, the leading alternative radio station in New York at the time, subsequently published in *Art News*,[11] the two artists elucidated many of the aesthetic ideas of what would soon become known as minimalism, and Judd said that he avoided compositional effects because "those effects tend to carry with them all the structures, values, feelings of the whole European tradition. It suits me fine if that's all down the drain." This could equally describe the approach of Foreman, who was looking for a theatre that would substitute formal structures for the emotional constructs and artificial relationships of more conventional drama.

Minimalism rejected the intense emotionalism of abstract expressionism. Critic Richard Wollheim – who coined the term in a 1965 essay[12] – contrasted minimalist art with the work of painters such as Jackson Pollock and Willem de Kooning and described the new form as having "a minimal art content: in that either they are to an extreme degree undifferentiated in themselves and therefore possess very low content of any kind, or else the differentiation that they do exhibit, which may in some cases be very considerable, comes not from the artist but from a nonartistic source, like nature or the factory."[13] Art critic Barbara Rose, in an *Art In America* essay later the same year, traced the origins of the new form to Duchamp's "ready-mades" and Kasimir Malevich's "Black Square" (1913), both of which, in different ways, challenged the accepted notions of art objects and content.[14] She also cited the repetitive structures of Erik Satie's musical compositions as a precedent. One significance of Rose's essay lay in her expansion of this movement beyond the visual arts to music, dance and performance, and even to the novel, especially the work of Allain Robbe-Grillet. By the ostensible elimination of content, the artist threw the focus onto the structure of the work. Judd in particular wanted to minimize composition – the arrangement of elements within an art work – because composition, by emphasizing internal relationships, drew focus away from the art work as a whole. In many of the works of Judd and Stella, the emphasis was on the frame, the symmetrical arrangement of space within the frame, or the echoing of the outer shape of the painting or sculpture within the frame.

Sculptor Robert Morris related the new art to phenomenology. The apparent simplicity of shape, he argued, freed spectators to become aware of their own relationship to the object and to the space in which the sculpture existed. Rather than presenting a pleasing aesthetic or explicating an idea, the sculptural object elucidated the space of the gallery or viewing environment, thereby forcing the spectators to become aware of their own process of viewing. Interestingly, a critic of minimalism, Michael Fried, objected that such art became a form of theatre because it created spectators who were more aware of their function as audience than of the object itself.[15] Literalist art, as Fried called it, had "a kind of stage presence" which "demands that the beholder take it into account, that he take it *seriously.*" He saw theatre and art as opposing forces because theatre inevitably transformed the art object and made the spectator complicit in the work. Whereas Fried saw this negatively, theatre artists such as Foreman and Wilson saw in the minimalist aesthetic a chance to rescue theatre from the emotional identification and manipulation typical of most dramatic endeavors. It could be seen, in fact, as an aesthetic version of Brecht's dialectics – making the audience aware *not* of its relation to a particular set of ideas but to the performance itself.

Whereas minimalism in art and sculpture could be manifested through repeated structures in space, live performance achieved an equivalent effect through repeated actions and motifs through time.

Erik Satie's *Vexations*, a piano piece from the early part of the century whose directions state that the 80-second musical composition is to be played 840 times, is in some ways the *ur*-minimalist performance. In 1963, John Cage organized the first performance of this work at the Pocket Theatre in New York. It lasted eighteen hours. What became clear was that the piece was no joke, as some had assumed; it took on a meaning and hypnotic effect, Cage observed, "far beyond what any of us had anticipated."[16]

Postmodern dance

In the early 1960s, a new movement, eventually called postmodern dance, began with performances at Judson Church. The most immediate lines of influence could be seen from Duchamp, Satie, and Stein, all filtered through Cage to Merce Cunningham and then on to the young choreographers and dancers, including, notably, Yvonne Rainer. Rainer performed a solo work entitled *The Bells* at the Living Theatre in 1961. "I remember thinking that dance was at a disadvantage in relation to sculpture," she noted,

> in that the spectator could spend as much time as he required to examine a sculpture, walk around it, and so forth – but a dance movement – because it happened in time – vanished as soon as it was executed. So in … *The Bells* I repeated the same seven movements for eight minutes. It was not exact repetition, as the sequence of the movements kept changing. They also underwent changes through being repeated in different parts of the space and faced in different directions – in a sense allowing the spectator to "walk around it."[17]

Similar structures could be found in many of the postmodern dances through the 1960s, reaching an apotheosis of sorts in the first act of Wilson's *Einstein on the Beach* (1976) with the mesmerizing performance of Lucinda Childs, who performed a repetitive dance on a diagonal line across the stage for nearly one hour.

One aspect of repetition in performance, as opposed to painting or sculpture, as Rainer understood, was the necessity of change. Any action repeated by a live performer inevitably went through some sort of transformation, which meant, as Gertrude Stein explained,

There can be no repetition because the essence of that expression is insistence, and if you insist you must each time use emphasis and if you use emphasis it is not possible while anybody is alive that they should use exactly the same emphasis. And so let us think seriously of the difference between repetition and insistence. Anybody can be interested in a story of a crime because no matter how often the witnesses tell the same story the insistence is different. That is what makes life that the insistence is different, no matter how often you tell the same story if there is anything alive in the telling the emphasis is different.[18]

Over the next several years dancer-choreographers such as Trisha Brown, Joan Jonas, Steve Paxton, David Gordon, Lucinda Childs, and others created works that rejected the "dancerly" qualities of even the late modern work of Cunningham and contained nothing that could be intentionally interpreted as meaning, mood, or musicality. As Michael Kirby, who coined the term "postmodern dance," explained, "The view is an interior one: movement is not pre-selected for its characteristics but results from certain decisions, goals, plans, schemes, rules, concepts, or problems. Whatever actual movement occurs during the performance is acceptable as long as the limiting and controlling principles are adhered to."[19] Minimalism may be understood as an art work reduced to its most fundamental and efficient elements – the ultimate manifestation of Robert Browning's dictum "less is more." Postmodern dance, which often reduced choreography to simple movements and patterns, and sometimes no movement at all, fulfills this popular conception. But minimalism, in its emphasis on outward structures, could be rich, complex, and dense, especially in the theatrical creations of Foreman and Wilson. Whereas Happenings, performed most often in art galleries, were looked upon as a performative permutation of visual art, postmodern dance took the ideas of Cage and Stein clearly into the realm of live performance and created the first template for formalist performance in the 1960s.

Jack Smith and New American Cinema

The one constant, however, the key to understanding this neo-formalist theatre – perhaps the lynchpin of the avant-garde – was filmmaker and performance artist Jack Smith (1932–1989). Best known for his notorious film *Flaming Creatures* (1962), Smith also presented live performances from the 1960s into the 1980s as well as performing in the early works of Wilson and the Ridiculous Theatrical Company. Smith's films and performances were seen by a wide range of avant-garde theatre and performance artists, filmmakers, dancers, and visual artists almost all of whom acknowledged his influence.[20] *Flaming Creatures* was described, a bit hyperbolically, in a *Film Culture* article as echoing "with ancient ritual chant, with Milton and with Dante ... for the very scope and scale of sin becomes demonic in a Miltonian sense, and *Flaming Creatures* might be subtitled *Pandemonium Regained*, a paean not for the Paradise Lost, but for the Hell Satan gained."[21] The film's notoriety derived from its scenes of male and female nudity, orgies, transvestism, masturbation, and homo-eroticism. The underground film festivals and theatres that presented *Flaming Creatures*, often at midnight showings, were frequently closed by the police (especially as New York city was attempting to clean up its image for the 1964 World's Fair; this was also the period in which comedian Lenny Bruce was arrested for indecency), and on at least one occasion the presenters were arrested. There were similar disruptions in Europe, and when the film was banned from a Belgian festival it was shown in a hotel room, where Jean-Luc Godard, Agnes Varda, and Roman Polanski watched it.[22] Its showing on college campuses across the country coincided with the aftermath of the free speech movement and the beginnings of the anti-war protests, and as a result, the banning or police disruption of showings often led to riots, one of the largest occurring at the University of Michigan. The film even became prime fodder in the Republicans' campaign against Abe Fortas, who had been nominated as Chief Justice of the Supreme Court by President Lyndon Johnson. Fortas' liberal rulings on pornography were the ostensible issue, and *Flaming Creatures* was shown in the Senate office building and graphically described in the *Congressional Record* of September 4, 1968.

Yet the response of a variety of serious artists to the film was not based on prurient interest. There was a high camp sensibility to the film, drawing consciously on the films of Maria Montez and other B movies, as well as on the exotic creations of Josef von Sternberg and the films of Busby Berkeley. As film historian P. Adams Sitney has noted, Smith foregrounded what was "latent in those films – visual texture, androgynous sexual presence, exotic locations," while completely abandoning any sense of narrative composition. The funda-mental structure of film (and, arguably, drama) was under attack. "He utterly transforms his sources and uncovers a mythic center from which they had been closed off," continued Sitney.[23] The movie consisted of

Plate 10 Scene from Jack Smith's film *Flaming Creatures*, with Mario Montez in the foreground.
Photo: ©: The Plaster Foundation, Inc.

ten loosely connected scenes, including three orgies in which the characters ("creatures") die and are reborn in a perverse reading of mythological scenarios. There was a soundtrack of American and Latin pop, rock 'n' roll, bullfight music, and a Chinese song. This sort of eclecticism, strongly informed by popular culture, would have a significant impact on subsequent forms of theatrical performance. Smith used a hand-held camera, which created uneven and jerky movements and odd framings (conventionally effective in the orgy scenes, disconcerting in others). Much of the film stock was past its expiry date, leading to discontinuities in texture and image quality; scenes were over- or underexposed and filmed at different speeds. The movie was shot on a rooftop against a painted theatrical backdrop, adding to the crude effect of the imagery. Foreman has acknowledged that the self-consciously home-made quality and lack of attention to technical polish – in direct opposition to the technical sophistication of commercial film – had a profoundly liberating effect on him as a theatre artist.

Critic Susan Sontag declared that the film was not about ideas in the conventional literary sense: "there are no ideas, no symbols, no commentary on or critique of anything in *Flaming Creatures*. Smith's film is strictly a treat for the senses ... *Flaming Creatures* is that rare modern work of art: it is about joy and innocence."[24] She went on to extol its joyous sloppiness, looseness, and arbitrariness, qualities that by flouting the prevailing sensibilities of the art world and intellectual criticism would inform the work of Richard Foreman, who described the film as "a Blakean vision come into three-dimensional, concrete life."[25]

Along with Smith, works of avant-garde filmmakers Maya Deren, Stan Brakhage, Ken Jacobs, Kenneth Anger and others were shown regularly in the 1960s at the Charles Cinema on Avenue B in the East Village. Richard Foreman was a regular member of the audience, but Wilson and others also saw the works. Aside from the undermining of slickness, the films rejected psychological motivation and Aristotelian plot – the fundamental bases of most twentieth-century film and theatre. Most important, they shifted the locus of the work of art from the content not simply to the form but to the raw elements of the creative process. The movement of the camera, the manipulation of the film stock itself (scratching the film was a favorite technique), the mixing of color with black and white, foregrounding of editing techniques, repetitive shots, long periods of narration over black screens, and so forth, drew attention to the filmmaker, to the medium, and to the process of watching the film rather than the traditional elements of composition, content, or form. Within the films, there was a constant rupture of continuity, as in Gertrude Stein. Pioneer avant-garde filmmaker Maya Deren stated it almost mystically when she wrote about her film *At Land*: "Today, the rules are ambiguous, the adversary is concealed in aliases, the oracles broadcast a babble of contradictions."[26]

Another form of avant-garde film influential for avant-garde theatre artists, notably Robert Wilson, was the "trance film," in which action, according to film historian Parker Tyler, is seen "as a *dream* and the actor as a *somnambulist*," and the film conveys "the magic of seeing while 'dreaming awake'; the world in view becomes that of poetic action pure and simple: action without the restraints of single level consciousness, everyday reason and so-called realism."[27] Jean Cocteau's films, particularly *Le Sang d'un poète*, in which events were placed outside time or within an instant of time, were particularly significant. Similarly, the repetitive images and self-reflective camera movements and editing of the films of Stan Brakhage, noted Sitney, evoked the narrative strategies of Gertrude Stein – an acknowledged influence for these filmmakers – and therefore provided another introduction to her work for the nascent theatre artists in the audience.

But for theatre artists, one of the most significant elements was the

Plate 11 Jack Smith's *The Secret of Rented Island* (1976), an adaptation of Ibsen's *Ghosts*, showing Smith as Oswald.

Photo: ©: The Plaster Foundation, Inc.

very breakdown of the elemental structures of showing film. In Jacobs' *Blonde Cobra*, for instance, the opening images were followed on the soundtrack by the voice of Ginger Rogers singing one line of "Let's Call the Whole Thing Off," after which the film became a scratchy leader strip and the sound track ended. There were then two sudden bursts of sound from live radios in the theatre, rapid changes from color to black-and-white imagery, and an onscreen character announcing, "We will now start all over again" as he writes out the film's titles.[28]

Smith's theatre performances appeared equally haphazard. His first, *Rehearsal for the Destruction of Atlantis*, was in November 1965 at Jonas Mekas' New Cinema Festival. Subsequently, he presented performances at his loft on Greene Street, which served as both living and performing space. Arriving at the fourth-floor space, one might or might not be let in; there might or might not be performers – audience members were frequently recruited for the performances, which could last long into the night, typically till 3 or 4 a.m. Nothing started on time. An eclectic mix of phonograph records played as Smith spent inordinate amounts of time arranging a phenomenal array of objects on the stage area. Stefan Brecht catalogued the detritus used in

Withdrawal from Orchid Lagoon: broken bottles, a votive screen, a toilet with a broken doll, old Christmas trees, feathers, netting, colored lights, a ladder.[29] Despite the impression of disorder, Smith was meticulous about everything. He would constantly interrupt the performance to redirect actors. The performance frequently ground to a halt, seemingly over, only to restart. Not surprisingly, it was Foreman who realized that the apparent chaos was, if not exactly calculated, singularly effective in reordering the whole perceptual approach to understanding theatre. "To watch Jack Smith perform," proclaimed Foreman,

> was to watch human behavior turn into granular stasis, in which every moment of being seemed, somehow, to contain the seed of unthinkable possibility. It was endlessly fascinating ... Jack extended the wait between lines of dialogue to five, ten, twenty, minutes ... the wait was exhilarating ... That extended slowness, combined with the continual (and somewhat calculated) going wrong of every performance, brought the audience into a state of present attention that is precisely what other theater avoided in order to affect (i.e., manipulate) its audience. The theater generally hypnotizes; it pulls one into a dream that imitates a place in which the spectator would like to be. (Even Wilson falls into this habit.) The theater of Smith, along with other manifestations that took place in those days of Cinematheque performance, avoided that through building into performance various "confounding" devices – in Smith's case the great slowness informed by a feeling that "everything was going wrong," which made it hard for the audience to remember what was happening at the same time that it was fascinated by what was, indeed, happening in a time rhythm that both spectator and performer were experiencing in sync.[30]

What Foreman perceived in Smith's work, and what was occurring in the films and, importantly, film showings of other underground filmmakers, was a creative and performative vocabulary that seems remarkably similar to what would become known as postmodernism. Key elements of postmodernism – rupture, discontinuity, disjuncture,[31] the structural strategy of what Frederic Jameson calls "pastiche,"[32] or Ihab Hassan's concept of "present-ification" or the "presence of the past" within a work – were all to be found in the new American cinema before the ideas were codified by post-structuralist theorists. I suggested earlier that Foreman's work was moving away from modernism. It was, in fact, one of the earliest examples of post-modern theatre in the United States, but the roots of his postmodernism could be found in Stein, Cage, Artaud, and mostly strikingly, the new American cinema.

Robert Wilson

Wilson's journey to theatre was almost accidental. Growing up in Waco, Texas, he demonstrated some artistic ability as a youngster and evinced a unique imagination. By his own account, when asked in second grade what he wanted to be when he grew up he replied, "The King of Spain."[33] After winning first prize in a children's art contest in sixth grade he was asked by the local newspaper, "Now tell us, Bob Wilson, What do you think is the Nicest Thing in the Whole World? And I said a big thick cat's paw!!"[34] (One wonders how many of these incidents are literally true. Wilson, best known for creating seemingly non-narrative plays, has carefully woven his own narrative portrait of the artist as a young man. Whatever the truth, his first major production was entitled *The King of Spain*, and its primary image was of a huge cat traversing the proscenium, but seen only as four cat's legs – the implied body of the cat looming over the theatre.) Wilson also suffered from a severe stuttering problem, which was largely cured during his teen years by work with a teacher named Mrs Bird Hoffman, a name he applied with slight variation to his theatre: the Byrd Hoffman School of Byrds. In 1963, he moved to New York to attend the Pratt Institute, an art and architecture school. During this time he also studied in Paris with abstract expressionist painter George McNeil, created the doll costumes for the "Motel" portion of the Open Theatre's *America Hurrah*, and sat in on choreographer Martha Graham's classes.

In addition to the performance work he was beginning to do, Wilson created a major outdoor sculpture in 1968, similar to the earth works of artists like Robert Smithson. It was created out of 676 telephone poles placed in a twenty-six-foot square in an open field in Loveland, Ohio. Described by Wilson as a "theatre sculpture play environment," the poles rose in a stepped arrangement from two and a half to eighteen and a half feet above the ground.[35] By calling it a "play environment," he was anticipating one theme of his subsequent work: when asked what his plays were about he sometimes responded, "nothing" – but he likened this to a child engrossed in private play who, when asked by his mother what he is doing, replies, "Oh, just

Plate 12 Robert Wilson's *The King of Spain* at the Anderson Theatre, 1969, showing the cat's legs.

Photo: Martin Bough. Courtesy the Byrd Hoffman Foundation.

nothing."[36] "On Broadway," he mused, "they always do the big huge obvious things and I thought wouldn't it be Fantastic if there was a superbig space and a huge cast doing tiny but projected little things little individual things."[37]

By 1968, he was performing with avant-garde dancer Kenneth King and director Meredith Monk. He also came to the attention of choreographer Jerome Robbins, who began to provide some financial support for Wilson's projects and invited him to teach movement classes at his American Theatre Laboratory. Of particular note, however, was his work from the mid-1960s in both Texas and New York as a teacher of art and theatre to young people in special education classes. Especially in New York, he worked with learning disabled and brain-damaged children and iron-lung patients. A turning point came in 1968 when he began to work with Raymond Andrews, a deaf-mute eleven-year-old whom he encountered while teaching in New Jersey. Convinced that Andrews' inability to communicate was a result of pre-verbal thinking, Wilson encouraged him to communicate through drawing. Wilson's approach with Andrews, and later with an autistic teenager, Christopher Knowles, was to adapt to his way of seeing and communicating rather than to attempt to change the behavior of the individual to fit societal norms. In the workshops at what was known as the Byrd Loft (from 1968 there were workshops at the loft every Thursday night), the participants would try to imitate the movements, gestures, and sounds of Andrews. It was, seemingly, a variant on the sound and movement exercises of the Open Theatre, which had been done in that very loft, but now instead of focusing on concentration and transformation, the Byrds, as they were known, were using it as a means of understanding alternative forms of perception and communication. Several of the movement patterns wound up choreographed into subsequent productions.

Wilson was not a theatre person in the sense of having much background or experience in theatre, although in addition to "Motel" he created decor for two dance pieces for the Murray Louis Company at the Henry Street Settlement. Especially in the early productions, the fact that they happened at all seemed a combination of sheer will power and serendipity. His description of the production of *The King of Spain*[38] is a free-associative narrative of poor planning, financial incompetence, narrowly averted disasters, and achieving the technically impossible (such as the cat's legs – ultimately constructed of salvaged fabric and giant Slinkys) simply because he did not know better. His performers were drawn largely from the people he worked with in workshops or in classes – they were all non-professionals. The designers and technicians – notably set designer Fred Kolouch (Kolo) and lighting designer Richard Nelson – fortunately, were willing to attempt anything, and they usually succeeded. What was clear from the beginning was that Wilson was able to attract devoted and dedicated individuals who recognized that something important was being created. Stefan Brecht has likened the Byrds to disciples.[39] They often gave up outside artistic endeavors and jobs to become full-time participants, and in this way they often became financially dependent on the Byrd Hoffman Foundation. One journalist described them as part of a psychodrama:

> They all seem not only dedicated to the Wilson way of theatre life but to be getting something back that is deeply personal and psychologically very rewarding to them. None of them seem to think like actors at all. They do not aspire to play Hamlet or Saint Joan, nor do they seek a Hollywood contract or their name in lights. They live and work together more as members of a commune than as members of an ambitious theatrical company.[40]

In this they could be seen as somewhat analogous to the Open Theatre or Performance Group, perhaps, but the focus was almost completely inward, as opposed to the theatre-oriented work of the others. The Byrds were perhaps closer to a cult than a commune.

The Life and Times of Sigmund Freud, which incorporated much of *The King of Spain*, was performed at the Brooklyn Academy of Music (BAM) in December 1969. BAM was not yet the chic venue it would become in the 1980s as home to the annual Next Wave Festival, and relatively few people attended. The production introduced many of the motifs of Wilson's future work. It was four hours long and consisted of a series of largely non-verbal *tableaux* and painstakingly slow movement, thus placing a burden on the spectator to develop a new means of watching. This required a different form of concentration than either a conventional realistic narrative play or even the relatively action-filled creations of the more experimental groups of the 1960s (although it bore some vague resemblance to the work of the Bread and Puppet Theatre). This was not, Wilson took pains to note, slow motion, but "natural time" as opposed to the "accelerated time" of conventional theatre. "I use the natural time that helps the sun to set, a cloud to change, a day to dawn," he explained. "I allow the audience time to reflect, to meditate on other things besides those which are happening on the stage; I allow them time and space to think."[41] In its reliance on "non-performers," it shifted the emphasis from the slick performance of a set of conventional skills and attitudes associated with "theatre" to the performer as self. However, Wilson carefully cultivated the particular and often stunning skills of the performers he worked with. Sheryl Sutton, for instance, who began to work with him in *Deafman Glance*, was able to "float," by which she meant an ability to move so slowly and effortlessly that the movement seemed almost imperceptible;[42] Andy de Groat was able to do whirling dances, one of which would comprise a nearly one-hour segment of *The Life and Times of Josef Stalin*. But unlike the typical theatre groups of the 1960s, whose work on physical training was intended to develop a physical virtuosity, Wilson aimed at a kind of sensitivity training for the actors, what he described as "raising your energy and sitting on it."[43] Performer Cindy Lubar recalled a workshop for *Deafman Glance* that consisted of walking "back and forth across the room for the entire workshop, just walking in parallel lines. We walked in tracks back and forth across the room for two or three hours, and there was a tape of someone talking in the background."[44]

It seems fitting that Richard Foreman wrote the first major piece on a Wilson theatre work when he reviewed *The Life and Times of Sigmund Freud* in the *Village Voice*. In the review, he drew attention to this use of "found" performers and found objects:

> Wilson also seems to transcend the popular notion of theatre as universally centered upon the talents of the specially trained and developed performer, and returns us to a healthier "compositional" theatre in which the directorial effort is not a straining after more and more intense "expression" of predetermined material, but is a sweet and powerful "placing" of various found and invented stage objects and actions – so placed and interwoven as to "show" at each moment as many of the implications and multi-level relations between objects and effects as possible.[45]

In a certain sense, the use of "found" or everyday objects and performers and the repetition of images in Wilson's work can be seen as an aspect of Pop Art as typified by the work of artists such as Roy Lichtenstein and Andy Warhol, who transformed the prosaic and commercial into subjects of high art. The images used by these artists were to be found on television, film, and in newspapers and magazines – the familiar iconography of our daily lives – and the constant repetition of these images created a rhythmic structure, just as the images themselves were repeated in newscasts, commercials, magazine ads, and the like. In art, this repetition created a new visual structure that replaced older compositional relationships;[46] in the theatre of Robert Wilson, it mimicked the visual iconography and rhythmic patterns of daily life. By emphasizing structure over content, however, it resembled neither conventional drama nor popular culture. The structural element was reinforced on many levels. The stage for *The Life and Times of Sigmund Freud*, for instance, was broken into seven horizontal "layers of zoned activity," and performers and their actions were confined to their particular zones. Foreman's review provides such a lucid description of this early Wilson work that it is worth quoting at length:

> The play itself proceeds as a series of "tableaux vivants," in silence or against occasional sound backgrounds. Act one is a sort of beach scene with real sand covering the vast Brooklyn Academy stage, a cloud-flecked sky behind. Performers start slowly crossing the stage, performing simple activities like sowing seed, running, crawling over the sand, as if the "cells," the building blocks of life (simple bodily resources), are laid out for us. A big turtle is slowly pulled across the stage. Freud and his wife walk across the sand, and what is slowly developed is a profound sense of the *true* rhythm of life, which builds not through the exercising of the will in moments of crisis and decision, but in the slow accretions that are spun around the human animal as his body and mind chew and re-chew on the materials of his mental and physical space. (And Freud walks through, musing on this slow accretion!) The act ends with one of the performance's many fantastic images: as performers start whirling and kicking up sand, we see Wilson himself as an over-stuffed black mammy – suddenly, fantastic! – joined by a chorus of 20 or 30 over-stuffed mammies (they look like birds with puffed-out bosoms and asses), and they all shuffle over the sand as the sky darkens.
>   Act two, a vast drawing room with an up-center entrance through which, at long intervals, people enter – I mean people! not *performers*! A collection of all shapes, sizes, ages. They really walk across the stage, and plop down into chairs, and one realizes that few directors have ever before composed their stage time-space so that bodies and persons emerged as the impenetrable (holy) objects they really are, rather than the usual virtuoso tools

used to project some play's predetermined energies and meanings. Then more impenetrable objects and acts – 30-foot-high hairy animal legs stride across the stage and the assembled guests solemnly file out after the beast. I relate this presentation of the impenetrable (self-sufficient) body and act to Heidegger's profound observations on art: "The earth appears openly illuminated as itself only when it is perceived and preserved as that which is essentially undisclosable." (I think Wilson demonstrates what might be deduced from Heidegger (and Gertrude Stein too) – that profundity and holiness re-enter the theatre through the proper articulation of the landscape aspect of the drama, filling the stage-space with real (i.e., impenetrable) objects in such a way that they are impenetrable, and that very *impenetrability* as what satisfies as it produces awe and delight. This is the goal of drama, rather than working on the audience's head and gut with mere "pretend" objects and acts that are little more than stimulants to our habitual, conditioned, emotional patterns and brain-sets.

For me the last act was most powerful of all. Wild animals (15 or so) slowly enter a cave one by one, and lie down in the straw. Beyond the mouth of the cave, in the sunlight, half-naked boys and girls run, exercise, and play. As the animals enter, iron bars slowly fall over the cave opening, separating animals from the world outside.

Finally Freud enters, and sits at a little table amidst the resting wild beasts, and a small boy cries at his feet. This takes half an hour or so, and it is slow and gigantic and wonderful, and the emotion that arises in viewing this 20th-century nativity scene is not the emotion that the theatre usually evokes (those emotions that bind us ever more firmly to what we have been conditioned to be) – it rather evokes the whole spectrum of feeling tone that is our biological and spiritual given – and having that whole *spectrum* of feeling awakened in us is the freedom-bestowing aim of art on the highest level.[47]

After this, the work with Raymond Andrews led to the creation of *Deafman Glance*, the production that brought Wilson international attention. Working with Andrews, and subsequently with Christopher Knowles, Wilson evolved his idea of interior and exterior screens. Most people's understanding of the world coincides with the external reality perceived through the eyes, ears, and other senses. But, Wilson believed, brain-damaged individuals, or those with disabilities that

Plate 13 Deafman Glance at the Brooklyn Academy of Music, 1971.
Photo: Martin Bough. Courtesy the Byrd Hoffman Foundation.

affected sight and hearing, perceived the world on an "inner screen," something that the majority of people experience only while dreaming or under the influence of drugs. Thus, the great length of Wilson's productions, the incredible slowness, and the trance-like music that began to accompany the pieces (most notably by Michael Galasso in the earlier works, and Philip Glass starting with *Einstein on the Beach*), were part of a strategy to induce a trance-like or hallucinatory state in the spectators so that they would begin to intermix interior and exterior perception. This was the logical extension of the surrealists' strategy of tapping into the unconscious to release trapped layers of creativity and understanding – something recognized by surrealist writer Louis Aragon, who, in response to the Paris production of *Deafman*, published an essay in the form of a letter to his late colleague André Breton, the founder of surrealism, who had died many years earlier and to whom Aragon had not spoken for years before that.

> The miracle was produced, the one we were waiting for, about which we talked ... The world of a deaf child opened up to us like a wordless mouth. For more than four hours, we went to inhabit this universe where, in the absence of words, of sounds, sixty people had no words except to move. I want to tell you right away, André, because even if those who invented this spectacle don't know it, they are playing it for you, for you would have loved it as I did, *to the point of madness.* (Because it has made me mad.) Listen to what I say to those who have ears, seemingly not for hearing: **I never saw anything more beautiful in the world since I was born. Never never has any play come anywhere near this one, because it is at once life awake and the life of closed eyes, the confusion between everyday life and the life of each night, reality mingles with dream, all that's inexplicable in the life of deaf man.**[48]

Arthur Holmberg provides a concise description of the opening of the play that Aragon rhapsodized over:

> *Deafman Glance* ... begins with a silent prolog: on a white platform, her back to the audience, a mother ([Sheryl] Sutton dressed in a black Victorian gown) stands next to a bottle of milk on a high, white table. Reading a comic book, a little boy sits on a low stool. On the floor, a little girl sleeps, covered by a white sheet. The mother, wearing red gloves, puts black gloves over them. In

extreme slow motion (the prolog takes forty-five minutes), she pours milk, gives it to boy, returns to table, picks up knife, gently stabs boy, wipes knife clean. Stage left, an older brother (Raymond Andrews) witnesses the event. He screams. The ritual … is repeated on little girl. Older brother screams again. The mother puts her hand over his mouth. Traumatized by witnessing the murders, he loses the gift of speech. Gray drop, showing a cracked wall, goes up, revealing a magic forest with a pink angel walking backwards. Nine ladies, elegantly clad in white Victorian gowns with white birds on their fingers, listen to "The Moonlight Sonata." The boy enters this dreamworld. Wonders ensue: A giant frog – dapper in velvet smoking jacket and cravat – lounges at a banquet table, sipping martinis nonchalantly. Men with yellow fish on their backs float across a red river. A magic bench flies the boy through the air. A giant bee and giant bunny wiggle and bump to the pop tune "Mutual Admiration Society." An ox swallows the sun, his stomach glows, his head falls off. Nine apes crawl up from the ground. As Fauré's *Requiem* sounds, apes pick up red apples. George Washington and Marie Antoinette stroll in. The queen's parasol bursts into flames. Apples float into space. Stars fall from the heavens. Drop comes down as a banjo strums "When You Are in, Love, it's the Loveliest Night of the Year."[49]

All Wilson's works through the early 1970s were, from a verbal standpoint, silent spectacles – the few words that occurred were simply part of a sound score. Yet this could not really be seen as another version of Artaud-inspired non-verbal communication. Rather, it was visual art come to three-dimensional, kinesthetic, and temporal life; it was pre-verbal communication operating on a level of consciousness normally available only in dreams.

The first part of Wilson's career culminated in the December 1973 production of *The Life and Times of Josef Stalin* at the BAM Opera House. This twelve-hour opera consisted of seven acts, with the formal structure of Act I mirrored in Act VII, Act II in Act VI and so on, with Act IV as the unique midpoint. The opera was not merely an aesthetic culmination but also a summation, since much of the production was an anthology of sorts of Wilson's earlier work. Acts I–III incorporated *The Life and Times of Sigmund Freud*, which itself had subsumed *The King of Spain*; Act IV was developed from *Deafman Glance*; Act V contained excerpts from *Program Prologue Now: Overture for a Deafman* (1971); Act VI contained fragments of the 168-hour *KA*

MOUNTAIN AND GUARDenia TERRACE, which had been performed in Shiraz, Iran. Act VII was newly created – including a dance for 100 actors in ostrich costumes mirroring the Act I dance of the black mammies – as were the "knee plays," so called because they were the joints between the acts. The sheer size of the work – truly operatic on a Wagnerian scale – dwarfed anything the avant-garde had ever attempted. The cast included 140 performers, all with multiple and complex costumes, and elaborate settings that filled the Opera House stage. That the four performances over two weekends came off at all was something of a miracle.

Wilson also created chamber pieces ranging from *The $ Value of Man* (a large production by Off Broadway standards, but small for Wilson) to works like *DIA LOG* (1975) – a language piece between Wilson and Christopher Knowles. The work with Knowles moved Wilson into an exploration of language – not as a means for narrative communication but as a structure to be explored, broken apart, and used for alternative forms of communication. One of the language pieces, *A Letter for Queen Victoria*, was actually presented for three weeks on Broadway in 1974. (The use of professional performers contributed to the end of the Byrd School as a collaborative organization.) The major work of the mid-1970s, however, was *Einstein on the Beach* (1976), written with composer Philip Glass. This five-hour piece premiered at the Avignon Festival in France, toured Europe and was given its American premiere in two performances at the Metropolitan Opera House in New York. While *Einstein* had no clear-cut message or linear story, it nonetheless played upon the dichotomy of Einstein the scientist versus Einstein the dreamer, and with its recurrent images of a train, a trial, and a spaceship it seemed to question the effects of the march of science upon society. Yet the production could be appreciated solely on a formal level with its rigid structure, elaborate scenographic interplay of space, line and form, the repetitive phrases and slow modulations of Philip Glass' music, which received its first widespread hearing with this production, and hypnotic patterns of movement. With its appealing imagery, seemingly transparent message, trance music, and a length only slightly greater than that of many traditional operas, the piece achieved a status as a modernist hit.

Because no theatre or arts foundation in the United States was willing or able to support Wilson's grandiose vision, much of his subsequent work was done in Europe, mostly in Germany and France. In 1983, he began an epic undertaking, *the CIVIL warS*, a multi-part performance created in sections in Rotterdam, Cologne, and Rome, which received performances of the various sections in several European cities. The entire monumental work was to come together at the 1984 Los Angeles Olympics, but the organizers were able to raise only half of the $2.6 million budget and the event was canceled; the complete work has never been performed. In addition to his original pieces, Wilson has directed operas at major houses in Europe, including La Scala; directed classic plays at the American Repertory Theatre in Cambridge, Massachusetts; and, most notably, worked on several highly successful productions with the late German playwright Heiner Müller – whose postmodern deconstructions of mythological and classical texts and social and philosophical explorations of culture made him one of the most dominant German playwrights since Brecht. It was as if, after twenty years of deconstructing the theatrical experience and creating a new vocabulary of performance, Wilson, starting in the mid-1980s, was willing to return to classical theatre and opera. However, his stagings of the classics were always filtered through his unique vision.

Wilson has often been classified as a postmodernist, but the pervasiveness of the iconic symbol, the constant striving for the beautiful image, and the harmonious and unified structure of his works places Wilson's *mise en scène* firmly within the modernist framework. His texts, however, with their use of pastiche, quotation, and self-referential content, certainly relate him to the postmodern movement, as his affinity for Müller demonstrates.

Richard Foreman

Richard Foreman's work is a remarkable nexus of wide-ranging intellectual investigations into the nature of being and modes of perception manifested through rigorous formal dramatic structures, together with staging practices that exhibit elements of vaudeville, film noir, grande guignol, cabaret, slapstick, expressionist film, the carnivalesque (both in Bakhtin's sense of the term and in the literal embodiment of a funhouse), and perhaps a dose of Meyerhold. Although most of his plays have been published, to read them outside the context of performance is to miss a crucial element, and to describe the performances without the text or some sense of the underlying theory risks trivializing the event. These are pieces of total theatre.

Foreman began his career fairly traditionally. Coming from an upper middle-class background in the suburbs of New York, he attended Brown University, where he participated in theatrical productions, and studied playwriting at Yale with the legendary John Gassner. He began his career by writing bedroom farces, one of which was optioned for Broadway though never produced. But even at Yale he had become unhappy with the structure and content of conventional drama. Foreman saw the majority of theatre as simply reinforcing the expectations and understandings with which the audience entered a theatre. Even a theatre that presented new social or political ideas most often did so through conventional dramatic structures. Foreman, however, felt that the purpose of art was to present something that could not be experienced in the quotidian world.

Foreman wanted to disrupt the process of viewing and challenge the preconceptions of the spectator. "Character, empathy, narrative – these are all straitjackets imposed on the impulse so it can be dressed up in a fashion that is familiar, comforting, and reassuring for the spectator," he declared. "But I want a theatre that frustrates our habitual way of seeing and by so doing frees the impulse from the objects in our culture to which it is invariably linked."[50] He was not, it should be emphasized, trying to bring the spectator to a particular ideological point of view. Unlike Brecht, who was an early inspiration, he did not have a political agenda and was not leading his audience toward some form of social action. But in the process of altering perceptual mechanisms, there would undoubtedly be some change in the way the spectator saw the world, and in this sense his theatre could be seen as political. Foreman saw his own process of writing as an attack on habitual patterns of understanding:

> The sentences I write, which proliferate into a play, are individual doses of acid, hurled against coagulated thought, coagulated feelings, which all stand as a wall blocking perception, hiding paradise. What I am trying to do is get to the grain of thought and feeling. The free-possibilities of the primary process usually coagulates in us into codes, into ever more deeply cut channels, rendering all the more interesting and complex maneuvers and transformations no longer possible. I try in my work to take dictation from the non-coagulated, still granular source: paradise.[51]

Foreman compares the process to a form of psychoanalysis in which a problem is solved by reframing it: "My plays propose an art that focuses on changing the perceptual environment within which we see objects and problems; I refuse to analyze objects and problems using the terms insisted upon by our socially enforced perspectives."[52]

When he began to produce plays in 1968, he somewhat capriciously chose the name Ontological-Hysteric Theatre for his theatre, inspired by Austrian artist Hermann Nitsch's "Orgien Mysterien Theater," which had been performing at the Cinematheque. As Foreman acknowledged, the name was off-putting to some early audiences – sounding pretentious and indicative of the worst excesses of experimental theatre. But it summed up his preoccupations: "I'm taking nineteenth-century naturalistic triangles and other psychological situations, which I believe are basically hysterical at their roots, in terms of classical psychiatry, the hysterical syndrome," he explained. "And I'm trying to redeem them, and open up holes by which more ... *cosmic* perceptual concerns bleed through, that are really ontological concerns in the Heideggerian sense."[53]

Foreman's "Manifesto III" (1975) reads in large part like a response to Heidegger's *Being and Time*. Heidegger suggested that inherent in the concept of understanding is a "forestructure" that guides interpretation through a set of assumptions and beliefs. "We do not *know* what 'Being' means," claimed Heidegger. "But already when we ask, 'What *is* being?' we stand in an understanding of the 'is' without being able to determine conceptually what the 'is' means."[54] This philosophy is echoed by Foreman:

> The task of art is to serve understanding ... by trying to create a field which is isomorphic with what
> > *stands-under*
>
> experience – which is not experience itself.
>
> Now, what stands-under experience cannot be experienced, experience is not the mode by which we can know it.
>
> What *stands-under* experience are the laws (processes) of perception and other laws-of-configuration of the universe.[55]

Foreman's goal, like that of the minimalist artists, was to refocus the process of viewing onto the structure of the event and the process of creation to create what he called "reverberation machines."

Foreman's early productions were typified by somnambulistic movement, monotone delivery of lines mixed with prerecorded dialogue and his own commentary, lights shining in the eyes of the audience, and sudden loud and abrasive sounds that would jolt spectators out of the trance-like state induced by the pacing. The stage was criss-crossed with strings, sometimes connecting two objects or a performer and an object, sometimes simply bisecting the space. Actors would often strike awkward or grotesque poses, movement would be distorted or exaggerated, and there would be frequent, mostly female, nudity (usually in juxtaposition to elaborately dressed performers). Hand-made props and set pieces filled the stage, which was most often a monochromatic field of somber tones hiding shadowy depths and recesses suggesting a frightening dream. The stage could become chaotically filled – with miniature set pieces, Victoriana, furniture, fabric and curtains, Renaissance paintings and frames, lamps and chandeliers, and the aforementioned strings, suggesting a cross between an old attic filled with family memorabilia and a child's room following some theatrical endeavor – only to become suddenly empty, like the mind jumping from cluttered thoughts to clarity. The self-referential dialogue, especially when abstracted from the context of performance, seems almost childlike. Certain "characters" – Rhoda (always played by Kate Mannheim, whom Foreman later married), Max (played by filmmaker Bob Fleischner), Ben, Sophia – recurred through most of the early work, although these characters had no narrative or psychological basis; they could have no independent life outside the performance. (Foreman was often accused of treating his actors as puppets – Craig-like übermarionettes – yet the intense and distinctive acting of Mannheim in particular was powerful and energetic, reminiscent of the great German expressionist performers.) The text is best understood as Foreman having an ongoing dialogue with himself, questioning his thoughts and ideas and commenting on what has just been said. A section of text from *Rhoda in Potatoland*, dealing with the process of writing, exemplifies this pattern. (In the following, the indented text is generally spoken in taped voice-over.)

It should be easier than this.
> What.
> (*Pause.*)

Writing good.
> Don't you know? There's nothing to it.

What.
> Writing good.

What makes me think writing is important.
> (*Shrugs.*) Everybody does it all the
> time so it must be important.

Plate 14   *Rhoda in Potatoland* (1975–76). Note lights aimed at audience, miniature painted set upper left, and strings. With Camille Foss (foreground), Cathy Scott (kneeling), and Kate Mannheim.

Photo: Arnold Aronson.

    She doesn't do it.
Who. (*Pause.*)Rhoda? She's always writing. Everybody is always writing.
    RHODA
    (*Enters.*)
Hello.
    VOICE
She wrote it.
    RHODA
Am I late.
    VOICE
She wrote it.
    RHODA
She said it.
    VOICE
Look, look compare her to a typewriter.
    SOPHIA
    (*Enters.*)

Hello.
  (*Pause.*)
  RHODA and SOPHIA
Hello.
  (*They squeeze together.*)
  RHODA
What are you doing.
  SOPHIA
Writing.
  RHODA
I'm comparing myself.
  SOPHIA
Don't push.
  RHODA
She likes it.
  SOPHIA
  (*Arms around her. They collapse.*)
Oh Rhoda, what a good writer you are.
  RHODA
Would you get this sack of potatoes off my body?
  WAITER
  (*Enters.*)
What'll it be?
  MAX
  (*Pause.*)
Potatoes.
  (*RHODA and SOPHIA get up and plop on his table.*)
  RHODA
Don't read while you eat.
  SOPHIA
Here's a potato.
  "They don't really compare themselves to potatoes but he
  does."
  RHODA
I wish I was growing someplace.[56]

The repetitions, simple syntax, interchangeability of characters, and mixture of nonsense and profundity are reminiscent of Gertrude Stein, one of Foreman's major influences.

Foreman's work seems related, if not necessarily indebted, to that of the artist Joseph Kosuth. Influenced by Wittgenstein's discussion of the tautologous nature of mathematical propositions and their function as a picture of the world, Kosuth declared that "a work of art is a tautology in that it is a presentation of the artist's intention, that is, he is saying that that particular work of art is art, which means is a *definition* of art."[57] In his "Art as Idea as Idea" series, in which Kosuth paid homage to artist Ad Reinhardt, who had stated that "art is art as art," Kosuth would display an object, a photograph of the object, and a photostat of a dictionary definition of the object, thus calling into question the nature of reality (which is the "real" object?), art, and representation. Just as Rhoda in *Rhoda in Potatoland* says that "comparison will be the basis of my life," [58] Foreman's plays are filled with Kosuth-like contrasts in which miniaturized models of larger objects on the stage are presented for comparison, in which analogous yet different objects are juxtaposed (a boat and a shoe, for example – both means of transportation), and in which the omnipresent strings force the spectator to draw comparisons between ostensibly unrelated items, all of which calls into question assumptions about how we perceive and understand the world. Embedded within a particular setting could often be found smaller versions of the set (or sets already seen or soon to be seen). These might be painted on walls or exist as models placed at points within the set. Thus the spectator was allowed to view the same space from various perspectives and in different ways, and even in a sense to move through time not by narrative device but through visual manipulations and juxtapositions, all the while remaining in a fixed location. While sound, light, and gesture was often used to frame an action, object, or image, the stage was often filled with literal frames that evoked Renaissance paintings while at the same time segmenting and focusing spectator attention. The proscenium-style arrangement of most of his productions allowed an amazing control and manipulation of space, depth, and focus. Foreman set out to accomplish nothing less than a nearly total revision of modes of perception learned by most audiences through the whole modern tradition of Western theatre.

Through 1972, the Ontological-Hysteric Theatre productions were presented at the Cinematheque or at Theatre for the New City in the East Village. Starting with *Vertical Mobility* in 1974, Foreman worked in lofts in Soho. *Rhoda in Potatoland* was presented in a fourth-floor loft that was fairly narrow but eighty feet deep. Foreman placed the audience on bleacher seats at one end and used the great depth of the loft to play with spatial and depth perceptions, constantly altering the depth of the space through Baroque-style sliding flats and the use of lighting. There was a home-made quality to the sets and lights (the latter, in typical Off Off Broadway style, tending to be a mixture of dime-store clip-on lights and "tin-can spots" – PAR lamps housed in old coffee cans). Yet it was not amateurish by any means. The scenography was complex and sophisticated; it merely eschewed the slickness of the commercial world, as did the acting. This was not a company in the sense of the Performance Group or Open Theatre. While some actors worked frequently with Foreman, Kate Mannheim was the only regular, appearing in nearly every production through the mid-1980s. None were professionals. Foreman sought a quality that was at once unaffected and non-narcissistic, yet that required intense concentration, rigor, and presence. By the early 1970s, rehearsals would generally occur over a period of three months, with Foreman meticulously directing every movement and stance. This was not a theatre for actors who wished to improvise or to contribute to the process of developing the play.

With *Pandering to the Masses* (1975) and *Rhoda in Potatoland* (1975–76), Foreman moved out of the hypnotically paced meditative works into a more energetic style. The latter piece, though still with its quiet moments, was suffused with 1930s jazz, grotesque dances, rapid shifts of action, and both slapstick and intellectual humor. The title inevitably evoked thoughts of *Alice in Wonderland*, and certainly Rhoda (an aspect of Foreman) was lost in a world where normal rules did not apply, narrative and linearity were thwarted at every turn, and great works of literature and philosophy were comparable to potatoes, which appeared in the production in forms ranging from the actual object to actors in potato costumes. In a 1997 colloquium on Foreman's work, philosopher Arthur Danto contrasted the French concept of the absurd with the Anglo-American concept of nonsense as embodied by Lewis Carroll's *Alice in Wonderland* and placed Foreman's work – admiringly – in the latter tradition. "Your plays," Danto said to Foreman, "have nothing to do with logic, with reason, or the denials of those things . . . but display a kind of constantly unfurling creative nonsense, which is pretty heady."[59] But "it ALWAYS makes sense," as Foreman had pointed out in 1977:

> Sense *can't* be avoided. If it first seems to be non-sense, wait: roots will reveal themselves. Anything that is produced, that 'arises' on the scene of our on-going human discourse of mutual lived lives, comes from 'someplace,' from some source – and that

fact kept in mind is what orients one to the latent 'sense.' The sense is what the 'arrived' or produced item is translated into by OTHER on-going modes of discourse. So sense is always available, simply a transformation of the 'arrived' fact (which makes us see that several 'senses' are always mutually available, as several transformations can always be worked upon the 'arrived.')[60]

Unlike Wilson, Foreman fought against trance and against the audience losing itself in the performance. Every element of an Ontological-Hysteric Theatre production worked to throw the audience back on itself, as it were – forcing the spectator to confront the text and the performance and to constantly question modes and methods of perception. The plays eschewed the meta-narrative of modernism for the disjunction of postmodernism. The works were constantly commenting on themselves and their creation – a truly postmodern example of irony.

Foreman had the financial luxury of not needing to work to support himself. In addition, he became adept at securing grants from the National Endowment for the Arts, the New York State Council on the Arts, and other foundations. Because he was a director, playwright, designer, and producer, he could often secure funding separately in each category, which meant that, for Off Off Broadway productions, the works were usually well supported. The box-office income thus went to the actors.

In addition to his Ontological-Hysteric work, Foreman also created several musicals with composer Stanley Silverman. While considered avant-garde in comparison with the usual musical theatre fare, the pieces were nonetheless melodic and entertaining, and some, notably *Dr. Selavy's Magic Circus* (the title a homage to Duchamp's "R. Rose Selavy"), achieved a moderate Off Broadway success. Joseph Papp, producer of the New York Shakespeare Festival, also began to hire Foreman as a director, and in 1976 he directed a highly successful, if somewhat controversial, production of Brecht's *Threepenny Opera* at the Vivian Beaumont Theatre at the Lincoln Center. (Some critics complained about the incorporation of many of Foreman's visual trademarks – strings, Victoriana, lamps, and the like – but even more disturbing for New York audiences, who still remembered the sentimentalized Theatre de Lys production of the 1950s, was the eerily detached acting and stylized movement, which created an alienation effect for the 1970s.)

Right up to the present day, Foreman has continued to produce at least one Ontological-Hysteric Theatre play a year in addition to productions for the Public Theatre or a regional theatre, and even the occasional opera (he scandalized Paris in 1983 with full frontal nudity at the Paris Opera production of *Die Fledermaus*). Certainly, the productions exist on a continuum with those of thirty years ago and, especially to the more casual observer, the productions retain the trademark qualities: feverish pacing, manic juxtapositions, grotesque imagery, and challenges to the viewer (a clear Plexiglas wall between stage and auditorium has generally replaced the harsh lights shining in the viewers' eyes). But the recent plays have taken on a much more introspective, and even accessible, tone. Filled with contemplations of mortality and the frustrations of knowing how much will never be known or accomplished, the plays are strangely wistful – the work of an artist entering a mature part of his creative life. "I think perhaps the sadness," Foreman explained, referring to his work in the late 1990s, "the pathos . . . increasingly documents the problematics of trying to carry out the program that, as a younger man, I thought would be exciting."[61]

Foreman and Wilson continue to produce on a regular basis more than thirty years after their start – Foreman annually at the Ontological-Hysteric Theatre at a downtown venue (since the mid-1990s at St Mark's-in-the-Bouwerie Church – one of the few Off Off Broadway organizations with a permanent home), Wilson primarily in Europe, though with regular appearances at the Next Wave Festival in Brooklyn and frequent productions at ART in Cambridge, Massachusetts. It is perhaps hard to call their works avant-garde after all that time. In a sense, they have, each in their own way, institutionalized the avant-garde, transforming it into a style. In Foreman's case, the work is still rigorous and unique. If it is no longer avant-garde in the sense that it is relatively familiar, even comforting to long-time supporters, it still has the power to challenge, surprise, even to shock. Wilson has had greater popular success, and he has most definitely established a style that has had an impact upon fashion advertising, music video, and even decorative arts (chairs and tables designed for productions have been manufactured as stylish furniture). It is perhaps not surprising that more recent work has been done in collaboration with rock composers Tom Waits (*The Black Rider*) and Lou Reed (*Time Rocker*). These works are highly mannered, replete with astonishing images, yet seem to lack the structural rigor of the earlier productions. Foreman and Wilson, in fact, are not unlike the aging rock stars who also emerged in the 1960s and who continue to tour and record with great success. A bit of nostalgia is involved in their continued popularity, yet while many have followed in their wake, none seems to have equaled their originality and talent.

Plate 15   *I've Got the Shakes* (1995). More than twenty-five years after
his first Ontological-Hysteric production, many of Foreman's
distinctive visual elements remain. The more horizontal
space of the theatre at St Mark's-in-the-Bouwerie Church
(as opposed to the deep space of the earlier lofts) leads to
a more static (and cluttered) set.

Photo: © Paula Court.

Chapter 6

Performance art (and the origins of the Wooster Group)

I'm so involved with form I could put anything into a structure. It has no personal meaning for me.

Elizabeth LeCompte[1]

The social and political tone of the country began to change in the early 1970s and with it, not surprisingly, the approaches to the creation of theatre and its style and content. The political assassinations of the 1960s took their toll on the national psyche, as did the shootings of student protesters at Kent State University in Ohio and Jackson State University in Mississippi in 1970. As the war in Vietnam dragged on, the social fabric of the country was increasingly torn apart; the revelations of Watergate and the resignation of President Nixon further eroded belief in national institutions and fostered growing cynicism. The ideals of community, self-sacrifice, and working for the common good, which was probably more prevalent in the romantic imagination than in practice anyway, began to give way to what ultimately became known as "identity politics," in which particular social or political constituencies focused on their more narrowly defined needs, often creating conflicts with former allies. The civil rights and feminist movements, for instance, once supported by a broad coalition, now gave way to more militant approaches to change and to a growing emphasis on separatism; exclusionary tactics replaced inclusionism as the respective movements sought to establish their particular identities. Various social, ethnic, political, and economic groups followed suit. The trend was abetted, if not entirely caused, by a deteriorating economy. The spirit of community and altruism crumbled under the pressure.

Faced with the failure to end the war, eradicate poverty, advance the cause of civil rights, and other attempts to effect large-scale social change, and faced with exclusion from movements that had once welcomed them, many people began to look inward. Several approaches to personal well-being that had begun to emerge in the 1960s – meditation, spiritualism, holistic medicine, and various psychological therapies – now came to take precedence over communal action. "The personal is the political" became the new slogan as the individual became the measure for social change. How social, political, or economic factors affected oneself became as important as how such factors affected whole classes of society. But such a shift in attitude also had the inevitable potential for replacing compassion with self-indulgence and selflessness with greed. Author and social observer Tom Wolfe dubbed the 1970s the "me decade," which he character-ized by a desire to talk about "me" and the search for self-fulfillment.[2]

If the baby-boom generation needed any confirmation that the communal spirit of the 1960s was over, it could be found in the disin-tegration of the rock groups that had dominated the period, most notably the Beatles. The similar disintegration of many of the major theatre collectives may not have had so profound an effect upon the larger cultural landscape, but it certainly marked a shift in the evolution of the avant-garde and even had effects upon mainstream theatre. Already by 1968, the monodramas of Richard Foreman, say, suggested a turning inward for creative inspiration instead of looking to the surrounding world, although Foreman's indebtedness to a vast intel-lectual arena elevated his works well beyond a mere solipsistic enterprise. But a new form of performance began to emerge, centered around the individual and concerned primarily, if not entirely, with the self. As with comparable trends in society at large, this introspective theatre ranged from a healthy starting point for the generation of complex and innovative new material, as with the work of the Wooster Group, to self-indulgent forms of display in some, though certainly not all, of what became known as performance art.

Spalding Gray and Elizabeth LeCompte

Spalding Gray, who had joined Richard Schechner's Performance Group in 1970, acting in *Commune* and *The Tooth of Crime* (1972), was appearing as the character Swiss Cheese in the group's 1974 production of *Mother Courage* when he began to attend the Byrd Hoffman open houses and participate in Robert Wilson's workshops. Although Schechner's approach to acting had always emphasized the Brechtian dialectic between actor and character, there was still an emphasis on "psychological honesty and full, emotive expression of feeling," as Gray described it.[3] But Wilson's workshops triggered a new response. "I began to have a flow of feeling that I could not name because the flow, which was directly connected to the physical flow of body movement, happened so quickly and in a continuum that it was more difficult to pin down and name. There was only direct unmediated expression," which seemed to change in response to the movement of others in the room.[4] In other words, there was a perceived shift from the outward expression of emotion to a deeper connection with inner emotions. Elizabeth LeCompte, who had also joined the group with Gray in 1970 (she and Gray were a couple at the time) as assistant director and sometime actor, was likewise becoming disenchanted with Schechner's approach but primarily because the work seemed to her to lack an intellectual and aesthetic commitment. As a graphic artist, she sought an artist's sense of distance from the work. "I think *Dionysus in 69* definitely bridged the gap between the theatre world and the art world," she explained.

> Structurally it was non-linear and it broke open a lot of ideas about theatre space. That piece should have been a bridge, but I think the aspirations of the people who were involved were theatrically-oriented. The performers wanted to be great actors but they had no sense of or interest in the meaning of the piece, its concept.[5]

She was more drawn to the musical and geometric structures of Wilson's *Deafman Glance* and the abstracted gestures of Richard Foreman's work.[6] So, during *Mother Courage*, Gray, LeCompte, two other group members and a few friends began their own workshops to explore a more personal approach to performance – one in which the exploration was, in Gray's words, "a dialectic between ... life and theatre rather than between role and text."[7]

The workshops culminated in two productions in 1975: *A Wing and a Prayer* by Ellen LeCompte (Elizabeth's sister) and *Sakonnet Point*, "composed and directed" by Gray and Elizabeth LeCompte. The latter was the first production of what would become the *Rhode Island Trilogy* (including *Rumstick Road*, 1977, and *Nayatt School*, 1978 – titles all taken from locales of Gray's childhood) and which would lead to the formation of the Wooster Group in 1980. (Once the Wooster Group had been formally established, all the work created by its members since 1975 was retroactively referred to as part of the Wooster Group *oeuvre*.) *Sakonnet Point* was a radical break from the

Performance Group style and, indeed, from almost any other form of contemporary American theatre. In these pieces, the group merged the personal and autobiographical inspiration of a single performer (Gray) with the spirit of ensemble creation, and with the singular creative vision and control of an artist-director (LeCompte). LeCompte functioned as a plastic artist, taking found material – at first Gray's autobiographical contributions and subsequently classical dramatic texts – deconstructing it, and then shaping, molding, and arranging it into theatrical performance. As she described her process at the time:

> Spalding sits for a portrait that I paint. [The other group members] assist me in this painting at one moment, and at another I include them in the composition with Spalding. There is a dialogue between the sitter and the painter. The portrait, the persona that emerges, is an amalgam of the sitter's image of himself and the vision of him/her that the painter sees and constructs. When the painter and the one painted *both* recognize themselves in the final portrait, it is a perfect collaboration. The persona named Spalding Gray is made from this kind of collaboration.[8]

This was the crux – just as Gertrude Stein shaped a literary persona for Alice B. Toklas in *The Autobiography of Alice B. Toklas*, so LeCompte created a theatrical persona out of the real Gray. The process of creating a text from "found objects" created something new, which might be called collage theatre.

Beyond Foreman and Wilson, it was the work of Meredith Monk – a director, composer, filmmaker, and singer – that exerted the most significant influence on Gray and LeCompte. Monk began creating performances in the mid-1960s and in 1968 founded a collective of performers called the House, which pioneered site-specific work. Many of Monk's pieces explored the idea of memory, often contrasting perceptions of the past with understandings of the present. In *Education of the Girl Child* (1972–73), for example, six women discover a "relic," which turns out to be a living woman dressed in Peruvian clothing. The women train her to become part of their culture, thereby highlighting the nature of the cultural construction of womanhood. The images in these performances – often created around mundane objects such as a coffee cup, a pair of glasses, a suitcase, a model house – seemed to be drawn from Monk's personal memories, and yet the pieces were not ostensibly autobiographical. As described by dance historian Sally Banes, "Monk creates temporal palimpsests where layers of past, present and future mingle."[9] The landscape-of-memory structure of Monk's productions, and her evocative use of objects, found their way into *Sakonnet Point* and what followed.[10] (The use of simple, found objects was also a factor in Happenings and was, in the early 1970s, being exploited in the idiosyncratic performances of Stuart Sherman, whom LeCompte also acknowledged as an inspiration.[11])

Despite the strong physicality and ritualistic aspect of much of the ensemble work of the 1960s, there was still an underlying literary text and a strong thematic content that referred to issues in the world beyond the theatre. In the work of LeCompte and Gray, however, meaning constantly spiraled back inward to the source of creation – the self – and was totally and inextricably bound up in performance. *Sakonnet Point* was essentially an abstract sound-and-movement piece with almost no dialogue; it was an ethereal, impressionistic evocation of childhood luxuriating in the languorous rhythms of idle summers. Gray, dressed only in a green bathing suit, seemed to be returning to memories of youth as he flew a toy airplane around the dimly lit space of the Performing Garage (the performing area, a kind of theatre-in-the-round, was surrounded by scaffolding left over from *Mother Courage*) and played games with an eight-year-old boy, who was, perhaps, Gray as a child. A red tent, illuminated from within, sat ten feet above the stage on one of the scaffolds, and Tchaikovsky's Piano Concerto #1 emanated continuously from the tent throughout the entire one-hour performance, as did whispering from figures seen inside in silhouette.[12] The contemplative mood was pierced by moments of heightened activity, but it always returned to stillness. At the end, four of the performers spread out a blanket on the floor and lay down as if at the beach or on a picnic; bed sheets were slowly stretched above them on clothes lines; and the play concluded with a seven-minute fade out as the performers lay motionless.

The presence of the actor behind the character was well established by the mid-1970s, but the *Rhode Island Trilogy* productions took the idea of "character" into new realms, and in the process altered the relation of the audience to the character and, hence, the performance. Schechner, explained Gray, had "emphasized the performer, making him more than, or as important as, the text ... The way that I interpreted Schechner's theories was that I was free to do what I wanted, be who I was, and trust that the text would give this freedom a structure ... I began to question the whole idea of enacting a role at all ... [and] I discovered that text and action could exist separately and be

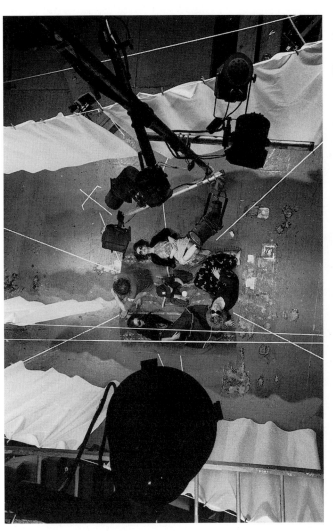

Plate 16 Sakonnet Point near the end of the performance as photographed from directly above. The audience, not visible in the photo, sat on scaffolds around three sides of the space.

Photo: Ken Kobland. Courtesy the Wooster Group.

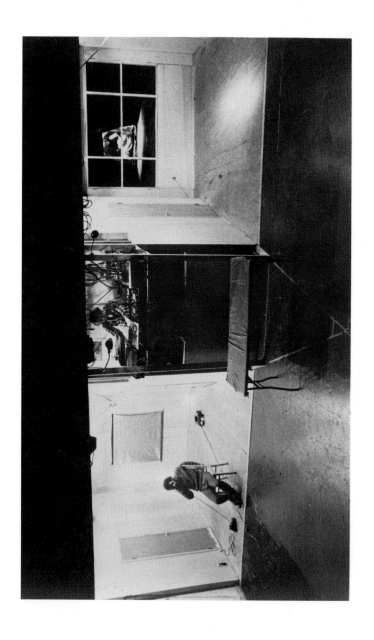

Plate 17 (opposite) The three trapezoidal spaces of *Rumstick Road* (the side spaces and the enclosed technical booth), which would become the basis for many future ground plans of Wooster Group productions. Spalding Gray talks on the phone to his mother's psychiatrist (heard on tape from a recorded phone conversation). Bruce Porter is in the control booth facing the audience (he can see the action reflected in a mirror in front of the audience). Libby Howes is in the red tent seen through the window. The doors in the sides of the control booth opened to a connecting passage; when the doors were open, the spectators could see the interior action on mirrors on the inner side of the doors.

Photo: Clem Fiori. Courtesy the Wooster Group.

understood."[13] Gray described his work in a painterly metaphor: "The 'figure' became myself in the theatre, and the 'ground' was the contingency of everyday time out of which this timeless, and therefore 'saved,' figure grew."[14]

Following *Sakonnet Point*, the Performance Group toured India with *Mother Courage*. The tour seemed to be a catalyst for a spiritual and emotional crisis for Gray, who was still haunted by his mother's suicide in 1967. Upon returning home he and LeCompte decided to channel that distress into performance. Whereas *Sakonnet Point* was, as LeCompte stated, not about the past *per se* but "really about us thinking about the past,"[15] *Rumstick Road* incorporated explicitly personal and autobiographical artifacts. The production used projections of family photographs and tape recordings of discussions between Gray and his two grandmothers, his father, and his mother's psychiatrist – all of which contributed to an uproar in some of the press about questions of privacy, appropriation of materials, and, in the case of the psychiatrist's tape, unauthorized use of a confidential conversation – the first of many controversies in which the group would become embroiled. This was not a documentary play, any more than *Long Day's Journey into Night*, say, is a documentary account of Eugene O'Neill's family or *Glass Menagerie* an autobiographical account by Tennessee Williams. The tension between the poignant and painful material (the psychiatrist's tape in particular, regardless of the ethics of using it, was harrowing in its apparent insensitivity) and the way in which the performers and LeCompte structured that material into a performance about madness contributed to the mixed and sometimes confused response by audiences and critics. Gray's description of the process of creating *Sakonnet* applies equally well to *Rumstick Road*:

A series of simple actions developed out of this process that created a series of images like personal, living Rorschachs. These images were not unlike the blank, white wall in Zen meditation, nor were they unlike the mirror reflection of a good therapist. Often, what the audience saw was the reflection of their own minds, their projections.[16]

Furthermore, Gray noted, *Rumstick Road* "was a confessional act. It was an act of distancing. At last I was able to put my fears of, and identification with, my mother's madness into a theatrical structure. I was able to give it some therapeutic distance."[17] But because the work was created in part through improvisation with other company members, and because it was formed by LeCompte, this could not be autobiographical in any conventional sense – this was not an enactment of Gray's script or Gray's life.

Rumstick Road also began another kind of autobiographical performance, one that might be called "group autobiography." It involved the conscious reuse of props, set pieces, costumes, scenographic shapes, and motifs from one production to the next. The red tent, which had served LeCompte and Gray as a temporary living space in the Performing Garage before they moved into their loft a few blocks from the theatre, phonographs, and telephones were recurring props. The ground plan of *Rumstick Road* was inverted and seen from a different angle in *Nayatt School*; the medical examination from *Rumstick* became a farcical breast examination in *Nayatt*, and so on. Many of these images and motifs carried over into *Point Judith (An Epilog)* in 1979 and many of the works to follow. Although any theatrical group carries its own history with it in each production, this continuity is generally seen and understood as a company's *style*; each production is a discrete enterprise, and any sense of continuity comes primarily from the presence of the actors and the space. But the Wooster Group did something virtually unknown in theatre history: it created an ongoing body of work that flowed from one production into the next and that was consciously self-referential and reflexive. Each of the Wooster Group's productions was, in a sense, part of an evolving and integrated theatrical self-portrait. A 1987 press release declared that its "texts stand as an alternative theatre language which redefines the traditional devices of story-line, character and theme. Each production reflects a continuing refinement of a nonlinear, abstract aesthetic which at once subverts and pays homage to modern theatrical 'realism'."[18]

Nayatt School began moving the group toward what would become its signature style – the appropriation and deconstruction of classical dramatic texts, the manipulation of spatial relationships both onstage and between the audience and the stage, and the syncopation of quiet or intense scenes with manic and frantic ones. The audience was placed on a high bank of bleachers whose lowest tier was about ten feet above the main performing space. As the play began, Gray and the four other adult performers (there were also four children in later scenes) sat at a long table directly facing the lowest rung of the bleachers. Wearing a white lab coat, Gray began talking about his experiences as an actor, particularly in a production of T.S. Eliot's *The Cocktail Party*. He played an excerpt from a Sir Alec Guinness recording of the play and then began an almost affectless reading of a scene from Act II with another performer, Joan Jonas (better known as a postmodern dancer). As the scene progressed, all the actors became increasingly active, while disco music filled the theatre, creating a tumultuous transition as the actors descended into the main playing area. Three scenes of seemingly farcical medical encounters ensued – though they were vaguely related thematically to Eliot's play and certainly referred back to *Rumstick Road*. Most of the action of these scenes occurred inside a trapezoidal soundproof room (the same shape as the side spaces from *Rumstick Road*). The audience looked into it through a window and a clear Plexiglas roof and heard dialogue through microphones, thus creating a sense of voyeurism as well as spatial dislocation. The play headed toward its conclusion – a manic, destructive version of the final scene of *The Cocktail Party* – with several of the guests played by children in oversized costumes (all from previous plays). A film was projected in the soundproof room showing Celia Copplestone, while actor Ron Vawter as Edward played a phonograph. Record players on the table in front of the audience were used to play records that had been played in *Rumstick* and *Sakonnet*. LeCompte described the scene, emphasizing the connections to the two previous parts of the *Trilogy*:

> Props and images are now doubled and tripled. One telephone becomes three, one red tent becomes three tents, one room becomes three rooms, one record player becomes six record players. More and more records emerge and are played simultaneously. The children begin to break the glasses and scream. The Man shoots Peter Quilpe, and he pretends to be dying. Julia falls asleep and is carried out and laid on the floor. Alex is covered with a sheet and laid on the floor. Lavinia pretends to die in Edward's

arms. She is shaken and laid on the table with her head in the tent. She doesn't wake up. Spalding [Sir Henry Harcourt Reilly], the Man, and the Woman ascend on ladders to the upper audience platform. They sit in front of the three record players. They first play and then destroy the records by scratching them, cutting them up, and finally burning them. They descend to the floor. The Man and the Woman climb up the back wall behind large sheets of white paper that traverse the space. They walk across the wall and disappear. Spalding returns to the soundproof room. He plays the Bach Partitas on the Fanola [a child's phonograph].[19]

In *Rumstick Road*, the play began with Gray introducing himself to the audience and reading a letter; in *Nayatt School* he developed a

Plate 18 Spalding Gray in *It's a Slippery Slope* at the Lincoln Center, 1997. Although the venues became more mainstream and larger – hence the microphone – the format of a simple table, glass of water, and notebook remained constant.

Photo: © Paula Court.

whole monologue, which was presented, almost lecture style, to the audience from behind a table. While both monologues segued into the structured performances that followed, they were important steps for Gray, who increasingly wanted to communicate directly with the audience. Beginning in 1979, he developed a series of explicitly autobiographical monologues. While engaging and funny – Gray is a master storyteller – they are deceptive. Delivered while sitting at a simple table facing the audience, the stories seem to be wry, thematically interwoven anecdotes about his childhood, past experiences, and neurotic encounters with the vagaries and peculiarities of late twentieth-century life and the idiosyncratic characters whom he encounters along the way. The monologues are delivered with simplicity and intimacy, as if by a charming dinner guest. Yet every gesture, every tic, every seemingly casual and spontaneous sip of water is a carefully choreographed and structured part of the performance. And the anxiety-riddled and angst-driven character who searches for a "perfect moment" or agonizes over buying a house in these monologues, though closely modeled on himself, was nonetheless a character, and the difference between Gray the person and Gray the character created a certain kind of Brechtian alienation and aesthetic distancing. In a fragmentary story by Jorge Luis Borges, "On Exactitude in Science,"[20] cartographers create a map of an empire so accurate and detailed that it completely covers the country "point for point" (until the empire fades and the map frays and disintegrates). Gray's onstage persona, and those of several other autobiographical performance artists, are equivalent to Borges' map – they are simulacra placed on top of the original. But no matter how exact the fit it is still a cover, not the original, and the audience experiences a strange sense of dislocation, causing part of the focus to fall not simply on the engaging stories or upon the storyteller but upon the gap between the two. Furthermore, his narratives confront audiences with material that is familiar, titillating, even embarrassing – adolescent sexuality, flirtations with homosexuality, the tug-of-war between guilt over the genocide in Cambodia and the desire for personal gratification – and to listen is to become complicit in guilty pleasures and voyeuristic journeys into someone else's psyche. Gray's monologues created the cognitive dissonance typical of some avant-garde performance but disarmed the audience through the charming guise of a raconteur.

As the dynamics of the group were changing, and especially as it became clear that Gray was moving in new directions, an epilogue to the *Trilogy* was written, called *Point Judith*. LeCompte envisioned it as

"Spalding's" (the character, though the actor as well) farewell. The piece incorporated a play called "Rig" by Jim Strahs, specifically written for the group, about men on an oil rig; a movie by Ken Kobland called "By the Sea" about the daily life of four nuns (played by group members, including Gray); and a thirteen-minute version of O'Neill's *Long Day's Journey into Night*.

The production marked another significant transition. At the same time that *Point Judith* was being developed, Schechner was workshopping a production of Genet's *The Balcony* involving several of the same actors as well as non-group actors. Tensions ran high, and it was clear that much of the core of the Performance Group now aligned itself with LeCompte instead of Schechner. As Schechner described it, the Performance Group actors (Gray, Vawter, Willem Dafoe, Libby Howes) "jobbed in: they arrived, learned their lines and blocking, and performed the play."[21] Following the two productions in 1980, Schechner left the Performance Group and the remaining collective assumed the name the Wooster Group, which had always been the official corporate name.[22] The Performing Garage was transferred to the new group as part of this arrangement. As one of the only theatre companies in New York to own its space, it had a stability and security few others had, and this contributed to its longevity.

Performance art

Given the critical acclaim that the Wooster Group was receiving by 1979, and Gray's instant rapport with the audience, his monologues gained immediate attention and popularity. In so doing they galvanized a public awareness of a phenomenon that had been underway for some time – self-created solo performance pieces that were known as performance art.

The artist is always present in some way in the work of art, but at least some artists throughout history have felt the urge to be more directly present in their art and, particularly in the twentieth century, some have attempted to eliminate the mediating effect of the art work altogether as a means of erasing the boundaries between art and life and to confront the spectator directly. It was an attempt by artists, explained art historian Kristine Stiles, "to reengage both themselves and spectators in an active experience by reconnecting art (as behavior) to the behavior of viewers."[23] There was also a desire, particularly in the postwar decades, to subvert the commodification of art. The artists stepped out from behind the canvas, as it were, presenting themselves or their actions as the art work, thereby substituting process or action for a tangible product that could be bought and sold.

Because the term encompassed two essentially different disciplines – performance (i.e., theatre) and art – it has been notoriously difficult to define. The term is a critical appellation that did not gain widespread usage until the 1970s – the artists themselves often referred to their work as live art, body art, action art, art performance, or, simply, performance. As critic RoseLee Goldberg observed, "Each performer makes his or her own definition in the very process and manner of execution."[24] Even the normally precise editor of *The Drama Review*, Michael Kirby, was unsuccessful at grappling with the phenomenon. Coining the awkward term "autoperformance" for a 1979 issue devoted to the subject, he described it as "presentations conceived and performed by the same person" but then went on to admit that some such presentations could involve several performers; furthermore, according to Kirby, the presence of Robert Wilson in his own productions qualified those works as autoperformance, as did Richard Foreman's conductor-like presence at his performances.[25] Such a broad definition loses any real utility, because its sweeping inclusiveness encompasses material that no serious observer of the avant-garde would classify as performance art, such as stand-up comedy, dramatic monologues, or any dance in which the choreographer appeared. And yet, to complicate matters maddeningly, some of those very works, such as the conceptual and idiosyncratic comic routines of the late Andy Kaufman, the dramatic character sketches of Eric Bogosian, and much of the work of postmodern dancers often *were* identified as performance art. Although there were formal similarities between the performance art generated by visual artists and that produced by theatre artists, each group generally had differing reasons and intentions for the creation of their performances, and thus definitions and understanding of performance art depended to a degree on the orientation or artistic origin of the performer or critic. Straining to avoid absolutes, art critic Linda Novak seemed to suggest that performance art was more a means of approaching an intellectual problem than a readily identifiable genre: performance art, she declared, was "a mode of discourse (a process of reasoning and talking about a subject), rather than … a category of exclusively formal properties."[26]

Despite such evasions and vagaries, performance art does have some clearly definable characteristics. More often than not, it *is* characterized by a solo performer presenting a self-created performance (as opposed to a text written by someone else). Such performances tend to take the form of autobiographical monologues, such as those by Holly Hughes or David Cale; the presentation of characters drawn from both life and the imagination, as well as those functioning as the performer's alter ego, as in the creations of Ethyl Eichelberger, Penny Arcade, or Eleanor Antin; or the enactment or embodiment of conceptual ideas in the tradition of conceptual art or concrete poetry, as in the performances of Chris Burden, Vito Acconci, or Stuart Sherman. A performance art piece could also employ several performers, as in the works of Suzanne Lacy or Sherman's later work, but in such cases the performers functioned not so much as collaborators but as raw material for the artist's vision. Whether a solo or group presentation, it is the singularity of the idea or subject that typifies performance art, as opposed to the complex interweaving of multiple layers of theme, narrative, character, language, action, and imagery in much traditional theatre, or the interplay of line, form, color, texture, and image in most traditional visual art. Performance art, by and large, derived its form and meaning from a singular and overriding concept or idea and, at least in solo work, the unifying and centering presence of the performer (and the autobiographical matter that was often the principal material of much theatre-based performance art). Furthermore, the performer consciously strove to undermine the traditional actor–audience relationship by regularly splitting focus between the content and the performer/performance while constantly making the audience question its relationship to the performer and the material. It is this "attitude" that allows the stand-up comedy of Kaufman or Lenny Bruce, for example, to be called performance art. And, finally, while there were exceptions – notably in the work of Laurie Anderson – performance art was often typified by a technical and physical simplicity that foregrounded concept and the performer over elaborate scenography or *mise en scène*.

(It is for all these reasons that I exclude most of the work of Foreman and Wilson from the category of performance art, although some critics include them. While it is true that these works represent a singular conceptual vision in which all elements are under the absolute control of the artist-director, they are richly complex, multi-layered, multivalent creations whose meaning and effect cannot be easily contained within a single concept or reduced to one central idea, and in which the artist, whether present or not, is neither the focal point of meaning nor the prime agent for conveying the content. Wilson's "chamber" works, such as the *DIA LOG* pieces with Christopher Knowles or *I was sitting on my patio this guy appeared I thought I was hallucinating* with Lucinda Childs, might qualify, although the focus seems to be more on language and movement than on conceptual presentation.

It is impossible to designate a specific set of influences or stimuli for the postwar trend toward performance. In some way it was certainly a response to the horrors of World War II, the Holocaust, and the atomic bomb. As art historian Paul Schimmel has pointed out, much postwar performance was based on a dialectic between creation and destruction.[27] By emphasizing the individual over the commodified object there was an attempt to reinstill a kind of humanity in art; by privileging the act over the object there was an apparent affinity with existentialism. The reintegration of life and art was implicitly a critique of society. By the 1970s, however, the impetus seemed more attuned to the self-absorption of the "me generation" than to larger socio-political concerns. There was also an economic factor in the rise of performance art, especially in the theatre world of the 1970s and 1980s. Increasingly high rents for both living and performance space in New York and other urban areas and the high cost of maintaining theatre companies and mounting productions fostered a return to simplicity and minimal means and a reliance upon the self. As performer Deb Margolin explained:

> [the] conventions that attend conventional theater: curtains, proscenia, fancy costumes and makeup, and all the trappings that make an actor invisible beneath his or her character ... were out of reach for a lot of us, and performance art allowed us a kind of postmodern license to perform anywhere and without such conceits, making it immediately into a kind of poor folks' theater.[28]

For visual artists, the key factor in performance was the body and the presence of the artist. In "live art" the artist's body became the site of the art, or the medium through which the art was realized, as in Vito Acconci's *Rubbing Piece* (1970), in which he rubbed his arm for an hour to produce a sore, thereby transforming his body into a sort of canvas, or the conceptually similar *Reading Position for Second-Degree Burn* (1971) by Dennis Oppenheim, in which the artist lay naked in the sun for five hours with only his chest covered by a book, thus using the sun to "paint" his body. But for performance artists who emerged from the theatre world, the emphasis was different. The performer was already present in the performance. What was missing for some theatre artists, however, was the real and tangible idea of the self. Playwrights have historically appeared as actors in their own works or functioned as directors, but in doing so they were becoming characters in their work or aiding in the realization or interpretation of their own art work, hidden by a real or metaphorical mask or remaining invisible backstage. Just as visual artists stepped out from behind the canvas, theatre artists stepped out from behind the "mask," and performance art became increasingly autobiographical and unmediated.

Some scholars have seen precedents for performance art as far back as ancient Greece and Renaissance Italy.[29] But any immediate influence upon contemporary performance art must be sought in the more recent historical avant-garde from Alfred Jarry, who transformed his daily life into art by assuming the identity of his dramatic creation Père Ubu, to the work of the futurists, dadaists, surrealists, and, to an extent, the theatre workshop of the Bauhaus. The artists of these movements often attempted to blur or eliminate the boundaries between life and art – the artists became living embodiments of their art work, which extended in a continuum from their daily lives through their passage through the street to formally conceived performances. Art was not a manufactured object but a state of mind or way of life.

There is also a history of action-based art – work that emanated from painting and sculpture but that required the live and active presence or participation of the artist and/or the spectator. In this, the history of performance art is similar to that of happenings. A prime example is Jean Arp's sculpture entitled "Planche à Oeufs" (Egg Board) of the 1920s, which consisted of a board with a hole (navel) in it and a set of instructions: "first, chop several eggs; second, split some wood; third, ring the bells; fourth, masturbate; and last, throw the egg in the navel."[30] But it was primarily Marcel Duchamp, with his "readymades," who most significantly reordered the basic understanding of the nature of art. By taking existing objects and reframing them through the act of labeling them as art, he not only drew attention to the aesthetic values of prosaic objects but also shifted the definition of art from a predetermined set or category of objects to an essentially linguistic definition. Art was now something – anything – that was designated as art: a fundamentally Wittgensteinian notion that language is fluid and subject to reordering through usage. Duchamp had "created" art by the simple act of signing his name to existing objects, thereby emphasizing the notion of the power of the artist over the actual work of art and the fact that the artist's signature serves to frame a work, thus removing it from the utilitarian and everyday world. In the late 1940s and 1950s, French artists Yves Klein and Ben Vautier and Italian artist Piero Manzoni, by signing nude models, a globe, and even the sky, declared that everything from human beings to the universe could be a personally created work of art.[31] While there was an element of parody in these actions, it did effectively interrogate the nature of art while dematerializing the object. Art was no longer something to be acquired and hung on a wall but rather life itself. It also suggested that the artist was more important than the individual creation.

The action painters, meanwhile, beginning with Jackson Pollock, established that process – and therefore the act of the artist – was the point of art, not the image or object that was incidentally created. The object became "merely" a by-product of a series of actions. (Subsequent scholarship has demonstrated that Pollock's action paintings were much more carefully conceived than they appear. Nonetheless, the popular conception inspired subsequent generations of artists.) Wittgenstein, as Kristine Stiles noted, raised a relevant question: "When I raise my arm, my arm goes up. And the problem arises: what is left over if I subtract the fact that my arm goes up from the fact that I raised my arm?"[32] Performance art, especially in the 1950s and early 1960s, was in essence about what happens if the object produced is subtracted from the action that produced it. Once the emphasis shifts to the artist, he or she becomes a performer, complete with all the elements of voyeurism, exhibitionism, and eroticism that attend theatrical performance. As art critic Barbara Rose has observed, it was the photographs of Pollock at work by Hans Namuth that helped to create the mythology of the artist as performer, "the artist as an inspired shaman," "the artist as actor."[33] From the foregrounding of the artist as actor it was a only small step for performance itself to take precedence over the production of a tangible art work.

Although artists have, presumably, always wanted their art work to be seen, a painting or sculpture, unlike theatre, can exist independently of an audience. The emergence of performance art, however, required an audience, and in many cases the desire to transgress the boundaries of life and art resulted in varying degrees of audience participation. Any art that includes a performer and an audience is, by definition, theatre. Among the earliest practitioners of performative and participatory art in the postwar era were members of the Gutai Group of Japan, founded in 1954, and Japanese-born artist Yoko Ono, who lived in the United States. For Ono's *Cut Piece* (1964), for example, she sat calmly on a stage dressed in elegant evening clothes and invited the audience to cut away her clothing with scissors. The elements of physical danger and eroticism in this piece anticipated the "body art" of performance artists such as Chris Burden a few years later.

In the United States, nowhere was the critique of materialism and the desire to integrate life and art better realized than in the work of the Fluxus Group, a loose association of international artists. Strongly influenced by John Cage, Dada, the situationist movement, and *Le Nouveau Realisme*, the group crossed boundaries of art, music, and literature. The term "Fluxus," coined by George Maciunas in 1961, was intended to embody a flow of shifting impulses and actions. "With a Fluxus work," explained Dick Higgins,

> there is a conceptual fusion – 'intermedia' is the term I chose for such fusions, picking it up from Samuel Taylor Coleridge, who had used it in 1812. Virtually all Fluxus works are intermedial by their very nature: visual poetry, poetic visions, action music and musical actions, happenings and events that are bounded, conceptually, by music, literature and visual art, and whose heart lies in the middle ground among these.[34]

While happenings tended to be fairly complex in their conception and execution, Fluxus events tended toward more unitary and simple actions that embodied an underlying concept. "When happenings were broken up into their minimal constituent parts, they became events," Higgins stated. "When events were minimal, but had maximum implications, they became one of the key things which Fluxus artists typically did (and do) in their performances."[35] Furthermore, as other commentators noted, "Fluxus is an attempt to get an essence ... The execution does not *voice* the conception, as in Conceptual Art, but *activates* it, so that the interpretation of a concept is as important as the concept itself."[36] The simple and singular nature of Fluxus events would likewise become a hallmark of much performance art.

Among the more influential American members of the group was George Brecht, whose work often consisted of plain white cards on which were printed a set of instructions or almost *haiku*-like phrases that could be interpreted in various ways. For *Motor Vehicle Sundown* (1960), a number of vehicles were to be arranged in an open space. The "performers" – one per vehicle – went to their vehicles, started the motors and then performed twenty-two actions based upon instructions from a set of twenty-two cards (out of a possible forty-four) that had been dealt to them. While each action was of an equal length, different actions would happen in each vehicle depending on the cards and order each performer was dealt. *Three Aqueous Events* consisted of a card that read:

THREE AQUEOUS EVENTS
- ice
- water
- steam[37]

This raises several questions. Is the "event" the card itself? Is it the idea(s) evoked rather poetically by the words on the card? Is it the realization of the words/ideas and if so, just how (and by whom) are these "instructions" to be carried out? There are many possible answers, especially to the last question, but clearly this is a conceptual performance that may exist solely in the mind of the performer; and even if it exists in real time and space it does not necessarily have cognizant spectators. Happenings creator Allan Kaprow, unhappy and frustrated with audience participation or even passive spectating in happenings, had in fact proposed the elimination of the audience as a means of creating a new art form (or "art/life genre") that was "distinct from any known genre."[38] "All the elements – people, space, the particular materials and character of the environment, time – can in this way be integrated. And the last shred of theatrical convention disappears."[39] Kaprow suggested turning to everyday life for inspiration. "Doing life, consciously, was a compelling notion to me," he declared.[40] Perhaps the exemplary manifestation of this idea was in the work of California artist Linda Montano, much of which she designated as "Living Art," which she described as "time spent artfully alone or not alone."[41] A period of time, ranging from hours to years, was designated for the artists to live and work together, and all the "time and activities which the artists perform are intended to be art."[42] For example, in 1973, when she began her living art pieces, she handcuffed herself to fellow artist Tom Marioni for three days, declaring that all aspects of their life for that time were art. The idea was continued in several living art pieces over the next two decades. The pieces were meticulously documented in notebooks, tape recordings, and photographs, but there were no formal "spectators." Another "life artist" who incorporated the everyday in his performances was Tehching Hsieh. Montano joined him in his one of his grueling and rigorous endurance works, entitled "One Year Performance" (1983–84), in which the two were tied with a rope at the waist for a year.

However, if theatre is the performing of an action in front of an audience, and if – Wittgenstein-like – we remove the audience (the act of perceiving), what is left? What is left, according to Michael Kirby, is no longer theatre but the activity. He described this form as one in which the tangible work of art has "moved inside the body, so to speak. The actions of the person himself become the object of his own attention. This work of art can only be seen by one person, and it can only be viewed from within."[43]

But performance can only be complete in the response of an audience. And while the desire by some artists to fight the commodification of art and to eliminate the passive spectator was strong, the desire to perform proved stronger (or more necessary) for others. And the desire to perform, quite logically and understandably, moved performance art from the somewhat distant and aesthetic conceptual realms of Yves Klein and George Brecht to works that were often more theatrical, personal, confrontational, or shocking, largely because the body became the central focus. Dionysian and shamanistic ritual and Artaudian theory mixed with Dada and minimalism to create performances in which the body was celebrated, but also abused and mutilated, and in which anatomy and bodily functions became part of public display.

Body art

In the United States, outside of Fluxus, it was primarily Carolee Schneemann – artist, performer, filmmaker – who had the largest impact on the transition from visual art to performance and who, by explicitly placing her body at the center of the work, also might be considered the first American "body artist." She was strongly influenced by Artaud, whom she first read in 1960, and believed that works of art should stimulate all the senses and create "conditions which alert the total sensibility – cast it almost in stress – extend insight and response, the basic responsive range of empathetic-kinesthetic vitality."[44] Also like Artaud, she saw live performers as just one potential medium: "performers or glass, fabric, wood … all are potent as variable gesture units: color, light and sound will contrast or enforce the quality of a particular gesture's area of action and its emotional texture"[45]

Schneemann's crossover from visual art to performance began with *Eye Body* (1963), which had begun as a loft environment in 1962 and was then manifested as a series of photographs. "I wanted my actual body to be combined with the work as an integral material," she explained.[46] In the photos, Schneemann is seen in the midst of the environment, her body completely naked (as it was in much of her subsequent work) and painted with ritual-like designs. "Covered in paint, grease, chalk, ropes, plastic, I establish my body as visual territory," she declared. "Not only am I an image maker, but I explore the image values of flesh as material I choose to work with. The body may remain erotic, sexual, desired, desiring but it is as well votive: marked, written over in a text of stroke and gesture discovered by my creative female will."[47]

In 1964, with sculptor Robert Morris, she created *Site*, a seminal work that literally transformed art into performance through a re-enactment of Manet's 1863 painting, *Olympia*. The painting of a nude, provocative in its own time, had lost its ability to shock a century later. By turning the two-dimensional image into a live figure staring at a live audience, elements of both eroticism and danger re-emerged.[48] Performance art, with its use of intermedia and emphasis on temporality and the necessity of an audience, has been acknowledged as one of the turning points between modernism and postmodernism. *Site*, with its essentially postmodern use of pastiche and quotation, serves as an early step along the way. Manet is being quoted, but the work is transformed from a fetishized art object into an element within a performance, emphasizing the role of an artist in the production of an art work.

Schneemann's Dionysian, ritualistic 1964 creation *Meat Joy* remains one of her most famous works. Initially created for a festival in Paris and then restaged in London and at Judson Church in New York, it used nine performers, including the artist. The piece was highly structured, with general movement patterns worked out in precise geometrical forms. The score consisted of fourteen contemporary "top 40" songs and a recording of Parisian street sounds. The actors began the performance dressed in street clothes but eventually undressed each other or stripped down to bikini underwear. Movement patterns ranged from languorous to frenetic through an environment of paper and plastic, with various actions of touching and coupling. Although the actors were choreographed, the specific movements and actions, such as painting each other's bodies, were improvised. Near the end of the one-hour performance, the "Serving Maid enters, carrying a huge tray of raw chickens, mackerel, strings of hot dogs ... Slowly, extravagantly she strews fish, chickens and hot dogs all over the bodies."[49] The piece ended with women throwing buckets of paint on the men and the performers burying each other in a five-foot high pile of paper.

It had, in her words, "the character of an erotic rite. Excessive, indulgent, a celebration of flesh as material."[50]

While *Meat Joy* had obvious affinities with happenings and postmodern dance, Schneemann's subsequent work kept moving on a path toward performance art, as in the more overtly political *Interior Scroll* (1975). Schneemann painted her naked body to emphasize its contours, and she assumed various poses on a table as she read from her own text, "Cézanne, She Was a Great Painter." The performance culminated with the reading of several texts written on a scroll that she unwound from within her vagina. Schneemann described this in terms of "interior knowledge," which had to do with "the power and possession of naming – the movement from interior thought to external signification, and the reference to an uncoiling serpent, to actual information (like a ticker tape, torah in the ark, chalice, choir loft, plumb line, bell tower, the umbilicus and tongue)."[51] In almost any work of art we accept that the product is a concrete expression of emotions that emerge from some mysterious place within the artist. Schneemann, and those who followed her lead, made this expression literal and explicit, forging visual and metaphorical connections not unlike those created by the strings in a Richard Foreman production, which are at once obvious and revelatory.

American body artists were also influenced by the Viennese Action Group (*Wiener Aktionsgruppe*), a group of Austrian artists who began performing in 1962 and formally joined together in 1965. These artists created ritualistic works involving the disemboweling of animal carcasses that drew inspiration from Catholic rites, the cult of Dionysus, and the psychoanalytical theories of Freud, Jung, and Wilhelm Reich. Some members of the group ventured into areas of apparent masochism and self-mutilation. Günter Brus, for instance, while dressed in women's lingerie, would slash himself with scissors, defecate onstage and then eat his feces. Rudolph Schwarzkogler created what he called "Aktions," which were, in essence, fictional documentary actions – carefully constructed images staged for a camera. In one of the photos, the "actor" held a gutted fish over his penis, creating a grotesque illusion of mutilation. Schwarzkogler died in 1969, but his work did not become well known in the USA until an exhibition in 1972. By that time, the images had fueled a rumor that the artist had died as a result of the gradual self-amputation of his penis – a rumor given widespread authenticity by art critic Robert Hughes in *Time* magazine[52] – which seemed to inspire acts of self-abuse among a new generation of performance artists.

The first wave of American performance artists were typified by elements of masochism and self-abuse, and they even subjected themselves to life-threatening danger. One of these artists, Rachel Rosenthal, felt that performance art was

> strongly related to masochism, if not actually masochistic in content. Performance artists have, at various times, cut, bitten, imprisoned themselves; caused themselves to be shot, buried, nailed down; have starved, force-fed, slashed, castrated themselves; eaten puke, eaten shit, drunk till they passed out, hurled themselves against walls, crawled naked on broken glass and razor blades ... just to name a few. When performance is not dangerous to the body, it is dangerous to the ego. Performers are exposed, naked. Artists have made themselves repulsive, have revealed their weaknesses, their personal lives, have gone out on the limb politically, have deal[t] with subjects too painful for most people to apprehend. Performance artists also place themselves at the mercy of time, chance, open-ended developments and the kindness of strangers ... Some of us seek pain. Not as [an] end in itself. As a technique, a trigger, a channel. As a path. Pain may be a path to orgasm, to the dissolution of ego, to growth, understanding, spiritual enlightenment, moral well-being and the feeling of being somewhat special and superior in the culture.[53]

One of the artists she alluded to was Vito Acconci, whose *Seedbed* (1972) was his most notorious work. In the Sonnabend Gallery in Soho, Acconci constructed an inclined ramp rising from the entrance to the rear wall of the gallery and placed himself under the ramp so that he was unseen as the audience walked above him. Twice a week, six hours a day, he lay under the ramp and, supposedly, masturbated while talking into a microphone – describing his fantasies, which were in turn fueled by the sounds of the people in the gallery. Despite the prurient aspects of the performance, it actually raised significant issues for those willing to confront its implications. Acconci became the actor at the center of the performance, yet despite his presence, he remained invisible or absent, like the artist/author who is present in any work yet also invisible. The ramp of the starkly empty gallery became a stage, transforming the audience into actors. The performer and audience were in one sense intimately conjoined, yet prevented from any meaningful interaction. Any theatre, with its exhibitionism and voyeuristic qualities, is erotic on some level, yet this is usually sublimated; here

Plate 19 Vito Acconci performing *Seedbed* at the Sonnabend Gallery in New York in January 1972.
Photo: Courtesy Barbara Gladstone Gallery.

Acconci was making the erotic, even pornographic, relationship of spectator to artist explicit. Furthermore, the audience of *Seedbed* could not remain passive spectators – their very presence at the gallery made them complicit in the event.

Another artist referred to by Rosenthal was California sculptor Chris Burden, who came to epitomize the masochistic branch of performance art. Beginning with *Five Day Locker Piece* (1971), in which he confined himself in a locker two feet high, two feet wide, and three feet deep for five days (the piece was done as his M.F.A. thesis at the University of California at Irvine), Burden created a series of more than sixty performance works in which he subjected himself to a range of dangerous or painful rigors, as in *Shoot* (1971), done at a Santa Ana, California, art gallery, in which a sharpshooter shot him in the arm with a rifle, or *Prelude to 220, or 110* (1971), in which he was bolted to the floor with copper bands while live electric wires were submerged in buckets of water on either side of him – if a spectator knocked over a bucket, Burden risked electrocution.

The Living Theatre, in *Seven Meditations on Political Sadomasochism* (1973), had graphically simulated the torture of political prisoners in Brazil in an attempt to challenge the social and moral assumptions of

Plate 20 Chris Burden strapped to the floor in *Prelude to 220, or 110*.
Note the two buckets of water and the live electric wires
leading into them.

Photo: Courtesy Chris Burden.

the spectators. But audiences understood the action as an illusion
within a theatrical framework and, much to the frustration of the
performers, rarely responded. Burden's works (and others like his), by
contrast, were disturbing because he presented spectators with the situation of a real person in real pain, danger, or deprivation, yet the
actions seemed arbitrary or at least stripped of any clearly identifiable
social or political reference. How was the audience intended to
respond? Burden chose to place himself in imminent danger; there was
no apparent reference to Vietnam, racism, or social injustice – the standard reference points for provocative and engaged art and performance
at the time. These were seemingly amoral actions. Burden claimed that
"my art is an examination of reality. By setting up aberrant situations,
my art functions on a higher reality, in a different state."[54] By abandoning the aesthetic distance that was a standard component of most
art, Burden created an immediacy that much art and performance
lacked. Yet, as one critic astutely noted:

The spectator, incapable of aesthetic detachment, was drawn into a ceremony where the moral implications were not clearly articulated. Hypnotized or repulsed by the tense proceedings and denied the release of a distinct and significant purpose, the viewer was unable to transcend the discreteness of the performance. With the meaning of his work eclipsed, Burden was framed in myth. Functioning simultaneously as a human being and as an object, his performances came perilously close to having their reason for being based on the hyperbole of a manufactured hero.[55]

Body art has continued as a major form of performance art into the 1990s, especially in California. One of the major practitioners is Los Angeles-based Ron Athey. In the context of ritual-like scenarios, Athey, whose body is almost completely covered by tattoos, and other performers would be pierced and scarified. In one of his most controversial pieces, *Four Scenes in a Harsh Life* (1994), a Saint Sebastian character was portrayed by a nude woman whose body was lanced with long needles, which Athey, as Saint Irene, removed. In a subsequent scene, an actor was strapped to a table and an African scarification pattern was carved on his back. The incisions were blotted by Athey with absorbent medical paper towels, which were then attached to clothes lines and pulled out over the audience. In a wedding scene, three brides had their cheeks pierced.[56] "What I do," claims Athey, "is to actually take these feats of the body as scenes in a play. I think there's something inherently spiritual in what I do that makes it a ritual. It's like a public sacrifice, I think. It is really parallel to doing penance."[57]

At a performance of the work in Minneapolis, it was the towels over the audience that alarmed a few spectators, who believed that blood might drip on them, putting them at risk for AIDS (though this was not possible). As a result, the performance led to a controversy over funding by the National Endowment for the Arts to the Walker Art Gallery, which had sponsored the performance.

California

It is not accidental that much of this work occurred in California. Although there had been pockets and fragments of avant-garde activity outside New York, the creation of avant-garde theatre had seemed to depend upon a close-knit theatrical and art community, a sense of connection to the European avant-garde, and the very energy derived

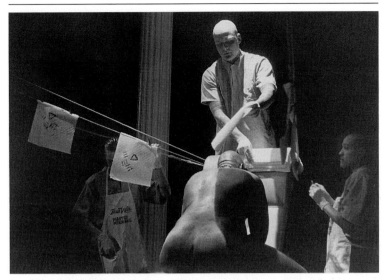

Plate 21   Four Scenes in a Harsh Life. After carving an African
scarification pattern on the back of Darryl Carlton (Divinity
Fudge), Ron Athey blots the marks with medical paper towels
and attaches them to lines and pulls them out over the
audience.

Photo: Dona Ann McAdams.

from the city itself. But performance art seemed to draw on different
energies. Several factors contributed. San Francisco already had some
tradition of avant-garde activity as home to a significant contingent of
Beat writers, as well as to the Actor's Workshop. It was also where, in
the late 1950s, Ann Halprin had her dance workshop, which was a
major factor in the development of postmodern dance. The very environment of California itself seemed conducive to the development of
performance art. Southern California in particular was sprawling and
decentralized and embodied newness, growth, individualism, and a
rejection of the establishment, especially anything associated with the
East Coast. Geographically, as well as economically and spiritually, the
region looked more to Asia than to Europe. The California climate
also created a culture devoted to the outdoors and to fitness, which,
when combined with Hollywood's emphasis on a manufactured ideal
beauty, and the various fads, cults, and movements exploring paths
toward spiritual and physical well-being that seemed to sprout everywhere in California, led to a cult of the body. California thus provided
an environment ripe for the creation of performance – the artist

substituting the body for the canvas and the street for the gallery or the theatre.

One component in the development of California performance was the willingness of many California academic institutions to incorporate performance within their curricula. Not only did this confer scholarly legitimacy on performance art but it also addressed one of the fundamental problems faced by performance artists: financial support. Without an object to sell (other than occasionally some form of documentation), performance artists had little financial support from their work. Some art galleries would fund installations and performances, and the National Endowment for the Arts and other arts foundations began to support performance artists on a limited basis (although this source of funding ultimately had political repercussions), but by and large, artists had to support themselves through "civilian" jobs or through teaching. At the same time, creating performance art within the security and confines of an academic institution sometimes dulled the edge that had attended the grittier and more difficult gallery or environmental performances, and this could lead to a more theoretical and rarefied type of production. Furthermore, the very act of legitimizing performance art in this way inevitably reduced its avant-garde-ness.

One of the first homes of performance art (and the place where the term finally gained acceptance) was the California Institute of the Arts, a conservatory funded by the Walt Disney organization that opened in 1961 in Valencia, about thirty miles north of Los Angeles. Although the Disney Studios had been a pioneer in the development of arts technology, it was a socially and artistically conservative organization, and as Cal Arts, as it was known, became increasingly avant-garde in the late 1960s, tensions sometimes developed between the school and the parent organization. Kaprow joined the faculty in 1969 after a year at Berkeley and served as a kind of Pied Piper, leading at least one branch of the avant-garde from New York to California. On the faculty were several Fluxus artists, including Nam June Paik, Alison Knowles, and Dick Higgins. And, in 1971, the separate program in feminist art at Cal Arts, headed by Judy Chicago and Miriam Schapiro, also began to offer courses in performance. Kaprow moved to the University of California at San Diego (actually in La Jolla) in 1974, along with several other performance artists, including Eleanor Antin and Linda Montano, thus establishing another locus of California performance. Performance was further legitimized later in the decade with the founding in 1978 of the monthly *High Performance*, the first magazine devoted solely to performance art. (The editors of the New York-based *Performing Arts Journal* began publishing the short-lived *Performance Art Magazine* in 1979.)

Conceptual performance

Conceptual performance did not disappear in the 1970s, but it became more theatrical as it became the domain of theatre- rather than art-based performers. The work of Stuart Sherman remains a paradigm of this mode. Sherman created a series of what he called "spectacles," a seemingly ironic designation given that the performances consisted of the metaphoric and symbolic manipulation of small objects – the kind easily bought at a "five and dime" store – often arranged on a small folding table. Sherman's works were exquisite miniatures – diminutive portraits that lasted barely longer than the thought that conceived them. Although Sherman's deadpan demeanor, his unchanging costume of rumpled clothes and tennis shoes, the use of toys, and the occasional visual puns gave the performances a whimsical quality, the pieces derived from his attempt to reconnect the abstract word to tangible and three-dimensional objects and then allowing various connections to be made between the objects through his actions. The performances were somewhat akin to surrealist "automatic writing," only now with objects supplanting words. In Sherman's hands, the commonplace and even the discarded objects of everyday life took on a mystical quality that could embody metaphysical thought. This description of part of the "Portrait of Toulouse/Lyon" section of his *Tenth Spectacle: Portraits of Places* provides a rough idea of what his performance was like, although mere verbal description belies the charm and effect of the piece.

Puts receiver on body of telephone

Picks up whole telephone, [news]papers and roller skate

  Returns to table and sets items on top of table telephone on right, papers on left, skate on top of papers, toe to audience

  With right hand on skate and left on receiver rolls skate once, lifts receiver horizontally about 4–5 inches, lifts skate from paper.

Turns head and reads aloud a few words chosen randomly

Replaces receiver

Crumples a page of the paper and tosses toward the three sheets already crumpled on the floor

Repeats this sequence twice, until the papers are gone[58]

For most spectators, the connection between the images/actions and the cities being depicted remained vague at best. (Sherman explained that the skate on the table suggested the bustling traffic around the city square in Toulouse, the rose represented the provincial quality, the newspapers suggested the detailed reports of world events, in contrast to a city where people seem oblivious to the events, and so on.)[59] The images and actions become embodiments of fleeting thoughts, giving weight, as it were, to the instantaneous nature of mental activity. Sherman's early spectacles were sometimes performed for invited audiences in his living room, but also on street corners and in parks in New York city, where he would sometimes attract crowds thinking they were about to see a magic act, only to be baffled by the abstract performance.

In the 1980s, Sherman began to produce deconstructions of established texts. *Chekhov* (1985), for instance, was a reduction of all of Chekhov's dramatic *oeuvre* to a fifteen-minute performance of emblematic images, actions and sounds leaving evocative essences and textures. Similar reductions were created around Strindberg and Brecht, as well as the plays *Hamlet, Oedipus,* and *Faust.* Most of these productions used several performers and employed relatively elaborate scenography.[60] *Chekhov* was neither an analysis of the plays nor a gloss on the playwright – it was an impressionistic response to the work that nonetheless raised questions about what it is that we respond to when we say that Chekhov's plays are a pillar of modern drama.

Laurie Anderson's first performances were not all that dissimilar to Sherman's. In *Duets on Ice* (1974 – New York and Genoa), Anderson stood on a street corner and played a violin (accompanied by tapes played through a speaker in the violin, thus allowing her to play duets with herself) while standing on ice skates embedded in two blocks of ice while discussing the similarity between playing a violin and ice skating. When the ice melted – when she lost her balance – the performance was over. But the element of technology expanded so that by the late 1970s she was creating large-scale, elaborate, and technically sophisticated productions incorporating electronic instruments, a

Plate 22 Stuart Sherman performing one of his "spectacles" on a New York city street *c.* 1975.

Vocoder – a kind of vocal synthesizer that transposed her voice into the male register while giving it a somewhat robotic quality – and complex slide and film projections. Music critic John Rockwell provided a description in his review of *United States* (1983):

> Miss Anderson herself [is] the center of attention, frail and grave in her black satin jacket and pants, her black shirt and tie, her red socks and black pumps, with her cropped punk hair and promi-nent cheekbones. Clever props, above all her violin, sometimes glowing in the dark or with a neon bow or the bow-hairs replaced by a tape that forms a sentence as the bow is passed over the body of the instrument. Sing-song speech, crisp and clear in its mid-American diction, recounting a child-like string of observations or

Plate 23   Laurie Anderson: *Duets on Ice* in Genoa, Italy. This was also performed on the street in New York.

Photo: Bob Bielecki. Courtesy Sean Kelly Gallery, New York.

a quirky allegorical tale. Musicians belting out a choppy, emphatic, art-rock instrumental, Taped background sounds from nature. Films and slides, sometimes directly illustrative of the words and sometimes moving parallel to them, evocatively.[61]

Starting in 1977, some of her songs were recorded as limited-edition singles or as contributions to collections of recorded poetry. In 1981, she released *O Superman* – inspired by Jules Massenet's "O Souverain" aria from his opera *Le Cid* – which reached the number two spot on the British pop charts; this was followed by *Big Science* in 1982, the first of many solo albums. Anderson thus crossed over from the rarefied world of avant-garde performance into the popular mainstream. Her performances took on the quality and structure of rock

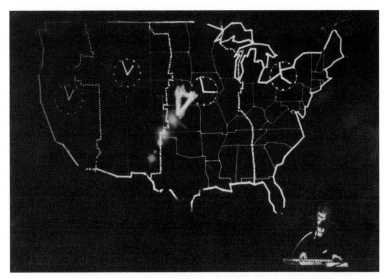

Plate 24 Laurie Anderson performs in front of a projection in *United States, Part II* at the Orpheum Theatre in New York, 1980.

Photo: © Paula Court.

concerts and played in venues normally devoted to mid-size rock concerts, such as New York's Beacon Theatre. They also employed rock-show technology. For the 1989 *Empty Places*, for instance, which toured fifty cities in the USA and Europe, there were two twenty-foot projection towers and three movable rear-projection screens, forty-five computer-controlled film and slide projectors in the towers and others in the auditorium. The technology also related Anderson to the body artists, although without the element of danger or self-abuse: body mikes allowed her to use her body as a resonator, so that by moving or touching different parts of her body she could create a percussive score.

The language structures of her monologue/songs were influenced by William S. Burroughs, who actually appeared in some of her concerts. Thematically, Anderson's work functioned as social commentary. The visual and verbal images were drawn from vernacular and pop culture and the banalities of everyday existence. By assuming a male-identified voice in many pieces, or shifting back and forth between voices, and by often wearing male-style or androgynous clothing, she was raising questions about gender and power as well as the role of technology in modern life. The 1979 "Words in Reverse," for instance, seemed to comment on the lack of communication between a man and a woman while raising essentially semiotic questions about the word "it."

She said: It looks. Don't you think it looks a lot like rain?
He said: Isn't it … isn't it just like a woman?
She said: It's really hard. It's just kind of hard to say.
He said: Isn't it … isn't it just like a woman?
She said: It goes. That's the way it goes. It goes that way.[62]

What keeps her monologues from being mere social observations or political statements is her essentially postmodern incorporation of contradiction and pastiche. "She presents a landscape of the ordinary," observed music critic John Rockwell, "made extraordinary through unexpected juxtapositions."[63] Anderson described her approach as a "stereo effect, a pairing of things up against each other and [I] see myself as a sort of moderator between things." She went on to emphasize that "sexuality is one of those things that I'm between."[64] Anderson's performances present multiple sign systems, which are presented in sometimes competing juxtaposition, with no attempt at reconciliation or resolution.

It is arguable that rock 'n' roll was the predominant and most original American art form of the postwar era. Laurie Anderson succeeded in grafting avant-garde performance onto the ultimate pop-culture medium, following in the footsteps of the Andy Warhol-associated rock group the Velvet Underground and laying the groundwork for such minimalist rock groups as Talking Heads.

There was an eruption of performance art in the mid-1980s, some of it conceptual, most of it, as in the work of David Cale, Lenora Champagne, Deb Margolin, and Tim Miller, of the autobiographical genre. Holly Hughes, however, epitomized the form. Her touching and witty autobiographical monologues were carefully crafted pieces of poetic narrative (though a poetry derived in part from the language of the streets and popular culture), often centered around her lesbian identity. She has also written plays that invert gender and sexual stereotypes. Hughes' monologue *World Without End* (1989) confronted, on a certain level, the same sort of material as *Long Day's Journey into Night*. Like Gray, she created a character, though somewhat more blatantly. Her costume for *World Without End*, for example, was a tacky cocktail dress – shiny, short, and strapless – with tasseled garters, stockings, and high heels. This may have reflected an aspect of her persona but was not Hughes *per se*. It contrasted strikingly at times

Plate 25 Holly Hughes in *World Without End.*
Photo: Dona Ann McAdams.

with the material. The monologue began with Hughes, alone onstage, describing a bird's nest under the eaves of her childhood home and how the same bird, or perhaps daughter of the bird, returned to the nest every year. She used this as a parallel to her own childhood:

> Okay! So the thing is: some nights my father'd come home drunk.
> There'd be the sounds of insults, breaking glass, you know.
> The usual family stuff, right?
> And I'd open the window very carefully because she might have a family.
> And I'd look at that nest.
> Sure looked like a piece of shit to me!
> But she came back every year.
> I thought that could mean this was a safe place after all.
> Or it could mean she didn't know any better. She didn't know what else to do but go on living in the mess her mother'd made.

We don't know.
We don't even know her name.
I bet my mother does. I'm going to ask her. When I get the chance.
She's always calling me, Jesus! Can you believe it!
I'm completely grown up and she's dead! What's there to say about it?
Get over it Mom![65]

O'Neill-like themes reverberated throughout, but while Hughes provided some aesthetic distance (through a simple set consisting of a wingback chair, end table, and vase of flowers; theatrical illumination; the costume) the interaction was not with characters in a fictionalized world but with the writer-performer in an intimate theatre. The presence of the artist and the minimal aesthetic distancing significantly limited the audience's ability to avoid the confrontation with the sometimes painful or emotional material. Though linguistically and narratively complex compared with most body art, and therefore engaging the mind and the senses in many different ways, it was nonetheless emotionally equivalent to the exposure and danger found in the works of Burden or Athey.

The crossover success of Anderson and Spalding Gray – he appeared in films and was recognizable enough to appear in a national television ad for an airline – combined to push performance art, and thus the avant-garde, into public consciousness and the media-saturated world of the 1980s and 1990s. Performance art thrives on the cult of the individual, which is in fact the mainstream preoccupation of the last part of the twentieth century. Although the majority of performance artists remain on the periphery of mainstream culture, nonetheless they have been made visible by cable and late-night television, by publications that interweave fashion with cutting-edge culture, and by the increasing array of media outlets. But unlike the historical avant-garde genres of the 1910s and 1920s, which were absorbed into the mainstream as stylistic and structural elements, the current avant-garde has maintained its superficial appearance while becoming one branch of contemporary culture. Performance art, if not the avant-garde in general, has become more a style than an approach to the creation of art.

Chapter 7

The Wooster Group, Reza Abdoh, and the end of the avant-garde

> Performance once more is ephemeral, the work of crazies, bourgeois-manques, bohemians: "artists." I regard the period, the people, the groups, the work in receding perspective: a parade passed, and still distantly heard piping.
>
> Richard Schechner[1]

Just as historian Fredrick Jackson Turner had famously declared the closing of the American frontier in 1893, Richard Schechner, in 1981, declared the end of the American avant-garde.[2] He argued that the demise of the avant-garde was largely precipitated by the rebellion of actors against the authority of the director and the shift of creative power from the director to the performer. As evidence he offered not only the case of the Performance Group – where the performers had rebelled against his authority – but also the rise of performance art. "Performance art flourishes but it … ought to be a sideshow," he argued plaintively, "not all the action there is."[3] The American avant-garde theatre could not survive, Schechner felt, if the introspective solo performer replaced the collaborative-creation model of theatre. While he rightly recognized a shift occurring in the experimental and alternative wing of theatre, his declaration was perhaps a decade early. Ultimately, there was a slight aura of sour grapes in Schechner's broadside. Recognizing that his position of leadership within the avant-garde was under siege, if not completely routed, he declared the game over.

In fact, there was in the 1980s a growing amount of alternative – though not necessarily avant-garde – theatre activity, especially in New York's East Village. Because this area of the city was filled with architecturally unattractive tenements, and much of the neighborhood was poorly served by public transport, it had resisted gentrification longer than other bohemian neighborhoods; at the same time, its very tawdriness gave it a certain cachet. Also, as the art market exploded in the 1980s, Soho quickly became unaffordable – either for living space or galleries – and the tenements and storefronts of the East Village provided a home for artists of the baby-boom generation and art dealers hoping to cash in on the lucrative market for new art. Limousines, boutiques, trendy bars, and well-dressed patrons incongruously began to appear in an area previously known for hippies and Polish and Ukrainian shops. Also, the decades of avant-garde and alternative theatre activity had exerted a pull on young people who once might have set their eyes on Broadway. But the rules for entering the world of theatre had changed. The idea of "paying one's dues" or joining an existing company now gave way to a do-it-yourself ethic. Because postmodern dance and performance art often emphasized simple and pedestrian action, expertise and virtuosity were often deemed unnecessary – even suspect. "Performance art surfed in on the wave of Punk Music in the late seventies," claimed Mark Russell, director of P.S.122, a converted schoolhouse in the East Village that had become the primary home for performance art. " 'Everybody can be a band' held for theatre and dance as well."[4] Or, as one young director stated in 1999, "I ... think anyone who wants to be a performer can be."[5]

The Drama Review, in an attempt to chronicle this new energy, devoted an entire issue to "East Village Performance," including the documentation of a range of performances on a single evening, November 30, 1984.[6] The amount of activity was prodigious. Tucked into dozens of clubs and unmarked storefronts amid the urban decay of the neighborhood, solo performances and iconoclastic theatre abounded. The majority of East Village performances were a mixture of performance art and more or less conventional plays, many with gay and lesbian themes and often performed with a strong camp sensibility. At their best, they were bold, provocative, energetic, funny, and poignant, but while perhaps oppositional to the mainstream, rarely were they avant-garde; with few exceptions, they bore little relation to the formalist or neo-expressionist theatre of the previous decades. If anything, they were descendants of the burlesques and travesties of Charles Ludlam's Ridiculous Theatrical Company of the 1970s (itself strongly influenced by Jack Smith). They were neither theoretically based nor intended to transform the idea of theatre. As one article in the *TDR* issue noted, "The new performers in the East Village have rejected minimalism and a structural emphasis and have returned to a focus on content. Their work comments on popular culture through

parody; it evolved from the Pop Art movement in the '60s."[7] Because
the main venue for this work was the clubs and bars in which the daily
patrons were also the primary audience, the emphasis was on entertainment, not esoteric, consciousness-altering art. In fact, the term
"avant-garde" was often rejected. Even Spalding Gray said he preferred
the term "backyard theatre" – in other words, a theatre in which,
simply, he could play by his own rules for his own satisfaction.[8]

This is not to say that there were no avant-garde performances.
Writer and filmmaker John Jesurun, for instance, created a "serial" – a
soap-opera-like play with a new episode every week – at the Pyramid
Club on Avenue A, called *Chang in a Void Moon* (1984), which not
only incorporated video but also created a sense of spatial dislocation
by physically mimicking cinematic shots such as overheads, pans, and
jump cuts.[9] (Particularly startling was a scene in which all the furniture
was attached perpendicular to the rear wall, with the actors strapped
into the chairs to prevent them falling out – to create the sense of a
camera looking down from the ceiling.) The melding of cinematic and
theatrical form created a fragmented and disorienting performance that
forced audiences to confront time, space, and narrative in new ways,
while the reference to pop culture still provided an entertaining spectacle.

In one sense, the East Village performances continued an almost
Cagean aesthetic. Just as much performance art reduced the borderline
between life and art, these performances, by occurring in clubs, bars,
and deep within marginal neighborhoods, created a sense of continuity
with daily routine. They became part of the "scene," part of the social
life of this neo-bohemian community. As Kirby stated in his introduction to the East Village issue of *TDR*, "It may be ... that the
sociological aspects of this performance phenomenon are more important than the esthetic ones. It is a theatre closely tied to the place in
which it is created and the socio-cultural milieu from which it is generated."[10]

The Wooster Group

There was also a sociological aspect to the traditional avant-garde (by
the 1980s, such an oxymoronic phrase seemed appropriate) to be
found in Soho, an area with trendy restaurants, major art galleries, and
designer boutiques. Unlike the rough-and-tumble neighborhood of
the East Village a few blocks to the northeast, the neoclassical cast-iron
façades of the old industrial district were more imposing, more formal

Plate 26 John Jesurun's *Chang in a Void Moon*, Episode 46, presented at
LaMaMa E.T.C. in 1995. The scene depicts a table as if in a
vertical shot. The character at the top is "sitting" at the
table, and the man is thus lying on the table.

Photo: © Paula Court.

and, as part of a designated historical district, more tied to the past. The same could be said of the theatre to be found there. Certainly, the work of the Wooster Group in Soho seemed to have much more in common with its historical precedents than with the East Village performances. Although the Wooster Group productions, like their East Village counterparts, drew upon popular culture, they did so in a highly selective and intellectual way. The group's productions were not parodying the culture or commenting on it through travesty; rather, they were acknowledging the presence of the past in shaping perceptions of the moment, and they made a clear case for the equality of "high" and "low" culture. In many respects, the Wooster Group was the last major exponent of the postwar American avant-garde movement.

Once Spalding Gray ceased to be an active participant, LeCompte and the Performance Group actors were freed from the limitations of his autobiography and imagination as text. In 1980, following a production of Genet's *The Balcony*, the Performance Group disbanded. LeCompte and the remaining actors made an arrangement with Schechner that in return for taking over the company's accumulated debt they would retain the corporate name – The Wooster Group – and ownership of the Performing Garage. This semi-new group could now proceed unencumbered in its explorations. The first production under the new organization would be *Route 1 & 9 (The Last Act)*, which opened in October 1981. Picking up on the element of textual deconstruction already present in *Nayatt School* and *Point Judith*, this and most of the group's subsequent work employed an existing play as a point of departure or as a framework for the creation of a text. In the case of *Route 1 & 9*, the starting point was Thornton Wilder's *Our Town*. The term "deconstruction" here means something different from the Derridean concept. The group literally dismantled – deconstructed – existing literary texts, extracting scenes, characters, dialogue, and images in order to reframe and reconfigure them. The results, however, were not entirely dissimilar to philosophical deconstruction. By breaking down the structure ("language") of a particular play, resituating it, and placing it in juxtaposition to other shards and fragments of culture (other "language systems" as it were), the underlying assumptions and social codes of the original texts were exposed, and new meanings and understandings emerged. In this way, classical works could be reintegrated into contemporary popular culture, but always through the prism of the collective vision of the Wooster Group. It was as if the group took a Brechtian sense of alienation from the Performance

Group, chance methodology from Cage, a minimalist emphasis upon the frame over content from the art world, and a non-hierarchical approach to culture from postmodernism, and then mixed it through the solipsistic and self-referential world of performance art.

This approach to canonical plays should not be confused with the twentieth-century directorial approach of resituating a play in a different historical era, or the approach popularized by Peter Brook and Andrei Serban of revitalizing a classic text through a process of stripping away dated and lifeless conventions while contemporizing the tone, energy, and look of the play. The Wooster Group saw the existing text as a part of the theatre's (and society's) cultural consciousness and vocabulary and as such treated it as raw material – no different from Spalding Gray's memories – that would become a building block within a new production. The classic literary text was, on some level, no different from a prop or an actor's gesture – that is, a decontextualized cultural signifier around which to construct a scene or an entire production. "When I choose texts," explained LeCompte, discussing the 1984 production of *L.S.D. (... Just the High Points...)*, "they're random in a way. I feel I could use any text ... I could pick anything in this room and make a piece that's just as complete as *L.S.D.*"[11]

The production of *Route 1 & 9* (the title refers to a stretch of highway in New Jersey that traverses deteriorating industrial sites, oil refineries, and urban blight – a negative, as it were, of Wilder's Grover's Corners), began in the upstairs space of the Performing Garage. The audience watched an "educational" video that was a reconstruction of a 1950s *Encyclopedia Britannica* film about *Our Town*. Actor Ron Vawter was the lecturer (Clifton Fadiman in the original). As author David Savran has pointed out, the lecture's friendly yet authoritarian tone implicated the spectator in a universalized response to the play.[12] The video seemed an ironic comment on Wilder's text, and Vawter's deadpan delivery fostered in the audience a sense of superiority – thus lulling them into an attitude of condescension and complacency that would be shattered in the subsequent scenes. Following the video, the audience moved to the downstairs space, where they sat along the length of the garage facing an expansive playing area with video monitors overhead. Two actors (Willem Dafoe and Ron Vawter) entered in grotesque blackface makeup and black glasses, rendering them essentially blind, to construct a skeletal house – a version of the structure from *Point Judith*, which in turn made reference to the soundproof room in *Nayatt School*, which itself derived from *Rumstick Road*; it would reappear again in *L.S.D.* behind the long, narrow table (itself first seen in *Nayatt School*) – as recorded dialogue from *Point Judith* played in the background. The routine had echoes of the radio and television show *Amos 'n' Andy*, and the context rendered it uncomfortable, even offensive. Two women (Kate Valk and Peyton Smith), also wearing blackface makeup and employing broad "ghetto" accents, entered the frame house and began telephoning fried chicken restaurants saying they were having a party and trying to get an order delivered to the theatre (occasionally they succeeded). This section was followed by a raucous reconstruction of a comedy routine by black vaudevillian Pigmeat Markham. This gave way to the elegiac final act of *Our Town* – not acted live but shown on video. The contemplative beauty of Wilder's play was undercut once again by the final part of *Route 1 & 9*, which contrasted two videos: an Andy Warhol-like film of a car riding down Route 1 and 9 (escaping New York) and a graphic home-made porno film.

On a thematic level, the production highlighted the gap between the apparently idyllic world depicted by Wilder and the urban reality of the contemporary United States, and it exploded the myth of a unified American culture. Structurally, the play emphasized the fundamentally postmodern notion that in 1981 *Our Town* could not be seen as it was in 1938 when it was first presented; it is part of a complex web of theatrical, cultural, socio-political, and personal associations. In a world in which media make the past continuously available in the present (and hence break down any hierarchical difference between past and present), any image or cultural artifact (such as a play) is suffused with its own history and associative context. Furthermore, because the web of associations will be different for each spectator, the modernist concept of a single ideal viewer and a unified art work must be abandoned in favor of a fragmented object available to different spectators in different ways. Although LeCompte claimed at the time not to have read any of the postmodern theorists, she was at least instinctively aware of the postmodern strategy of incompletion and of its historical artistic roots. She compared her methodology when creating a production to that of post-impressionist painter Cézanne: "He doesn't finish a line. He leaves the canvas showing here and there. It gives a space and an air; it doesn't solidify it into a form that's not breakable. I can't stand it when something becomes perfect, enclosed. I like to leave the system open."[13] For this reason, the Wooster Group productions are never complete but are billed as works in progress. They are developed and performed over months, even years, and are constantly evolving.

The use of blackface in *Route 1 & 9* caused the New York State

Council on the Arts (NYSCA) to rescind part of its grant to the Wooster Group in 1981. While LeCompte insisted, either naively or ingenuously, that she was baffled by the charges of racism – the intention, she insisted, was to explore theatrical concepts and conventions of mask and character as well as the racial divide in America – the use of blackface was so loaded, because of its associations with minstrel shows, and the depictions so caricatured that the production crossed the line from being merely disturbing and provocative to being, for many viewers, offensive and racist.

The group's next major production, *L.S.D. (...Just the High Points ...)*, used a condensed version of Arthur Miller's *The Crucible* in combination with excerpts of writings from the Beat poets and writers, the debates between Timothy Leary and G. Gordon Liddy,[14] interviews with and biographies of various personalities from the era, live and recorded music, dance, and video. While certain synchronic and thematic threads tied the seemingly disparate elements together – the cultural and political milieu of the 1950s and 1960s, themes of paranoia and government persecution, for instance – much of the content of both *L.S.D.* and *Route 1 & 9* was almost arbitrary. Of particular interest was the way in which they used their own process as text – not unlike their use of Spalding Gray's memories and recorded interviews. LeCompte videotaped a rehearsal of *L.S.D. (...Just the High Points...)* in which the cast was under the influence of the hallucinogenic drug LSD. That tape, in turn, became the text for one scene of the production in which the actors recreated the "stoned" rehearsal. This same self-reflexivity became even more pronounced when one of the actors, Michael Kirby, was unable to participate in part of a tour of the production, so his role was put on tape and he was replaced by his image on a video monitor. When he rejoined the production, the video was retained and Kirby interacted with his own image. For LeCompte, there is almost a circularity to the way in which the production creates its own text:

> I take that chance occurrence and say, that is the *sine qua non*, that is the beginning, that is the text. I cannot stray from that text. As someone else would use the lines of a playwright, I use that action as the baseline. I can't just erase it ... It's an action-text that may have nothing to do with any thematic thing we're working on. I call it chance work, like throwing a handful of beans up in the air. And when they come down on the floor, I must use that pattern as one pole against which I work my dialectic. I cannot alter it unless,

somehow, another structure, another bunch of beans that I throw up in the air, comes into conflict with the first. Then one bean must move, one way or the other. But only at that point.[15]

Blackface reappeared in *L.S.D. (...Just the High Points...)*. Valk played the black character Tituba from Arthur Miller's *The Crucible*, but here it raised little outcry; the makeup was clearly functioning as a mask. Miller's play was being quoted within the larger Wooster Group production, and the makeup was an unambiguous reference to a black character written by a white author. There was not the discomfort of a white person caricaturing a black person outside of any apparent context, but of a white actor assuming a black role in a play whose very authority was being questioned to begin with. Valk again used blackface in the production of O'Neill's *The Emperor Jones*, again with no protest.

Setting aside the social and political implications of the group's explorations, its investigation of mask and character was setting the avant-garde on a new direction in terms of acting. The Brechtian actor–character dichotomy had prevailed in the Living Theatre–Open Theatre–Performance Group nexus, while the formalist tradition of the avant-garde had stressed the use of an actor's unique qualities as raw material for the director-artist. But the Wooster Group members participated as co-creators of their works, and while the actors assumed characters, the basis was neither psychological nor emotional; rather, it was a semiotic approach – the creation of character through the accumulation of signs. In *Route 1 & 9*, social and cultural sign systems overwhelmed the aesthetic ones that the group hoped to emphasize, but in *L.S.D.*, LeCompte was able to revel in the possibilities. When the actress playing Tituba reappeared as Mary Warren, for example, she was still in blackface. The precipitating factor was the lack of time for the actress to remove her makeup, but it left the audience pondering questions of identity, racial politics, social commentary, and the simple mechanics of dramatic impersonation.

L.S.D. (...Just the High Points...) resulted in another controversy, however. Arthur Miller threatened to sue the group over its unauthorized use of his text.[16] In an attempt to get around the legal obstacles, the group first substituted gibberish for the Miller text within the production, and later, when that strategy did not appease, substituted a new text called "The Hearing," written by Michael Kirby, that was structurally identical to the fragment of *The Crucible* the group had appropriated. But ultimately, faced with the threat of legal proceedings

Plate 27 The *Crucible* sequence from the Wooster Group's *L.S.D. (...Just the High Points...)*. Note Kate Valk in blackface makeup. Upper level (l. to r.): Freya Hansell, Matthew Hansell, Peyton Smith, Willem Dafoe, Elion Sander, Ron Vawter; lower level (l. to r.): Tina Cohen, Anna Köhler, Kate Valk.

Photo: Nancy Campbell. Courtesy the Wooster Group.

the group shut down the production. "I want to use irony and distancing techniques to cut through to the intellectual and political heart of the *Crucible*, as well as its emotional heart," explained LeCompte in a letter to Miller when attempting to secure the rights. "I want to put the audience in a position as 'witnesses' – witnesses to the play itself, as well as witnesses to the 'story' of the play."[17] But *The Crucible* was not presented as merely an excerpt. It was done in a mixture of theatrical-historical costume and everyday dress, with one adult character played by a boy, and the lines mostly delivered at near incomprehensible speeds or in strangely detached intonations. Was this commentary, irony, parody, reinterpretation, or something else entirely? The Wooster Group has been dubbed a theatre of irony,[18] but irony rests upon an ultimately identifiable point of view. The controversies erupting out of the group's productions stemmed at least in part from an apparent lack of an identifiable framework that would allow a spectator to view the piece from a clearly defined vantage point. One could like or dislike, agree or disagree with earlier works of the avant-garde, but the relationship of the spectator to the performance was ultimately knowable. With the Wooster Group, that connection was not always clear. The work was strangely hermetic and self-referential – a strategy that worked with the monodramas of Richard Foreman, for instance, but that could collapse upon itself when the material depicted was not a personal and interior vision but charged images from the cultural and social landscape. The group's seemingly steadfast refusal to adopt a point of view – the apparent apoliticism in the context of politically volatile material – served, ironically, to provoke political responses and to create inflammatory reactions where none was necessarily sought.

In 1991, the group's work moved in a slightly different direction. *Brace Up!* was based on Chekhov's *The Three Sisters*, but now the original was no longer a mere fragment within a larger work – it was the main content of the production, albeit significantly reframed. Stanislavsky, referring to his original production, had said that he wanted the spectators to feel like guests at the Prozorov household. Spectators in 1991, however, with more than a century of naturalism and film behind them, were never going to have that response – and Chekhov's plays were encrusted with ninety years of cultural and social baggage – so the group sought other ways to make the play their own and to make it fresh for the audience. Spectators now became guests at the Wooster Group's "house." There was a "narrator" (played by Kate Valk), invented for this production, who greeted the audience, introduced the actors and their characters and set the scene.[19] This was no longer a classic play requiring the willing suspension of disbelief but an overtly theatrical production by the Wooster Group in which the actors – familiar to many – would present *The Three Sisters* by Chekhov. This was not an interpretation or adaptation of the play but a radical reframing in which the play was yanked out of its conventional moorings, mixed with (or placed in violent collision with) disparate and seemingly random cultures and traditions, and resituated within the ongoing *oeuvre* of the Wooster Group.

The audience sat on a steep bank of seats, filling about one-third of the theatre, facing an essentially square platform filling much of the remaining space and raised about two feet above the floor. A skeletal framework of metal tubing outlined the stage and served as a grid on which to hang the vertical panels of fluorescent lights stage left and right,[20] beyond which the walls and some backstage area of the garage were visible. On the floor at the rear of the stage was a long, narrow table whose top was just visible above the stage platform. Whereas the table had been in the foreground in *Nayatt* and *L.S.D.*, here it gave the impression of being in another room – the audience had to strain to see the action occurring around it – and some actors sat at it with backs to the audience. And in what has become a signature element of the Wooster Group, there were three television monitors, two of which moved on tracks in the stage floor. The overall effect, as in many of their productions, was of a slightly shabby industrial space into which some modern technology has been inserted; it was at once spartan and complex. The result was cool and somewhat distancing, a tone reinforced by line readings that could range from the dispassionate to the ironic to a riveting theatricality sometimes at odds with the expected naturalism of the dialogue. The use of microphones – either freestanding or of the headset variety – created another layer of distance as they not only amplified voices but sometimes also distorted or disembodied them.

In fact, the Wooster Group's use of technology was one of its most significant contributions to the avant-garde. Since at least the time of Erwin Piscator in the 1920s, theatre artists have made varying attempts to incorporate technology, specifically media, into their productions. But the results were generally disappointing. Either the technology was substitutional – projections in place of three-dimensional scenery, for example – or an attempt to incorporate the new gimmick of film or video into the theatrical matrix. But film and video have their own vocabularies, and the process of reading them is significantly different from reading a stage production. Most experiments had simply tried to subjugate media to the rules of theatre and, it is safe to say, most of the experiments did not succeed – even Laurie Anderson's productions sometimes fail to integrate the three-dimensional figure with the projected image. Robert Wilson is often discussed as a practitioner of "high-tech" avant-garde, but while he has employed elaborate sound systems and sometimes used projections, the "high-tech" look of his productions is precisely that – a "look" or, more accurately, a scenographic style, though certainly abetted by large budgets and sophisticated equipment. The Wooster Group, however, employed technology in the service of its unique theatrical vision. Even the simple platform stage sometimes moved on hydraulic lifts, as in *The Temptation of St. Anthony* (1988). (Although the Wooster Group, like all companies, has had its share of financial struggles, its success in grant and fund raising, in combination with the luxury of its own home, has allowed it to purchase technology beyond the means of most Off Off Broadway organizations.) In its use of technology, especially video and amplified sound, the Wooster Group succeeded, more than any other American theatre company, in simulating the sensory experience of contemporary life.

Chekhov's language and narrative made up the bulk of *Brace Up!*, yet the text was poured, as it were, into a new vessel. The sisters were intentionally cast with actresses who were older than the roles implied. Two of the sisters, Irina and Masha, were frequently placed in geriatric shower chairs and rolled on, off, and around the stage. The play's translator, Paul Schmidt, also played the role of Chebutykin and was occasionally called upon within the context of the performance to summarize scenes that had been cut or to explain character motivations or thematic elements. (A translator is always "present" in any translated production or work of literature – here it was made explicit.) Noh, Kabuki, and Asian folk dances were interspersed throughout, as were clips from Japanese *Godzilla* movies and a video adaptation of a documentary on Japanese Geinin troupes. Actors were seen as both live and taped images on the monitors. Some characters, such as Chebutykin, were seen almost exclusively on the monitors (Schmidt sat in a chair in the upstage left corner of the stage with his back to the audience and a video camera focused on his face). Others were seen on monitors as they recited their lines from offstage, where they were either invisible or only partially glimpsed. For the love scene between Natasha and Andrei, the audience saw Natasha's face only on the monitor. At other times, prerecorded images of the actors were played on monitors as the

Plate 28 (opposite)   *Brace Up!*, based on Chekhov's *The Three Sisters*.
Note the three video monitors, including two on
floor tracks. Note also samovar downstage left.
Vertical panels on stage right are lighting fixtures –
part of Jennifer Tipton's lighting design. In
foreground (l. to r.): Beatrice Roth, Roy Faudree,
Joan Jonas, Kate Valk; at rear (l. to r.): Peyton Smith,
Ron Vawter, Paul Schmidt (seated with back to
audience), who was also the translator of
Chekhov's text.

live actors performed a scene. Added to the mix were images from
Japanese films and American soap operas. The resultant impression was
of actors hovering around the edges of the stage – the center of the
stage was frequently empty – or of electronic images filling the space
while their corporeal bodies remained offstage. The video had the
effect of creating temporal and spatial dislocation; it had the ability to
create simultaneous yet conflicting images, and it forced the audience
to employ varying forms of concentration to decipher and decode
multiple framing devices and differing methods of reading images.

Whereas much of the work in the East Village performances, for
example, was based on the form and content of specific pop culture
sources such as Hollywood films of the 1930s and 1940s, the Wooster
Group worked from the new sensibilities fostered by the structures of
contemporary media. "There's no question that my work has been
influenced by MTV," declared LeCompte in 1984, "and specifically
before MTV by ads on TV – the cutting, editing, distancing, story-
telling, the combination of live characters and animation in
commercials, the quick pacing. Telling a sometimes disjointed story in
a very rapid way is definitely a great influence."[21] Contemporary audiences have become so accustomed to the disjuncture of a daily barrage
of rapidly shifting, discontinuous images that following a straightforward, slow-moving narrative has actually become more difficult, in
some cases, than comprehending a pastiche of conflicting representations. The Wooster Group, more than most other companies, has
mirrored this particular sensibility of the culture.

Reza Abdoh

The logical heir to the avant-garde tradition of the Wooster Group was
director Reza Abdoh, whose biography could almost stand as a
paradigm of late twentieth-century multicultural American society. Born

in Iran, he was educated in England and, briefly, the University of Southern California. He began directing as a teenager at school in England, but the style for which he became known emerged around 1990 with *Father Was a Peculiar Man* and *The Hip Hop Waltz of Eurydice*, followed over the next four years by *The Law of Remains* (1992), *Tight White Right* (1993), and *Quotations from a Ruined City* (1994). He died of AIDS in 1995. These plays ransacked popular culture, incorporating references and images ranging from "borscht-belt" night club acts to minstrel shows, from film quotations to hip-hop music to mass murderer Jeffrey Dahmer. As with the Wooster Group, dances were a major component of the works. Whereas MTV may have informed LeCompte's way of thinking, Abdoh directly lifted the form, structure, and manic pacing of music videos and video arcade games for his directorial approach. The pieces were loud, raucous, and frenetic – one emerged with a feeling of sensory assault and exhaustion. He adapted environmental staging practices, performing in lofts, warehouses, and site-specific locations (*Father Was a Peculiar Man* was staged in the streets of Manhattan's meat-packing district), surrounding the audience on all sides, forcing them to move during a performance – often rapidly to keep up with the action or to get out of the way. Whereas the Wooster Group confronted its audiences, both metaphorically and spatially, Dar a Luz, the company Abdoh founded in 1991, implicated them, making them physically and psychologically complicit in the action and thus forcing them to rethink a wide range of social attitudes.

If Abdoh's vocabulary was essentially similar to that of LeCompte and even Foreman and Wilson, there was a fundamental difference in that his works were clearly political – there was no ambiguity about intent, although specific meanings were not always clear. Abdoh was commenting on American society as seen from his perspective as an outsider living within the society. *Tight White Right* incorporated black and white characters, a Jewish wedding, an Austrian folk dance, neo-Nazi meetings, and a Ku Klux Klan scene, as well as a variety of images of sexuality. The plays often created profound mental discomfort as repulsive ideas and actions – racism, homophobia, rape, murder, etc. – were presented in the context of rich, sensuous, highly theatricalized imagery and action. While some references in the performances were obvious, others were obscure, and the rapid assault of image and sound worked against easy comprehension of word or idea while at the same time numbing the audience within a vortex of carnival-like activity. Sounding like a latter-day Artaud, Abdoh explained:

Plate 29 Scene from Reza Abdoh's *The Law of Remains*, 1992.
Photo: © Paula Court.

> Language is a ready-made tool of communication. It's a set of shared symbols, a form of repression. So, not to understand everything or not share all the symbols is perfectly OK for me; in fact, it helps my work because the work becomes more a puzzle rather than something that's easily digestible ... I don't want to just sort of bow gracefully to traditions. I take traditions and I break them. That's my whole philosophical and aesthetic engagement. I have to subvert the forms that I'm using and learning from. It's not a museum piece. It's alive. It's about now, it's about contemporary culture.[22]

At the same time, like many of his contemporaries, he rejected the label of "avant-garde." "I hate the word avant-garde," he declared. "I'm a populist. I think of my work as a popular entertainment."[23]

The postmodern detachment of the Wooster Group and others was a logical, perhaps inevitable, response to the loss of a political center after the Vietnam War and the scandal of Watergate. But the advent of AIDS in the 1980s refocused political consciousness and inspired a new social activism. It was hard to argue that art should remain disengaged from large-scale social issues in a world in which significant numbers of artists were dying from an epidemic disease that, at least initially, seemed to arouse little official response. But a political theatre, in order to be effective, must ultimately engage and persuade an audience, and to do so requires a degree of identification and enough familiarity that the spectators can focus on theme and content and not be absorbed in the decoding of complex structures. Holly Hughes made ironic reference to the art world's detached approach to political ideology in her monologue *World Without End*. In a segment in which she talks about battered women, she says,

> Oh, I know! This is not art! Believe you me, I wish I could be whipping out a haiku, or doing a little macramé demonstration – I wish I could be sharing some art with you right now. I'm just like everybody else. All I want to do is sleep.
>
> Oh I know the difference between politics and art! I went to art school ... and the first thing they said when they saw me coming through the door was: "Holly, don't hit them over the head. Art is not supposed to hit them over the head!"[24]

The moral distancing and linguistic ambiguity of postmodernism proved insufficient for the concerns of the age of AIDS, feminism, and the irrational violence of contemporary society. The call for a more direct confrontation with ideas and the attempt to rouse the audience to action would ultimately work against the traditional approaches of the avant-garde.

Forces of disintegration

Perhaps the single strongest force at work transforming the avant-garde was the changing economics of living and working in New York. Through the early 1970s, it was possible to live cheaply in the fringe neighborhoods of Manhattan, and at least some theatre could be produced on nothing more than box-office income or donations. But inflation and the gentrification of once inexpensive neighborhoods drove out struggling artists and precluded the rental of rehearsal and performing space. The avant-garde scene had thrived in part on the sense of community among artists, but as they were increasingly scattered all over the metropolitan area there was no sense of community, no core, and, for theatre companies, no artistic home. Theatre artists with no independent means of support had to spend increasing amounts of time working at non-theatre jobs in order to survive.

Theatre companies and creators became increasingly dependent on grants. The foundations, such as Ford and Rockefeller, that had been major benefactors in the 1960s and 1970s provided less and less funding through the 1980s and 1990s. Major private grants came through corporations such as Philip Morris (the tobacco company), American Express, or Seagram (the liquor company), which raised touchy political and ethical questions for those who accepted money from these sources; government funding came primarily from the National Endowment for the Arts (NEA), the National Endowment for the Humanities (NEH) and, in New York, NYSCA. By taking government subsidies, the artists or groups were then subject to a degree of government control and restriction. By the 1990s, government funding of the arts – never popular among conservative political factions and never abundant to begin with (the NEA's peak budget was $176 million in 1992) – came under increasing attack. Although the vast majority of NEA funding went to institutions such as museums, orchestras, and established dance and theatre companies, and to community arts organizations, a small percentage went to fund performance artists and various forms of avant-garde theatre. For conservative politicians, the sexually explicit material to be found in some NEA- and NEH-funded projects was excuse enough to attempt to dissolve the agencies. Legislation was introduced in 1989 prohibiting "depictions of homosexual or sadomasochistic activities, child pornography or individual sex acts." Among those singled out for attack were four performance artists, who became known as the "NEA Four": Karen Finley, John Fleck, Holly Hughes, and Tim Miller. The latter three included lesbian or gay themes or subject matter in their performances – mostly through language; Finley dealt with AIDS and the debasement of the female body in society, sometimes through performances in which she was nude and covered her body with substances such as chocolate sauce to simulate excrement. In 1990, although the four were awarded grants by a peer panel, the grants were subsequently vetoed by the National Arts Council, apparently for political reasons. Later that year, a federal law was passed that required the NEA to judge not only artistic excellence in awarding grants but also "general standards of decency and respect for the diverse beliefs and values of the American people." Any individual or organization accepting federal grant money had to sign an agreement pledging to abide by these standards.

The four fought their "defunding" in the courts for years. They received an out-of-court cash settlement in 1993, and in 1996 a federal appeals court ruled that the decency clause was unconstitutional. But in 1998, the Supreme Court overturned that ruling and upheld the decency clause. The laws and the court battles took their toll, if in no other way than by sapping the energies and focus of artists and theatre companies. (The four, and the theatres or museums that sponsored them, also received hate mail, harassing phone calls, and death threats.) Some theatres, out of principle, rejected NEA funding if it meant signing the decency agreement; other companies accepted the money, which in turn led to condemnation by some artists. Whether or not it had been their intended goal, the conservative legislators had succeeded to a degree in getting artists to fight among themselves. The atmosphere for creating politically or socially provocative work had been poisoned.

But even assuming for a moment that grants could come with no strings attached – no need to carry corporate logos on advertising and programs, no restrictions as to content, no community responsibilities – there is an inevitable question about the possibility of an avant-garde with corporate and government support. An oppositional art form funded and therefore implicitly condoned by the establishment becomes, *ipso facto*, an extension of that establishment. Corporations fund the arts because this provides them with a kind of cultural legitimacy, a seal of approval as it were. Theatre that is part of the establishment culture cannot, by definition, be avant-garde no matter how subversive it may try to be.

Another source of damage to the avant-garde may have come, ironically, from a well-intentioned academia. Since the late 1950s, European (mainly French) literary, linguistic, and philosophical theory – first structuralism, then post-structuralism and deconstruction – had come to dominate much of the humanities and some social sciences and inevitably made its way into the critical and analytical study of theatre. While opening fresh lines of inquiry and interpretation, such theoretical approaches also contained potential pitfalls for the theatre. On a superficial level, the esoteric and complex language employed to explicate these critical models could easily devolve into obfuscating jargon and, in fact, there was a proliferation of academic articles written in dense prose that often failed to find an audience among the practitioners and was of little use to non-specialist audiences seeking interpretations of difficult theatre. Apparently gone were the days when serious and rigorous critics could bridge the gap between scholarly exegesis and popular journalism. More problematic, though, was the attempt to apply post-structuralist theory to theatrical production.

Jacques Derrida's deconstructive analysis, for example, could be fruitfully applied to an essentially static work of art such as a novel, but it began to encounter complications when applied to a more complex and constantly modulating form such as theatre, with its multiple layers of "text," interwoven and sometimes conflicting sign systems, multiple "authors" (in the collaborative process), multiple simultaneous "readers," and the fluid and virtually ungraspable object known as performance. In a sense, "reading" theatre had always been a deconstructive exercise. Scholars attempting to apply literary theory to theatre sometimes lacked the necessary understanding of the dynamics of performance. The result was an ever-widening gulf between scholarly critic and practitioner, and theory was increasingly read not by artists but by other theorists. Popular journalism, on the other hand, often lacked the tools and vocabulary to deal with non-traditional forms of theatre in a meaningful way. Meanwhile, the dominant academic disciplines of the 1980s and 1990s – post-colonialism, cultural studies, feminist theory, new historicism, and the like – tended to fragment the field even further by observing the subject through a fairly narrow lens while sometimes attacking alternative points of view. The result was essentially two groups talking past each other – theoreticians having little impact on the creation of theatre, and practitioners, who had little use for scholarship or criticism, at least as it existed in theatre journals, while the public was left on the sidelines, excluded from any meaningful discourse that would allow the development of a committed audience engaged in the creation of new theatre.

Technology versus the avant-garde

While we have not yet achieved the technological utopia of science fiction, the explosive growth of technology – primarily related to computers – since the mid-1980s has had a profound effect upon society and, ironically, has also been a contributing factor in the decline of the avant-garde. Technology and media are simply outstripping the avant-garde – not just in terms of theatre's ability to absorb and incorporate new technical equipment and innovations (theatre can never equal the technical sophistication of rock concerts or create the equivalent of cinematic special effects and digital imagery) but also in the way in which computer technology is altering the way we think and the way we see the world. Hypertext and the World Wide Web have transformed the perceptual process so that we are now accustomed to leaping from idea to idea through associative links. Richard Foreman's ubiquitous strings, which drew connections between seemingly disparate objects, seem almost as quaint as nineteenth-century expositional monologues or the spotlight that guided a spectator's gaze, when compared with the rapid links and logistical leaps made by a simple click of a computer mouse. Similarly, devices such as the television remote control allow viewers to flip from image to image (and narrative to narrative) – to "surf" – at bewildering speeds, yet somehow keep dozens of anomalous images and texts in discrete mental compartments simultaneously. This rapid navigation through images and narratives is determined as much by coincidence, juxtaposition, and accident as by any coherent pattern or intention. Structures have dissolved; discrete images have evaporated; all images, all ideas, all thoughts, are equal; linearity is archaic, anachronistic.

Thus the century-long project of the avant-garde to undermine structures of linear thought, objective imagery, and psychological associations has been accomplished rapidly and almost effortlessly by technology and has been adopted almost casually by society at large. Within less than a generation, the Aristotelian–Renaissance model of the linear narrative and unified frame has been largely supplanted by an image-driven associative model of structure. This is what French philosopher Gilles Deleuze dubbed a "rhizomatic structure" – a non-hierarchical, ever-expanding network capable of sprouting a complete form at any point, a structure capable of almost infinite replication.[25]

A new drama is emerging out of this new sensibility, or at least showing its influences. American writers such as David Ives, Suzan-Lori Parks, and especially Mac Wellman construct plays in which linearity, narrative coherence, even the stability of characters from moment to moment, is irrelevant. Historical figures, fantasy, news events, and real life intermingle in works that are no longer bound by narrative structures, standardized acts and scenes, or even a socially agreed-upon duration. Playwright Paula Vogel has stated that in a postmodern play, "character, plot, language, and environment or plasticity as self-contained entities correspond fitfully, if at all, and only until the playworld fragments once again."[26] Much of this theatre has abandoned neoclassicism, romanticism, and naturalism for a flow of images and ideas that replicates the perceptual processes of contemporary audiences, who are shaped by the hypertextual world of electronic media.

In the 1990s, narrative theatre has been replaced by what might be called the "pastiche play," which creates a juxtapositional world of images and texts ransacked from the cupboard of cultural history and

Plate 30 Scene from *The Medium*, directed by Anne Bogart, with Ellen Lauren and Will Bond.

Photo: Richard Trigg. Courtesy the Saratoga International Theatre Institute.

pieced together into new shapes. One of the best examples may be found in the work of director Anne Bogart. Known for her deconstructions of classic texts and her work with Japanese director Tadashi Suzuki, she has also created original pieces with her company, the Saratoga International Theatre Institute, such as *The Medium*, based on the writings of Marshall McLuhan; *Small Lives, Big Dreams*, based on the writings of Chekhov; and *American Silents*, based on the early silent film industry. These are classic examples of Jamesonian pastiche – dramatic events created out of found texts, modern dance, Suzuki technique, popular culture, and the collaborative input of performers. Beginning with a theme or image, Bogart makes a theatrical collage of textual fragments, movements, and gestures, which are shaped into a performance – part theatre, part dance – which may even tell a story, though it mostly explores an idea. Part of Bogart's creative process consists of making actual collages of relevant images, which become a kind of *ur*-text for the performance. Bogart's production values are generally fairly simple, yet structurally they are as far removed from the realistic dramas of the first half of this century as neoclassicism was from medieval drama. They reflect a societal world view utterly transformed by current technological sensibility. To quote Bogart,

"Physicists now say that nothing touches, nothing in the universe has contact; there is only movement and change."[27] Her plays attempt to incorporate and convey this understanding of the world, which will be instinctively understood by audiences with no understanding of quantum mechanics.

But the fact that it is instinctively understood takes it out of the realm of the avant-garde. It is a theatre that reflects contemporary consciousness; it does not push ahead into uncharted and dangerous territory. Arthur Miller, in the introduction to his collected plays in 1957, stated his belief that theatre cannot introduce entirely new ideas or convince an audience of what it is not prepared to accept. A play, he declared, can only enunciate "not-yet-popular ideas which are already in the air"[28] – in other words, ideas for which an avant-garde of some sort has blazed a trail. The productions of Anne Bogart and others of the recent so-called "cutting edge" theatre are closer in spirit to Miller than to John Cage; they reveal to the audience what it already senses in the air, they take the audience where it is already prepared to go.

Conclusion

The avant-garde was a product of the romantic sensibility. It grew in part out of a belief in a utopian future arrived at through a spiritual quest led by those inspired individuals who forged new paths or tore down the old structures of society. The first avant-garde rode the wave of nineteenth-century futurism, but at the end of the twentieth century, Westerners, at least, seem unwilling or unable to look forward. The final decade of the century began with historian Francis Fukuyama's announcement of the "end of history",[1] which spawned a host of declarations of other "ends." Although Fukuyama was providing a debatable Hegelian reading of history – the conclusion of the Cold War, he believed, marked the culmination of the thesis–antithesis structure of human development – his phrase tapped into a popular sense of millennial doom ("the end is nigh," as the sign-carrying prophet had it in the old cartoons). Thus the impending new millennium sparked not utopian visions but rather retrospection, introspection, and a general loss of forward movement. Whatever the import for society at large, such an attitude undermined the ability of the avant-garde to function.

In the twentieth century, avant-garde performance strove toward a radical restructuring of the way in which spectators viewed and experienced the very act of theatre. Having emerged out of the romantic era, it was based on the Hegelian model: the avant-garde functioned as the antithesis of the status quo. Once the synthesis had been achieved – once the avant-garde had been absorbed into the mainstream – a new avant-garde emerged. But if the function of the avant-garde is to undermine habitual patterns and social norms, and if the avant-garde stands in opposition to the practices and postures of mainstream society, then there is very little in today's theatre that can be considered avant-garde. The so-called avant-garde no longer exists in opposition to established culture; it is a dynamic subset within the culture. The *raison d'être* of the avant-garde has fallen away – evaporated – leaving behind a kind of exoskeleton of style and form that has been subsumed within aspects of thriving popular culture.

One need look no further than the arts pages of newspapers and magazines. The cultural scene of *fin de siècle* New York and the United States in general is filled on an annual basis with works by Foreman, Wilson, the Wooster Group, postmodern dancers, and performance artists – in other words, by the avant-garde of the past forty years or so. Much of this performance can be found in arts centers, established theatres, well-equipped downtown venues, and even opera houses. Moreover, these same performers and directors are teaching university courses in writing and performance, thereby transforming an erstwhile avant-garde into a methodology equivalent to that of Aristotle or Stanislavsky. Many of the actors, directors, and writers from the fringe move fluidly between Off Off Broadway, Broadway, Hollywood, and television, further blurring any distinctions between genres and suggesting that there is no fundamental difference in styles. One can purchase a coffee-table book of photographs of performance art[2] or collections of performance art texts, while articles on artists and performances show up in newspapers and national magazines. In addition to the nearly two-decade-old "Next Wave Festival" at BAM, New York boasts half a dozen annual fringe-type festivals that have become "events" and tourist attractions, regularly written up in the Sunday "Arts and Leisure" section of the *New York Times* and given the same treatment as articles about Broadway productions, while the artistic directors of these events are heralded as the entrepreneurs of the next century.[3]

The avant-garde has become a kind of cultural establishment. In a sense, John Cage has triumphed: theatre, music, and dance have become intertwined and, in some cases, indistinguishable; and not only are few distinctions made between high and low art, but there are few barriers between what elements or components may or may not be used in artistic creation. Consequently, there is, in a sense, no establishment versus antiestablishment – only a monolithic culture scene with internal variations. It is not unusual, over the course of a season, for an individual spectator to patronize the opera, modern dance, Broadway, Off Broadway, the Next Wave Festival, a rock concert, a poetry slam, performance in a club, and an evening of performance art, and to attend movies, rent videos, and watch selected television shows regularly – activities and tastes that until recently would have been deemed largely incompatible. Even the term "avant-garde" has become somewhat passé, subsumed by the "downtown" aesthetic – a subgenre typified by an edgy, glossy, hip style with elements of the grotesque and perhaps a slightly jaded, distanced, ironic attitude or point of view. Perhaps exemplifying this trend is *The Donkey Show*, a popular 1999 adaptation of Shakespeare's *A Midsummer Night's Dream* in which the story is told entirely through 1970s disco music and is performed in a club. A *New York Times* article identifies the production as a harbinger of "downtown" theatre to come and cites such theatre as "the flying wedge of a downtown sensibility expressed most consistently in the previous decade through music and especially the visual arts."[4] The production appropriated the environmental staging of the Performance Group and Abdoh, but there was no iconoclastic aesthetic or political message – the audience was encouraged to dance with the performers, who gently parodied the disco world while presenting an exuberant, updated, and loving if highly condensed version of Shakespeare's play. This is avant-garde as a conflation of performance, entertainment, and social life. Of equal significance is the fact that the production reaches potential audiences as much through its website in cyberspace as through traditional media advertising.

With almost no boundaries, it is hard for an art to develop or to exist *outside* the mainstream. And, more important, with no sense of forward motion, there is nothing to be ahead of; one cannot be in the vanguard – the scouting party out ahead of the advancing troops – for a culture that is circling the wagons or looking backwards. Instead of a belief in the perfectibility of humankind, the end of the twentieth century has brought a distrust of science on the one hand (genetic engineering and nuclear energy, for instance), and a blasé attitude toward technological change on the other. The latter is manifested in faster computers, higher-definition televisions, digital sound – all elements of consumer electronics and thus all part of materialist culture. Technology, by creating both a demand for the new and a comfort with constant change, has deadened the landscape for the avant-garde. The new is no longer shocking; it is commonplace and expected. Moreover, the new is no longer associated with an ever-improving future for society, just with an ever-improving product to be purchased.

The publishing and fashion industries – with their constant search for new images, new ways of selling, or new ways of promoting culture – have contributed heavily to the mainstreaming of the avant-garde. Flipping through the pages of ads in the high-fashion magazines or watching music videos, one is seeing the strong influence of Robert

Plate 31 (opposite)   *The Donkey Show, A Midsummer Night's Disco* at the
Club El Flamingo, created and directed by Diane
Paulus and Randy Weiner. Action occurred on the
dance floor, on a raised stage (pictured to right),
on galleries above the dance floor, and a mezzanine
area (pictured at rear). Pictured: Rachel Benbow
Murdy, Dan Cryer, Quinn, Anna Wilson, Emily
Hellstrom, Jordin Ruderman.

Photo: Solomon Joseph. Courtesy Project 400 Theater Group.

Wilson, of director Martha Clarke, or of American-trained German choreographer Pina Bausch – a world of mannered performers gliding over intensely theatrical, high-concept stages, confronting the audience through the proscenium arch (equivalent to the fashion model looking either seductively or dispassionately at the camera). Except for ostensibly different objectives – selling clothes versus expressing ideas – there is little visual or structural difference between a Wilson opera and a fashion show.

The search for the new also means that artists do not have the luxury of developing ideas and work (and an audience) away from the pressure of constant surveillance. Whereas both popular and high art could, in the past, gestate and develop over time, now anything that catches the slightest public attention is immediately pounced upon and promoted by those in the media looking for the latest trend (a demand exacerbated by 24-hour news shows and a plethora of weekly style and entertainment magazines) and by producers or collectors hoping to get rich quick. Under such circumstances, most of the art and culture so generated is quickly consigned to oblivion. Well before new companies or artists can establish a reputation, be analyzed and explicated in journals, and evolve their work, newspapers and trendy magazines announce the next "must-see" event of the weekend. In such an environment, audiences begin looking for trendy events, not challenging encounters. Disposable culture has subsumed the arts as well as consumer products.

If anything, "avant-garde" has become a designator for a style or genre. But it is hard to find an overriding aesthetic. Avant-garde-ness has come to be equated with the quirky, the shocking, or the merely offbeat and unexpected, but, by and large, there is no theoretical underpinning for most of this work. The impetus to create comes not so much from a dissatisfaction with the intellectual basis of contemporary theatre as from the age-old theatrical impulse to entertain. Only now, not surprisingly, the structure and content for new theatre is

Plate 32 Theatre as fashion show: Robert Wilson's *Time Rocker*, 1997. Music and lyrics by Lou Reed, text by Darryl Pinckney.

Photo: Clörchen Baus-Mattar from the Thalia Theater (Germany) production.

derived from the ubiquitous imagery of popular culture, media, and cyber-technology. For those audiences still attuned to slow-moving linear narratives, psychologically based character, and thematically oriented material, i.e. traditional theatre, the new performance with its disjunctive, dissociative, alogical barrage of sound and image derived from videos, pop music, film, television, and cyber-media may indeed be disconcerting. But such theatre is not avant-garde – it is merely representative of the *fin de siècle* thought process. Insofar as self-consciously "edgy," trendy, even provocative theatre is labeled "avant-garde," it might better be thought of as the decadent avant-garde: a theatre of style *sans* substance.

So, in a sense, the goal of the avant-garde has been achieved. Structures of thinking and modes of perception have been – or are in the process of being – fundamentally altered. But it has happened largely through the ineluctable (and singularly untheoretical) combined forces of technology and popular entertainment. No longer locked in opposition to the mainstream, the avant-garde continues now as a form of classicism. The annual productions of the Ontological-Hysteric Theatre and near-annual works-in-progress of the Wooster Group, and the periodic creations of Robert Wilson (which are guaranteed media events) draw regular audiences – some of whom were not even born when these theatres began to produce – equivalent, in a way, to audiences who attend Shakespeare festivals. Meanwhile, the visual style and rhythmic structures of avant-garde theatre have been absorbed into and permeate fashion, music, graphic art, and a variety of media, which in turn feed back into multimedia performances, performance art, and the hybrid theatre of clubs and discos. It is all of a piece. Until and unless some form of recognizably traditional theatre re-emerges as a significant factor within the larger official culture, there will be no possibility of an avant-garde theatre rising in opposition. The American avant-garde that began in the late 1940s faded away in the 1990s.

Notes

Preface

1 See, for example, F. Orton and G. Pollock, '*Avant-Gardes* and Partisans Reviewed', in F. Frascina (ed.) *Pollock and After: The Critical Debate*, New York, Harper & Row, 1985.
2 C. Greenberg, 'Avant-Garde and Kitsch', *Partisan Review*, Fall 1939, VI.5, pp. 34–49.
3 L. Kronenberger (ed.), *The Best Plays of 1952–1953*, New York, Dodd, Mead & Co., 1953, p. 5.

1 Origins of the avant-garde

1 J. Cage, 'History of Experimental Music in the United States', in *Silence*, Cambridge, Mass., MIT Press, 1961, p.73.
2 J. Kalb, 'A Coupla White Guys Sittin' Around Talkin', *Village Voice*, May 26, 1992, p.110.
3 L. Strasberg, *Famous American Plays of the 1950s*, New York, Dell, 1962, pp.15–16.
4 *Ibid.*
5 T. Crow, 'Modernism and Mass Culture in the Visual Arts', in F. Frascina (ed.) *Pollock and After: The Critical Debate*, New York, Harper & Row, 1985, p.257.
6 Rockefeller Panel Report on the Future of Theatre, Dance, Music in America, *The Performing Arts: Problems and Prospects*, New York, McGraw-Hill, 1965, pp.33–4.
7 Cage, *op. cit.*
8 R. Motherwell, 'Painter's Objects', *The Collected Writings of Robert Motherwell*, S. Terenzio (ed.), New York, Oxford University Press, 1992, p.23.
9 *Ibid.*, pp.23–4.
10 J.F. Lyotard, 'The Sublime and the Avant-Garde', *Artforum*, April 1984, 22, p.39.
11 M. Kirby, *Happenings: An Illustrated Anthology*, New York, E.P. Dutton, 1965, pp.19–21.
12 D.D. Egbert, 'The Idea of "Avant-Garde" in Art and Politics', *The American Historical Review*, December 1967, LXXIII.2, pp.340–1. See also R. Shattuck, *The Banquet Years*, New York, Vintage Books, 1968.
13 Egbert, *op. cit.*, p.342.
14 *Ibid.*, p.343.
15 L. Trilling, *Beyond Culture: Essays on Literature and Learning*, New York, Viking Press, 1965, p.xiii.
16 Quoted in Trilling, *ibid.*, p.xvii.
17 C. Greenberg, 'Avant-Garde and Kitsch', *Partisan Review*, Fall 1939, VI.5, pp.5–6.

18 Lyotard, *op. cit.*, p.37.
19 K. Elam, *The Semiotics of Theatre and Drama*, New York, Methuen, 1980, p.7.
20 *Ibid.*, p.87.
21 K. Davy, *Richard Foreman and the Ontological-Hysteric Theatre* (1979), Ann Arbor, UMI Research Press, 1981, p.188.
22 Quoted in A. Camus, 'Art and Revolt', *Partisan Review*, May–June 1952, XIX.3, p.271.
23 Lyotard, *op. cit.*, p.37.
24 G. Stein, 'Plays', *Lectures in America* (1935), Boston, Beacon Press, 1985, pp.118–19.
25 Trilling, *op. cit.*, p.xii.
26 A. Huyssen, *After the Great Divide: Modernism, Mass Culture, Postmodernism*, Bloomington, Indiana University Press, 1986, pp.167–8.
27 R.H. Gabriel (ed.), *The Pageant of America: A Pictorial History of the United States*, 15 volumes, New York, United States Publishers Association, 1929.
28 L.A. Fiedler, *Love and Death in the American Novel*, Cleveland, Meridian Books, 1962, p.xxiii.
29 A. Ginsberg, *Howl and Other Poems*, San Francisco, City Lights Books, 1959, p.18.
30 J. Habermas, 'Modernity – An Incomplete Project', in T. Docherty (ed.) *Postmodernism: A Reader*, New York, Columbia University Press, 1993, p.99.
31 H. Rosenberg, *The Tradition of the New* (1959), New York, McGraw-Hill, 1965, p.32.
32 Letter of Walt Kuhn to Walter Pach, in J.W. McCoubrey (ed.) *American Art 1700–1960: Sources and Documents*, Englewood Cliffs, NJ, Prentice-Hall, 1965, p.189.
33 This process is superbly and painstakingly chronicled in S. Guilbaut's study, *How New York Stole the Idea of Modern Art*, A. Goldhammer (trans.), Chicago, University of Chicago Press, 1983. Guilbaut shows how the political connections – the rising and waning fortunes of communism and socialism and the artists' attempts to break free of dogmatic political domination – led to the development of abstract expressionism. Where Guilbaut is weak is in outlining the aesthetic and artistic precedents and influences. For this see M. Kirby's 'Introduction' to *Happenings: An Illustrated Anthology*, *op. cit.*
34 Quoted in Guilbaut, *op. cit.*, p.57.
35 'Our Country and Our Culture', *Partisan Review*, May–June 1952, XIX.3, p.293.
36 Quoted in Guilbaut, *op. cit.*, p.172.
37 Quoted in S. Guilbaut, 'The New Adventures of the Avant-garde in America', in Frascina, *op. cit.*, p.160.
38 Quoted in Guilbaut, *How New York Stole the Idea of Modern Art*, *op. cit.*, p.159.
39 W. C. Seitz, *The Art of Assemblage*, New York, The Museum of Modern Art, 1961, pp.88–9.
40 Ginsberg, *op. cit.*, pp.9–10.
41 Quoted in Guilbaut, *How New York Stole the Idea of Modern Art*, *op. cit.*, p.161.
42 *Ibid.*, chapter 3, *passim*.
43 *Ibid.*, pp.180–1. Guilbaut quotes various critics from *Art Digest, The World Telegram*, and *Life*, among others, to support this argument.
44 Quoted in Guilbaut, *How New York Stole the Idea of Modern Art*, *op. cit.*, p.181.

2 Theories and foundations

1 G. Hugnet, 'The Dada Spirit in Painting', in R. Motherwell (ed.) *The Dada Painters and Poets: An Anthology*, Cambridge, Mass., The Belknap Press of Harvard University Press, 1981, p.140.
2 P. Biner, *The Living Theatre*, New York: Horizon Press, 1972, p.72.

3   J. Cage, in R. Kostelanetz (ed.) *John Cage*, London, Allen Lane, 1974, p.149.

4   B. Brecht, *Brecht on Theatre*, J. Willett (ed.), New York, Hill & Wang, 1966, pp.37–8. Roger Copeland explores this point in some detail in 'Merce Cunningham and the Politics of Perception', reprinted in *What is Dance? Readings in Theory and Criticism*, New York, Oxford University Press, 1983, and again in 'A Community of Originals: Models of Avant-Garde Collaboration' in the *Next Wave Festival Catalogue* (1983).

5   G.W. Knight, *The Wheel of Fire: Interpretations of Shakespearean Tragedy*, London, Methuen, 1956, p.3.

6   M. Cunningham, in conversation with Jacqueline Lesschaeve, *The Dancer and the Dance*, New York and London, Marion Boyars, 1991, pp.17–18.

7   A. Kaprow, 'The Legacy of Jackson Pollock', *Art News* 57.6 (October 1958), p.26.

8   Aristotle, *Poetics*, S.H. Butcher (trans.), Francis Fergusson (ed.), New York: Hill & Wang, 1961, p.55 [chapter IV].

9   *The Writings of Marcel Duchamp*, eds. M. Sanouillet and E. Peterson, New York, Da Capo Press, 1989, p.8.

10 *Ibid.*, p.140.

11 *Ibid.*

12 His "Dust Breeding" serves as an example of the latter. Dust would be allowed to collect on a glass for four–six months, perhaps falling through a sieve, and then the resultant product would be encased in a transparency, thus becoming a work of art.

13 G. Stein, *Lectures in America*, Boston, Beacon Press, 1985, p.98.

14 *Ibid.*, p.99.

15 *Ibid.*, p.95.

16 *Ibid.*, p.104.

17 *Ibid.*, p.119.

18 *Ibid.*, p.122.

19 *Ibid.*, p.125.

20 R. Foreman, *Unbalancing Acts*, New York, Pantheon Books, 1992, p.79.

21 A. Artaud, *The Theatre and Its Double* Mary Caroline Richards (trans.), New York, Grove Press, 1958, p.81.

22 *Ibid.*, p.41.

23 See especially 'Metaphysics and the Mise en Scène', in Artaud, pp.33–47.

24 Artaud, *op. cit.*, p.53.

25 *Ibid.*, p.89.

26 *Ibid.*, p.96.

27 Cage, *op. cit.*, p.138.

28 R. Barthes, *S/Z*, R. Miller (trans.), New York, Hill & Wang, 1974, p.4.

29 Cage, *op. cit.*, p.11.

30 *Ibid.*, p.166.

31 Cage, 'Experimental Music: Doctrine', in *Silence*, p.14.

32 Michael Kirby and Richard Schechner, "An Interview with John Cage," *Tulane Drama Review* X,2 (Winter 1965): p. 58.

33 *Ibid.*, p.65.

34 Cage, *Silence*, p.14.

35 The original production of *Imaginary Landscape #4* took place at the McMillan Theatre at Columbia University in 1952. Because it was not performed until nearly midnight, most radio stations had gone off the air, so very little was actually "caught."

36 C. Tomkins, *Off the Wall*, New York, Penguin Books, 1981, p.71.

37 Cage, 'On Robert Rauschenberg', *Silence*, p.102.

38 Cage, 'History of Experimental Music in the United States', *Silence*, p.70.

39 Kirby and Schechner, *op. cit.*, p.50.

40 Cage, "On Robert Rauschenberg', *Silence*, p.100.

41 In 'A Dialogue about Acting', Brecht makes reference to "an audience of the scientific age." A few years later in 'Interview with an Exile' he declares:

> The theatre must keep up with the times and all the advances of the times, and not lag several thousand miles behind as it does at present ... Look at an airplane, then look at a theatrical performance. People have acquired new motives for their actions; science has found new dimensions by which to measure them; it's time for art to find new expressions.
>
> *Brecht on Theatre*, pp.26, 67

42 Brecht, *op. cit.*, p.71.
43 *Ibid.*, p.25.
44 *Ibid.*, p.136.
45 *Ibid.*, p.37.
46 *Ibid.*, p.41.
47 Schawinsky has described *Spectodrama* as "symphonic inter-action and effect; color and form, motion and light, sound and word, gesture and music, illustration and improvisation." M. Duberman, *Black Mountain: An Exploration in Community*, New York: E.P. Dutton, 1972, p.98. For *Danse Macabre* the audience wore masks, thus becoming part of the performance.
48 *Ibid.*, p.291.
49 *Ibid.*
50 Cage, in Kostelanetz, *op. cit.*, p.81.
51 This should not be confused with one of his later compositions, entitled "Theatre Piece."
52 Duberman, *op. cit.*, p.350.
53 *Ibid.*
54 See Duberman, pp.350–58.
55 Kirby and Schechner, *op. cit.*, pp.52–3.
56 D. Bell, *The Cultural Contradictions of Capitalism*, New York, Basic Books, 1976, p.7.

3 Off Broadway, Happenings, and the Living Theatre

1   Quoted in R. Kostelanetz, *The Theatre of Mixed Means*, (1967) New York, RK Editions, 1980, p.53.
2   J.D. Salinger, *The Catcher in the Rye*, New York, Signet Books, 1953, pp.114–15.
3   S.W. Little, *Off-Broadway: The Prophetic Theater*, New York, Coward, McCann & Geoghegan, 1972, pp.13–14.
4   J. Poggi, *Theater in America: The Impact of Economic Forces, 1870–1967*, New York, Cornell University Press, 1968, pp.173–4.
5   Quoted in J. Schevill, *Break Out! In Search of New Theatrical Environments*, Chicago, Swallow Press, 1973, p.12.
6   J. Beck, *The Life of the Theatre*, San Francisco, City Lights Books, 1972, section 7 [n.p.].
7   R. Foreman, foreword, in B. McNamara and J. Dolan (eds.) *The Drama Review: Thirty Years of Commentary on the Avant-Garde*, Ann Arbor, University of Michigan Research Press, 1986, p.x.
8   P. Biner, *The Living Theatre*, New York, Horizon Press, 1972, p.27.
9   K. Brown, *The Brig*, New York, Hill & Wang, 1965, p.87.
10 R. Motherwell, *The Collected Writings of Robert Motherwell*, S. Terenzio (ed.), New York, Oxford University Press, 1992, p.79.
11 *Ibid.*, pp.77–9.

12 J. Malina, *The Diaries of Judith Malina 1947–1957*, New York, Grove Press, 1984, p.50.

13 J.C. Holmes, 'The Philosophy of the Beat Generation', *Esquire*, February 1958, 49. Quoted in L. Phillips, 'Beat Culture: America Revisioned', *Beat Culture and the New America 1950–1965*, New York, Whitney Museum of American Art, 1995, p.28.

14 J. Beck, 'Why Vanguard?' *New York Times*, March 22, 1959, Arts and Leisure, p.1.

15 Beck, *The Life of the Theatre*, *op. cit.*, entry 9 [n.p.].

16 Malina, *op. cit.*, p.14.

17 *Ibid.*, p.72.

18 Material on the history of the Living Theatre is drawn primarily from J. Tytell, *The Living Theatre: Art, Exile, and Outrage*, New York, Grove Press, 1995.

19 P. and P. Goodman, *Communitas: Means of Livelihood and Ways of Life* (1947), New York, Columbia University Press, 1990, p.17.

20 J. Beck, 'Storming the Barricades', in Brown, *op. cit.*, p.7.

21 Quoted in W. Glover, 'The Living Theatre', *Theatre Arts*, December 1961, p.63.

22 Beck, 'Storming the Barricades', in Brown, *op. cit.*, p.21.

23 *Ibid.*, p.22.

24 M. Cunningham, in conversation with Jacqueline Lesschaeve, *The Dancer and the Dance*, New York, Marion Boyars, 1991, p.149.

25 This and subsequent quotes about the space from Beck, 'Storming the Barricades', in Brown, *op. cit.*, p.31.

26 J. Tallmer, review of *Many Loves* by William Carlos Williams, *Village Voice*, January 21, 1959, p.9.

27 J. Gelber, *The Connection* (1957) New York, Grove Press, 1960, p.17.

28 R. Brustein, review of *The Connection*, *The New Republic*, September 28, 1959, p.29.

29 Brown, *op. cit.*, p.27.

30 Gelber, *op. cit.*, p.53.

31 Tytell, *op. cit.*, p.157.

32 Gelber, *op. cit.*, p.7.

33 Beck, 'Storming the Barricades', in Brown, *op. cit.*, p.26.

34 Beck, *The Life of the Theatre*, *op. cit.*, section 7.

35 A. Ginsberg, interview, *All Things Considered*, National Public Radio, January 31, 1993.

36 R. Brustein *et al.*, 'History Now', *Yale/Theatre*, Spring 1969, 2.1, p.21.

37 M. Kirby, 'On Acting and Not Acting, *The Drama Review*, March 1972, 16.1, pp.3–15.

38 Brustein, 'History Now', *op. cit.*, p.18.

39 J. MacLow, *The Marrying Maiden*, unpublished ms, 1960, revised 1967.

40 Beck, 'Storming the Barricades', in Brown, *op. cit.*, p.29. J. Malina wrote the section of the essay dealing with *The Marrying Maiden*.

41 A. Kaprow, 'The Legacy of Jackson Pollock', *Art News*, October 1958, p. 26.

42 A. Kaprow, *Assemblage, Environments, & Happenings*, New York, Harry N. Abrams, 1966, p.165.

43 A. Kaprow, 'The Legacy of Jackson Pollock', *op. cit.*, pp.56–7.

44 Reprinted in M. Kirby, *Happenings: An Illustrated Anthology*, New York, E.P. Dutton, 1965, pp.54–65. Rutgers was then home to many emerging avant-garde artists. The same issue of the *Anthologist* included photos of works by Robert Whitman, George Segal, and Lucas Samaras.

45 *Ibid.*, p.71.

46 The total event is lucidly described in Kirby, *Happenings: An Illustrated Anthology*, *op. cit.*, pp.67–83.

47 *Ibid.*, p.21.

48 The interview, along with J. Beck's 'How to Close a Theatre', C.L. Mee Jr.'s 'Epitaph for the Living Theatre' and K. Brown's *The Brig* can be found in *Tulane Drama Review*, Spring 1964, 8.3.

49 *Ibid.*, 'The Living Theatre and Larger Issues', pp.195–7.

50 The work evolved over the years; the published version, which differs in several respects from the first production, dates from 1969. In J. Lahr and J. Price (eds.) *The Great American Life Show: 9 Plays from the Avant-Garde Theater*, New York, Bantam Books, 1974.

51 G. Rogoff, 'The Theatre Is Not Safe', *Yale/Theatre*, Spring 1969, 2.1, p.92.

52 Biner, *op. cit.*, p.93.

53 Rogoff, *op. cit.*, pp.98–9.

4 The 1960s: collectives and rituals

1 Y. Rainer, *Work 1961–73*, Halifax, Press of Nova Scotia College of Art and Design, 1974, p.8.

2 S. Beckett, *Endgame*, New York, Grove Press, 1958, p.44.

3 S. Sontag, *Styles of Radical Will*, New York, Farrar, Straus & Giroux, 1969, p.23.

4 Quoted in A. Poland and B. Mailman (eds.) *The Off Off Broadway Book*, Indianapolis, Bobbs-Merrill, 1972, p.xviii.

5 E. Blumenthal, 'Chaikin and Shepard Speak in Tongues', *Village Voice*, November 26, 1979, p.103. Quoted in B. Daniels (ed.) *Joseph Chaikin and Sam Shepard: Letters and Texts, 1972–1984*, New York, New American Library, 1989, p.1.

6 Quoted in G. Steiner, *Language and Silence* (1967), New York, Atheneum, 1986, p.52.

7 A. Artaud, *The Theatre and Its Double*, M.C. Richards (trans.), New York, Grove Press, 1958, p.7.

8 *Ibid.*, p.37.

9 *Ibid.*, p.60.

10 J.C. van Itallie, *The Serpent*, New York, Atheneum, 1969, p.ix.

11 J. Chaikin, 'The Open Theatre', *Tulane Drama Review*, Winter 1964, 9.2, p.193.

12 Steiner, *op. cit.*, pp.26–7.

13 J. Grotowski, *Towards a Poor Theatre*, New York, Simon & Schuster, 1968, p.77.

14 M. Gibson, 'Brook's Africa', *The Drama Review*, September 1973, 17.3, pp.46–7.

15 R. Wagner, *The Art-Work of the Future and Other Works* (1895), W.A. Ellis (trans.), Lincoln, University of Nebraska Press, 1993, pp.192–3.

16 Artaud, *op. cit.*, p.116.

17 J. Lahr, *Up Against the Fourth Wall: Essays on the Modern Theatre*, New York, Grove Press, 1970, p.160.

18 Artaud, *op. cit.*, p.26.

19 *Ibid.*, p.28.

20 Chaikin, 'The Open Theatre', *op. cit.*, p.191 (italics added).

21 For an in-depth examination of Chaikin and his work, see E. Blumenthal, *Joseph Chaikin: Exploring the Boundaries of Theater*, Cambridge, Cambridge University Press, 1984.

22 Quoted in R. Pasolli, *A Book on the Open Theatre*, Indianapolis, Bobbs-Merrill, 1970, pp.xiv–xv.

23 J. Chaikin, *The Presence of the Actor*, New York, Atheneum, 1972, pp.53–4.

24 *Ibid.*, p.20.

25 Pasolli, *op. cit.*, p.33.

26 *Ibid.*, p.50–51.

27 *Ibid.*, p.110.

28 R. Pasolli, 'The Genesis of 'The Serpent', *Village Voice*, February 20, 1969, p.50.

29 Lahr, *op. cit.*, p.166.

30 *Ibid.*, p.169.
31 R. Wetzsteon, 'Theatre Journal', *Village Voice*, March 6, 1969, p.44.
32 R. Schechner, 'An Interview with Joseph Chaikin', *The Drama Review*, Spring 1969, 13.3, p.144.
33 For a complete discussion of environmental theatre, see A. Aronson, *The History and Theory of Environmental Scenography*, Ann Arbor, UMI Research Press, 1981.
34 R. Schechner, '6 Axioms for Environmental Theatre', *The Drama Review*, Spring 1968, 12.3, pp.41–64.
35 R. Schechner, *Environmental Theater*, New York, Hawthorn Books, 1973, p.45.
36 *Ibid.*, p.44.
37 Initially the actors wore skimpy costumes for some scenes. Grotowski's response when he saw these costumes was that it was like strip-tease and suggested that the actors be either total naked or fully clothed – the group opted for nudity.
38 Schechner, *Environmental Theater*, op. cit., p.43.
39 *Ibid.*, p.82.
40 For a thorough study of Serban's work, see E. Menta, *The Magic World Behind the Curtain*, New York, Peter Lang, 1995.
41 R. Eder, 'Andrei Serban's Theatre of Terror and Beauty', *New York Times Magazine*, February 13, 1977, p.45.
42 Artaud, *op. cit.*, p.102.
43 P. Brook, *The Shifting Point*, New York, Harper & Row, 1987, p.108.
44 *Ibid.*, p.110.
45 Menta, *op. cit.*, p.14.
46 A. Serban, 'The Life in a Sound', E. Blumenthal (trans.), *The Drama Review*, December 1976, 20.4, p.26.
47 Menta, *op. cit.*, p.23.
48 Robb Baker, *Soho Weekly News*, July 3, 1974, quoted in Menta, *op. cit.*, p.23.
49 Menta, *op. cit.*, p.25.
50 *Ibid.*, p.26.

5 Smith, Wilson, and Foreman

1 R. Foreman, 'Ontological-Hysteric: Manifesto I', *Richard Foreman: Plays and Manifestos*, K. Davy (ed.), New York, New York University Press, 1976, p.72.
2 A. Holmberg, *The Theatre of Robert Wilson* (1996), Cambridge, Cambridge University Press, 1998, pp.2–3.
3 Libe Bayrak quoted in S. Brecht, *The Theatre of Visions: Robert Wilson*, Frankfurt-am-Main, Suhrkamp, 1978, pp.31–3.
4 T. Fairbrother (ed.), *Robert Wilson's Vision*, Boston, Museum of Fine Arts, 1991, p.110.
5 Foreman, *Richard Foreman: Plays and Manifestos, op. cit.*, pp.1–31.
6 *Ibid.*, p.xi.
7 *Ibid.*
8 K. Davy, *Richard Foreman and the Ontological-Hysteric Theatre* (1979), Ann Arbor, University of Michigan Research Press, 1981, p.141.
9 Foreman, *op. cit.*, p.70.
10 *Ibid.*, p.69.
11 *Art News*, September 1966, reprinted in G. Battcock, *Minimal Art: A Critical Anthology* (1968), Berkeley, University of California Press, 1995, pp.148–64.
12 See R. Wollheim, 'Minimal Art', in Battcock, *op. cit.*, pp.387–99.
13 *Ibid.*
14 B. Rose, 'ABC Art', in Battcock, *op. cit.*, pp.274–97.
15 M. Fried, 'Art and Objecthood', in Battcock, *op. cit.*, pp.116ff.

16 C. Tomkins, *The Bride and the Bachelors: Five Masters of the Avant-Garde* (1962), New York, Viking, 1968, p.104.

17 Quoted in B. Rose, 'ABC Art', in Battcock, *op. cit.*, p.290.

18 G. Stein, 'Portraits and Repetition', *Lectures in America*, (1935) Boston, Beacon Press, 1985, p.167.

19 M. Kirby, 'Post-Modern Dance Issue: An Introduction', *The Drama Review*, March 1975, 19.1, p.3. See also S. Banes, *Democracy's Body: Judson Dance Theater, 1962–1964*, Durham, NC, Duke University Press, 1993.

20 See E. Leffingwell, 'The Only Normal Man in Baghdad', in Leffingwell *et al.* (eds.), *Jack Smith: Flaming Creature: His Amazing Life and Times*, Long Island City, The Institute for Contemporary Art/P.S.1 Museum, 1997, p.70.

21 Ken Kelman, quoted in P.A. Sitney, *Visionary Film*, New York, Oxford University Press, 1979, pp.353–4.

22 J. Hoberman, 'The Big Heat: Making and Unmaking *Flaming Creatures*', in Leffingwell, *op. cit.*, p.162.

23 Sitney, *op. cit.*, p.353.

24 S. Sontag, 'Jack Smith's Flaming Creatures', *Against Interpretation and Other Essays* (1961), New York, Dell, 1969, pp.231–2.

25 Quoted in Leffingwell, *op. cit.*, p.25.

26 Sitney, *op. cit.*, pp.23–4.

27 Quoted in Sitney, *op. cit.*, pp.20–1.

28 *Ibid.*, p.331.

29 S. Brecht, *Queer Theatre*, Frankfurt-am-Main, Suhrkamp, 1978, p.12. See also J. Mekas, 'The End of Civilization', *Village Voice* July 23, 1970, p.45.

30 R. Foreman, 'During the Second Half of the Sixties', in Leffingwell, *op. cit.*, p.26.

31 See, for example, I. Hassan, 'Toward a Concept of Postmodernism', *The Postmodern Turn*, Columbus, Ohio State University Press, 1987, pp.84–96.

32 See F. Jameson, *Postmodernism, or The Cultural Logic of Late Capitalism*, Durham, NC, Duke University Press, 1991.

33 W.M. Hoffman (ed.), *The King of Spain*, *New American Plays*, Vol. 3, New York, Hill & Wang, 1970, p.246.

34 *Ibid.*, p.247.

35 Fairbrother, *op. cit.*, p.110.

36 Hoffman, *op. cit.*, p.257.

37 *Ibid.*, p.260.

38 *Ibid.*, pp.245–72.

39 Brecht, *The Theatre of Visions: Robert Wilson*, *op. cit.*, p.198.

40 B. Langton, 'Journey to Ka Mountain', *The Drama Review*, June 1973, 17.2, p.53.

41 Quoted in F. Quadri *et al.*, *Robert Wilson*, New York, Rizzoli, 1997, p.12.

42 Holmberg, *op. cit.*, p.4.

43 B. Simmer, 'Robert Wilson and Therapy', *The Drama Review*, March 1976, 20.1, p.103.

44 *Ibid.*, pp.103–4.

45 R. Foreman, review of *The Life and Times of Sigmund Freud*, *The Village Voice*, January 1, 1970, p.41.

46 See M. Archer, *Art Since 1960*, London, Thames & Hudson, 1997, p.11.

47 R. Foreman, review of *The Life and Times of Sigmund Freud*, *op. cit.*

48 L. Aragon, 'An Open Letter to André Breton on Robert Wilson's *Deafman Glance*', *Performing Arts Journal*, Spring 1976, 1.1, p.4.

49 Holmberg, *op. cit.*, pp.4–5.

50 R. Foreman, *Unbalancing Acts*, New York, Pantheon Books, 1992, p.4.

51 R. Foreman, 'Notes on the Process of Making It', Program for *Blvd. de Paris (I've Got the Shakes)*, New York, 1977, p.9.

52 Foreman, *Unbalancing Acts*, *op. cit.*, p.25.

53 Foreman, *Richard Foreman: Plays and Manifestos, op. cit.*, p.17.
54 M. Heidegger, 'Being and Time: Introduction', *Basic Writings*, D.F. Krell (ed.), San Francisco, Harper San Francisco, 1977, p.46.
55 Foreman, *Richard Foreman: Plays and Manifestos, op. cit.*, p.188.
56 *Ibid.*, pp.208–9.
57 Quoted in Archer, *op. cit.*, p.80.
58 Foreman, *Richard Foreman: Plays and Manifestos, op. cit.*, p.208.
59 C. Bernstein *et al.*, 'Beyond Sense and Nonsense: Perspectives on the Ontological at 30', *Theater*, 1997, 28.1, pp.28–9.
60 Foreman, 'Notes on the Process of Making It', *op. cit.*, p.8.
61 Bernstein *et al.*, *op. cit.*, p.26.

6 Performance art (and the origins of the Wooster Group)

1   E. LeCompte interview in *Performance Art Magazine*, 1979, 2, p.15.
2   T. Wolfe, 'The Me Decade and the Third Great Awakening' (1976), reprinted in *The Purple Decades: A Reader*, New York, Farrar, Straus & Giroux, 1982, pp.265–93.
3   S. Gray, 'The Making of a Trilogy: Playwright's Notes', *Performing Arts Journal*, Fall 1978, 33.2, p.88.
4   *Ibid.*
5   LeCompte, *op. cit.*, p.14.
6   D. Savran, *The Wooster Group, 1975–1985*, Ann Arbor, UMI Research Press, 1986, p.4.
7   S. Gray, 'About Three Places in Rhode Island', *The Drama Review*, March 1979, 23.1, p.33.
8   Quoted in J. Bierman, 'Three Places in Rhode Island', *The Drama Review*, March 1979, 23.1, pp.13–14.
9   S. Banes, 'The Once and Future Past: Meredith Monk's Visionary Archeology', *Meredith Monk: Archeology of an Artist*, exhibition catalogue, New York Library for the Performing Arts, 1996.
10 Gray, 'About Three Places in Rhode Island', *op. cit.*, p.36, acknowledges the direct influence of *Education of the Girl Child*, as well as the Living Theatre's *Frankenstein*.
11 Savran, *op. cit.*, p.4.
12 For a complete description, see A. Aronson, 'Sakonnet Point', *The Drama Review*, December 1975, 19.4, pp.27–35.
13 Gray, 'About Three Places in Rhode Island', *op. cit.*, pp.32–3.
14 *Ibid.*, p.33.
15 Aronson, *op. cit.*, p.35.
16 Gray, 'About Three Places in Rhode Island', *op. cit.*, p.36.
17 *Ibid.*, pp.38–9.
18 'A Brief History of the Wooster Group', New York Library for the Performing Arts, clipping file [n.d.].
19 E. LeCompte, 'The Making of a Trilogy: An Introduction', *Performing Arts Journal*, Fall 1978, 3.2, p.86.
20 J.L. Borges, *Collected Fictions*, A. Hurley (trans.), New York, Penguin Books, 1999, p.325.
21 R. Schechner, *Between Theater and Anthropology*, Philadelphia, University of Pennsylvania Press, 1985, p.263.
22 The Performance Group was the name decided upon by the original group members. When TPG was constituted as a non-profit, tax-exempt organization in the summer of 1968 it was known as The Wooster Group, Inc. [clipping files, New York Public Library].

23 K. Stiles, 'Uncorrupted Joy: International Art Actions', in R. Ferguson (ed.) *Out of Actions: Between Performance and the Object 1949–1979*, New York, Thames & Hudson, 1998, p.230.

24 R. Goldberg, *Performance: Live Art 1909 to the Present*, New York, Harry N. Abrams, 1979, p.6.

25 M. Kirby, 'Autoperformance Issue: An Introduction', *The Drama Review*, March 1979, 23.1, p.2.

26 L. Novak, 'The Degree of Oscillation: Why Performance Art Cannot Be Subsumed', in f-stop Fitzgerald (ed.) *DOC•U•MEN•TIA*, San Francisco, Last Gasp, 1987 [n.p.].

27 P. Schimmel, 'Leap into the Void: Performance and the Object', in Ferguson, *op. cit.*, p.17.

28 M. Russell (ed.), *Out of Character: Rants, Raves, and Monologues from Today's Top Performance Artists*, New York, Bantam Books, 1997, p.243.

29 See T. McEvilley, 'Diogenes of Sinope (*c.* 410 – *c.* 320 B.C.): Selected Performance Pieces', *Artforum*, March 1983; and A. di Felice, 'Renaissance Performance: Notes on Prototypical Artistic Actions in the Age of the Platonic Princes', in G. Battcock and R. Nickas (eds.) *The Art of Performance: A Critical Anthology*, New York, E.P. Dutton, 1984, pp.3–23.

30 G. Hugnet, 'The Dada Spirit in Painting', in R. Motherwell (ed.) *The Dada Painters and Poets: An Anthology* (1951), Cambridge, Mass., Belknap Press, 1981, p.161.

31 See T. McEvilley, 'Art in the Dark', *Artforum*, June 1983, p.63.

32 L. Wittgenstein, 'Philosophical Investigations', quoted in K. Stiles, 'Uncorrupted Joy: International Art Actions', in Ferguson, *op. cit.*, p.230.

33 B. Rose, 'Hans Namuth's Photograph and the Jackson Pollock Myth: Part One: Media Impact and the Failure of Criticism', *Arts Magazine*, 53.7, pp.112, 116.

34 D. Higgins, 'Fluxus: Theory and Reception', in K. Friedman (ed.) *The Fluxus Reader*, Chichester, John Wiley & Sons, 1998, p.222.

35 *Ibid.*, p.223.

36 P. Frank and K. Friedman, 'Fluxus: A Post-Definitive History: Art Where Response is the Heart of the Matter', *High Performance*, 1984, 7.3, p.58.

37 See A. Kaprow, *Assemblages, Environments & Happenings*, New York, Harry N. Abrams, 1966, p.273.

38 A. Kaprow, 'Performing Life', in C.E. Loeffler and D. Tong (eds.) *Performance Anthology: Source Book of California Performance Art* (updated edition), San Francisco, Last Gasp Press, 1989, p.x.

39 Kaprow, *Assemblages, Environments & Happenings, op. cit.*, pp.195–6.

40 Kaprow, 'Performing Life', *op. cit.*

41 Montano, *Art in Everyday Life*, Los Angeles, Astro Artz, 1981 [n.p.].

42 *Ibid.*

43 M. Kirby, 'The Activity: A New Art Form', *The Art of Time*, New York, E.P. Dutton, 1969, p.155.

44 C. Schneemann, *More Than Meat Joy*, B.R. McPherson (ed.), Kingston, McPherson & Co., 1997, p.9.

45 *Ibid.*, p.10.

46 *Ibid.*, p.52.

47 *Ibid.*

48 For a description, see J. Johnston, 'The Object', *Village Voice*, May 21, 1964, p.12, quoted in S. Banes, *Democracy's Body: Judson Dance Theater, 1962–1964*, Durham, NC, Duke University Press, 1993, p.206.

49 Schneemann, *op. cit.*, p.80.

50 *Ibid.*, p.63.

51 *Ibid.*, pp.234–5.

52 R. Hughes, 'The Decline and Fall of the Avant-Garde', *Time*, December 18, 1972, p.111.

53 R. Rosenthal, 'Performance and the Masochist Tradition', *High Performance*, Winter 1981–82, 4.4, pp.22–3.

54 C. Burden and J. Butterfield, 'Through the Night Softly', in Battcock and Nickas, *op. cit.*, p.223.

55 W. Enstice, 'Performance Art's Coming of Age', in Battcock and Nickas, *op. cit.*, p.146.

56 For a full description, see A.E. Shank *et al.* (eds.) '4 Scenes in a Harsh Life: Synopsis of Scenes', in 'A Casebook: Ron Athey', *TheatreForum*, Winter/Spring 1995, 6, pp.62–3.

57 J. Myers, 'An Interview with Ron Athey', *TheatreForum*, Winter/Spring 1995, 6, p.61.

58 T. Scott, 'Stuart Sherman's Singular Spectacles', *The Drama Review*, March 1979, 23.1, p.74.

59 *Ibid.*, pp.74–6.

60 See S. Sherman, *One Acts and Two Trilogies*, Imperial Beach, VRI Theater Library, 1987.

61 J. Rockwell, review of *United States*, *New York Times*, February 6, 1983, p.50.

62 L. Anderson, 'Words in Reverse', in J. Kardon, *Laurie Anderson: Works from 1969 to 1983*, Philadelphia, Institute of Contemporary Art, 1983, p.55.

63 Quoted in Kardon, *op. cit.*, p.24.

64 *Ibid.*, 25.

65 H. Hughes, 'World Without End', in L. Champagne (ed.) *Out from Under: Texts by Women Performance Artists*, New York, Theatre Communications Group, 1990, p.10.

7 The Wooster Group, Reza Abdoh, and the end of the avant-garde

1 R. Schechner, 'The Decline and Fall of the (American) Avant-Garde', *Performing Arts Journal*, 1981, 5.2, p.51.

2 *Ibid.*, 5.2, pp.48–63 and 5.3, pp.9–19.

3 *Ibid.*, 5.2, p.51.

4 M. Russell (ed.), *Out of Character: Rants, Raves, and Monologues from Today's Top Performance Artists*, New York, Bantam Books, 1997, p.vii.

5 Diane Paulus, quoted in W. Harris, 'The Bump in a Midsummer Night: Is It a Dream?' *New York Times*, August 15, 1999, Arts and Leisure, p.7.

6 *The Drama Review*, Spring 1985, 29.1.

7 U. Parnes, 'Pop Performance in East Village Clubs', *The Drama Review*, Spring 1985, 29.1, p.5.

8 S. Gray, 'Perpetual Saturdays', *Performing Arts Journal*, 1981, 6.1, pp.46–9.

9 See R.K. Fried, 'The Cinematic Theatre of John Jesurun', *The Drama Review*, Spring 1985, 29.1, pp.57–72.

10 M. Kirby, 'East Village Performance: An Introduction', *The Drama Review*, Spring 1985, 29.1, p.4.

11 D. Savran, *The Wooster Group 1975–1985: Breaking the Rules*, Ann Arbor, UMI Research Press, 1986, p.50.

12 *Ibid.*, pp.14–18.

13 Quoted in A. Aronson, 'The Wooster Group's *L.S.D. (...Just the High Points...)*', *The Drama Review*, Summer 1985, 29.2, p.72.

14 Leary was the "guru" who popularized LSD as a consciousness-expanding drug; Liddy was one of the Watergate burglars with an outspoken right-wing credo. In the late 1970s, after each had served time in prison, they toured the country as a sort of vaudeville team engaging in a series of "debates."

15 Quoted in Savran, *op. cit.*, p.51.
16 LeCompte had in fact written to Miller and his publisher on several occasions, and Miller had even seen an early performance and talked with LeCompte. Ultimately, he was concerned that the work would be seen as parody (a fear confirmed by Mel Gussow's *New York Times* review) and interfere with a "first-class" production in New York. See D. Savran, 'The Wooster Group, Arthur Miller and *The Crucible*', *The Drama Review*, Summer 1985, 29.2, pp.99–109.
17 *Ibid.*, p.102.
18 J. Leverett, 'The Wooster Group's "Mean Theatre" Sparks a Hot Debate', *Theatre Communications*, July/August 1982, 5.4–5, p.17.
19 For a detailed description of the production and its creation, see E. Arratia, 'Island Hopping: Rehearsing the Wooster Group's *Brace Up!*', *The Drama Review*, Winter 1992, 36.4, pp.121–42, as well as other articles in the same issue by Susie Mee and Paul Schmidt.
20 Beginning with *Brace Up!* the lighting was designed by Jennifer Tipton, one of the most innovative lighting designers of the last thirty years; the settings were created by James Clayburgh.
21 M.N. Levine, 'Interview with Elizabeth LeCompte', *Theatre Times*, August 1984, 3.8, p.13.
22 P. Wehle, Reza Abdoh and *Tight Right White*: 'Interviews with Philippa Wehle', *TheatreForum*, Fall/Winter 1994, 4, p.61.
23 *Ibid.*
24 H. Hughes, 'World Without End', in L. Champagne (ed.) *Out From Under: Texts by Women Performance Artists*, New York, Theatre Communications Group, 1990, p.25.
25 See G. Deleuze and F. Guattari, 'Rhizome', *On the Line*, New York, Semiotext(e), 1983, pp.1–65.
26 P. Vogel, 'Anne Bogart and the New Play', in A. Bogart, *Anne Bogart: Viewpoints*, M.B. Dixon and J.A. Smith (eds.), Lime, Smith & Kraus, 1995, p.95.
27 *Ibid.*, p.11.
28 A. Miller, 'Introduction to the *Collected Plays*', in R.A. Martin and S.R. Centola (eds.) *The Theater Essays of Arthur Miller*, New York, Da Capo Press, 1996, p.122.

Conclusion

1 F. Fukuyama, *The End of History and the Last Man*, New York, Avon Books, 1993.
2 D.A. McAdams, *Caught in the Act*, New York, Aperture, 1996.
3 See, for example, J. McKinley, 'Quirk after Quirk in Side-by-Side Festivals', *New York Times*, August 15, 1999, Arts and Leisure, pp.3, 6.
4 E.V. Copage, 'Not Your Mother's Musical, and That's the Point', *New York Times* September 6, 1999, p.E3.

Bibliography

In addition to the specific references below, I have also consulted reviews and articles from a wide range of sources, but notably the newspapers *New York Times*, *Village Voice*, and *Soho Weekly News*, and the journals *American Theatre*, *High Performance*, *Performing Arts Journal*, *TheatreForum*, *[Yale] Theatre*, and *The [Tulane] Drama Review*.

Anderson, L., *Stories from the Nerve Bible: A Retrospective 1972–1992*, New York, Harper Perennial, 1994.

Aragon, L., 'An Open Letter to André Breton on Robert Wilson's *Deafman Glance*', *Performing Arts Journal*, Spring 1976, 1.1, pp.3–7.

Archer, M., *Art Since 1960*, London, Thames & Hudson, 1997.

Aristotle, *Poetics* (1961), S.H. Butcher (trans.), F. Fergusson (ed.), New York, Hill & Wang, 1967.

Aronson, A., 'Sakonnet Point', *The Drama Review*, December 1975, 19.4, pp.27–35.

—— *The History and Theory of Environmental Scenography*, Ann Arbor, UMI Research Press, 1981.

—— 'The Wooster Group's *L.S.D. (…Just the High Points…)*', *The Drama Review*, Summer 1985, 29.2, pp.65–77.

Arratia, E., 'Island Hopping: Rehearsing the Wooster Group's *Brace Up!*', *The Drama Review*, Winter 1992, 36.4, pp.121–42.

Artaud, A., *The Theater and its Double*, M.C. Richards (trans.), New York, Grove Press, 1958.

Atkinson, B., *Broadway*, New York, Macmillan, 1970.

Auerbach, D., *Sam Shepard, Arthur Kopit, and the Off Broadway Theater*, Boston, Twayne Publishers, 1982.

Banes, S., *Democracy's Body: Judson Dance Theater, 1962–1964*, Durham, NC, Duke University Press, 1993.

—— *Greenwich Village 1963: Avant-Garde Performance and the Effervescent Body*, Durham, NC, Duke University Press, 1993.

—— 'The Once and Future Past: Meredith Monk's Visionary Archeology', *Meredith Monk: Archeology of an Artist*, exhibition catalogue, New York, New York Library for the Performing Arts, 1996.

Barthes, R., *S/Z*, R. Miller (trans.), New York, Hill & Wang, 1974.

Battcock, G. (ed.), *Minimal Art: A Critical Anthology* (1968) Berkeley, University of California Press, 1995.

Battcock, G., and R. Nickas (eds.), *The Art of Performance: A Critical Anthology*, New York, E.P. Dutton, 1984.

Baumol, W.J., and W.G. Bowen, *Performing Arts – The Economic Dilemma*, New York, The Twentieth Century Fund, 1966.

Beck, J., 'Why Vanguard?' *New York Times*, 22 March 1959, Arts and Leisure, p.1.

—— 'How to Close a Theatre', *Tulane Drama Review*, Spring 1964, 8.3, pp.180–90.

—— *The Life of the Theatre*, San Francisco, City Lights Books, 1972.

Beckett, S., *Endgame*, New York, Grove Press, 1958.

Bell, D., *The Cultural Contradictions of Capitalism*, New York, Basic Books, 1976.

Bentley, E., *The Theatre of Commitment*, New York, Atheneum, 1967.

—— *The Theatre of War: Comments on 32 Occasions* (1960), New York, Viking, 1972.

Bernstein, C., *et al.*, 'Beyond Sense and Nonsense: Perspectives on the Ontological at 30', *Theater*, 1997, 28.1, pp.23–34.

Bierman, J., 'Three Places in Rhode Island', *The Drama Review*, March 1979, 23.1, pp.13–30.

Bigsby, C.W.E., *A Critical Introduction to Twentieth Century American Drama, Vol III: Beyond Broadway* (1985), Cambridge, Cambridge University Press, 1988.

Biner, P., *The Living Theatre*, New York, Horizon Press, 1972.

Blumenthal, E., 'Chaikin and Shepard Speak in Tongues', *Village Voice*, 26 November 1979, p.103.

—— *Joseph Chaikin: Exploring the Boundaries of Theater*, Cambridge, Cambridge University Press, 1984.

Bogart, A., *Anne Bogart: Viewpoints*, M.B. Dixon and J.A. Smith (eds.), Lyme, NH, Smith & Kraus, 1995.

Borges, J.L., *Collected Fictions*, A. Hurley (trans.), New York, Penguin Books, 1999.

Brecht, B., *Brecht on Theatre* (1957), J. Willet (ed.), New York, Hill & Wang, 1966.

Brecht, S., *Queer Theatre*, Frankfurt-am-Main, Suhrkamp, 1978.

—— *The Theatre of Visions: Robert Wilson*, Frankfurt-am-Main, Suhrkamp, 1978.

Breton, A., *What Is Surrealism? Selected Writings*, F. Rosemont (ed.), New York, Pathfinder, 1978.

'A Brief History of the Wooster Group', New York Library for the Performing Arts, clipping file [n.d.].

Brook, P., *The Shifting Point*, New York, Harper & Row, 1987.

Brown, K., *The Brig*, New York, Hill & Wang, 1965.

Brown, N.O., *Love's Body*, New York, Random House, 1966.

Brustein, R., review of *The Connection*, *The New Republic*, 28 September 1959, 28, p.29.

—— *The Third Theatre*, New York, Alfred A. Knopf, 1969.

Brustein, R., *et al.*, 'History Now', *Yale Theatre*, Spring 1969, 2.1, pp.18–29.

Cage, J., *Silence* (1939), Cambridge, Mass., MIT Press, 1961.

—— *John Cage* (1968), R. Kostelanetz (ed.), London, Allen Lane, 1974.

Camus, A., 'Art and Revolt', *Partisan Review*, May–June 1952, XIX.3, pp.268–81.

Carlson, M. (ed.), *Theatre Semiotics: Signs of Life*, Bloomington, Indiana University Press, 1990.

Chaikin, J., 'The Open Theatre', *Tulane Drama Review*, Winter 1964, 9.2, pp.191–7.

—— *The Presence of the Actor*, New York, Atheneum, 1972.

Champagne, L. (ed.), *Out from Under: Texts by Women Performance Artists*, New York, Theatre Communications Group, 1990.

Copage, E.V., 'Not Your Mother's Musical, and That's the Point', *New York Times*, 6 September 1999, E3.

Copeland, R., and M. Cohen (eds.), *What Is Dance? Readings in Theory and Criticism*, New York, Oxford University Press, 1983.

Cordell, R.A., and L. Matson (eds.), *The Off-Broadway Theatre: Seven Plays*, New York, Random House, 1959.

Cunningham, M., in conversation with Jacqueline Lesschaeve, *The Dancer and the Dance* (1985), New York, Marion Boyars, 1991.

Daniels, B. (ed.), *Joseph Chaikin and Sam Shepard: Letters and Texts, 1972–1984*, New York, New American Library, 1989.

Davis, R.G., *The San Francisco Mime Troupe: The First Ten Years*, Palo Alto, Calif., Ramparts Press, 1975.

Davy, K., 'Foreman's *PAIN(T)* and *Vertical Mobility*', *The Drama Review*, June 1974, 18.2, pp.26–37.

—— *Richard Foreman and the Ontological-Hysteric Theatre*, (1979) Ann Arbor, UMI Research Press, 1981.

Deleuze, G., and F. Guattari, 'Rhizome', *On the Line*, New York, Semiotext(e), 1983, pp.1–65.

Docherty, T. (ed.), *Postmodernism: A Reader*, New York, Columbia University Press, 1993.

The Drama Review, Spring 1985, 29.1.

Duberman, M., *Black Mountain: An Exploration in Community*, New York, E.P. Dutton, 1972.

Duchamp, M., *The Writings of Marcel Duchamp* (1973), M. Sanouillet and E. Peterson (eds.), New York, Da Capo Press, 1989.

Eco, U., 'Semiotics of Theatrical Performance', *The Drama Review*, March 1977, 21.1, pp.107–17.

Eder, R., 'Andrei Serban's Theatre of Terror and Beauty', *The New York Times Magazine*, 13 February 1977, pp.42–60.

Egbert, D.D., 'The Idea of "Avant-Garde" in Art and Politics', *The American Historical Review*, December 1967, LXXIII.2, pp.339–66.

Elam, K., *The Semiotics of Theatre and Drama*, London, Methuen, 1980.

Fairbrother, T. (ed.), *Robert Wilson's Vision*, Boston, Museum of Fine Arts, 1991.

Ferguson, R. (ed.), *Out of Actions: Between Performance and the Object 1949–1979*, New York, Thames & Hudson, 1998.

Fiedler, L.A., *Love and Death in the American Novel*, Cleveland, Meridian Books, 1962.

Fitzgerald, f-stop, (ed.), *DOC•U•MEN•TIA*, San Francisco, Last Gasp, 1987.

Foreman, R., review of *The Life and Times of Sigmund Freud*, *Village Voice*, 1 January 1970, p.41.

—— 'Ontological-Hysteric Theatre: Third Manifesto', *The Drama Review*, December 1975, 19.4, pp.71–81.

—— *Richard Foreman: Plays and Manifestos*, K. Davy (ed.), New York, New York University Press, 1976.

—— 'How I Write My (Self: Plays)', *The Drama Review*, December 1977, 21.4, pp.5–24.

—— 'Notes on the Process of Making It', Program for *Blvd. de Paris (I've Got the Shakes)*, New York, 1977.

—— *Unbalancing Acts*, New York, Pantheon Books, 1992.

Frank, P., and K. Friedman, 'Fluxus: A Post-Definitive History: Art Where Response is the Heart of the Matter', *High Performance*, 1984, 7.3, p.58.

Frascina, F. (ed.), *Pollock and After: The Critical Debate*, New York, Harper & Row, 1985.

Fried, R.K., 'The Cinematic Theatre of John Jesurun', *The Drama Review*, Spring 1985, 29.1, pp.57–72.

Friedman, K. (ed.), *The Fluxus Reader*, Chichester, John Wiley & Sons, 1998.

Fukuyama, F., *The End of History and the Last Man*, New York, Avon Books, 1993.

Gabriel, R.H. (ed.), *The Pageant of America: A Pictorial History of the United States*, 15 volumes, New York, United States Publishers Association, 1929.

Gelber, J., *The Connection* (1957), New York, Grove Press, 1960.

Gery, A., and A. Gery, 'Linda Montano & Tehching Hsieh's One Year Art/Life Performance', *High Performance*, 1984, 7.3, pp.24–9.

Gibson, M., 'Brook's Africa', *The Drama Review*, September 1973, 17.3, pp.37–51.

Ginsberg, A., *Howl and Other Poems*, San Francisco, City Lights Books, 1959.

—— interview, *All Things Considered*, National Public Radio, 31 January 1993.

Gitlin, T., *The Sixties: Years of Hope, Days of Rage*, New York, Bantam Books, 1987.

Glover, W., 'The Living Theatre', *Theatre Arts*, December 1961, pp.62–4; 74–5.

Goldberg, R., *Performance: Live Art 1909 to the Present*, New York, Harry N. Abrams, 1979.

Goodman, P., and P. Goodman, *Communitas: Means of Livelihood and Ways of Life* (1947), New York, Columbia University Press, 1990.

Gray, S., 'The Making of a Trilogy: Playwright's Notes', *Performing Arts Journal*, Fall 1978, 33.2, pp.87–91.

—— 'About Three Places in Rhode Island', *The Drama Review*, March 1979, 23.1, pp.31–42.

—— 'Perpetual Saturdays', *Performing Arts Journal*, 1981, 6.1, pp.46–9.

Greenberg, C., 'Avant-Garde and Kitsch', *Partisan Review*, Fall 1939, VI.5, pp.34–49.

—— *Art and Culture: Critical Essays*, Boston, Beacon Press, 1961.

Grotowski, J., *Towards a Poor Theatre*, New York, Simon & Schuster, 1968.

Guilbaut, S., *How New York Stole the Idea of Modern Art*, A. Goldhammer (trans.), Chicago, University of Chicago Press, 1983.

Harris, W., 'The Bump in a Midsummer Night: Is It a Dream?' *New York Times*, 15 August 1999, Arts and Leisure, p.7.

Haskell, B., *Blam! The Explosion of Pop, Minimalism, and Performance 1958–1964*, New York, Whitney Museum of American Art, 1984.

Hassan, I., 'Toward a Concept of Postmodernism', *The Postmodern Turn*, Columbus, Ohio State University Press, 1987.

Heidegger, M., *Basic Writings*, D.F. Krell (ed.), San Francisco, Harper San Francisco, 1977.

Henderson, J.A., *The First Avant-Garde (1887–1894)*, London, G.G. Harrap, 1971.

Holmberg, A., *The Theatre of Robert Wilson* (1996), Cambridge, Cambridge University Press, 1998.

Hughes, R., 'The Decline and Fall of the Avant Garde', *Time*, 18 December 1972, p.111.

Huyssen, A., *After the Great Divide: Modernism, Mass Culture, Postmodernism*, Bloomington, Indiana University Press, 1986.

Jameson, F., *Postmodernism, or the Cultural Logic of Late Capitalism*, Durham, NC, Duke University Press, 1991.

Kalb, J., 'A Coupla White Guys Sittin' Around Talkin'', *Village Voice*, 26 May 1992, p.110.

Kaprow, A., 'The Legacy of Jackson Pollock', *Art News*, October 1958, 57.6, pp.24–6, 55–7.

—— *Assemblage, Environments, & Happenings*, New York, Harry N. Abrams, 1966.

Kardon, J., *Laurie Anderson: Works from 1969 to 1983*, Philadelphia, Institute of Contemporary Art, 1983.

Kernan, A.B. (ed.), *The Modern American Theater*, Englewood Cliffs, NJ, Prentice-Hall, 1967.

Kerr, W., 'What If Cain Did Not Know How to Kill Abel?' *New York Times*, 9 February 1969, Section 2, pp.1, 8.

Kirby, M., *Happenings: An Illustrated Anthology*, New York, E.P. Dutton, 1965.

—— *The Art of Time*, New York, E.P. Dutton, 1969.

—— 'On Acting and Not-Acting', *The Drama Review*, March 1972, 16.1, pp.3–15.

—— 'Autoperformance Issue: An Introduction', *The Drama Review*, March 1979, 23.1, p.2.

—— 'Post-Modern Dance Issue: An Introduction', *The Drama Review*, March 1975, 19.1, pp.3–4.

—— 'East Village Performance: An Introduction', *The Drama Review*, Spring 1985, 29.1, p.4.

—— *A Formalist Theatre*, Philadelphia, University of Pennsylvania Press, 1987.

Kirby, M., and R. Schechner, 'An Interview with John Cage', *Tulane Drama Review*, 1965, X.2, pp.50–72.

Knight, A., and K. Knight (eds.), *The Beat Vision: A Primary Sourcebook*, New York, Paragon House, 1987.

Knight, G.W., *The Wheel of Fire: Interpretations of Shakespearian Tragedy* (4th rev.), London, Methuen, 1954.

Kostelanetz, R., *The Theatre of Mixed-Means* (1967), New York, RK Editions, 1980.

Kronenberger, L. (ed.), *The Best Plays of 1952–1953*, New York, Dodd, Mead & Co., 1953.

Krutch, J.W., *"Modernism" in Modern Drama: A Definition and an Estimate* (1953), New York, Russell & Russell, 1962.

Lahr, J., *Up Against the Fourth Wall: Essays on the Modern Theatre*, New York, Grove Press, 1970.

Lahr, J., and J. Price (eds.), *The Great American Life Show: 9 Plays from the Avant-Garde Theater*, New York, Bantam Books, 1974.

Lampert, E.M., and R.W. Oliver (eds.), *Next Wave Festival Catalogue*, New York, Brooklyn Academy of Music, 1983.

Langton, B., 'Journey to Ka Mountain', *The Drama Review*, June 1973, 17.2, pp.48–57.

LeCompte, E., 'The Making of a Trilogy: An Introduction', *Performing Arts Journal*, Fall 1978, 3.2, pp.81–6.

—— interview, *Performance Art Magazine*, 1979, 2, pp.14–16.

Leffingwell, E., *et al.* (eds.), *Jack Smith: Flaming Creature: His Amazing Life and Times*, Long Island City, The Institute for Contemporary Art/P.S.1 Museum, 1997.

Leverett, J., 'The Wooster Group's "Mean Theatre" Sparks a Hot Debate', *Theatre Communicatons*, July/August 1982, 5.4–5, pp.16–20.

Levine, M.N., 'Interview with Elizabeth LeCompte', *Theatre Times*, August 1984, 3.8, p.13.

Little, S.W., *Off-Broadway: The Prophetic Theatre*, New York, Coward, McCann & Geoghegan, 1972.

Loeffler, C.E., and D. Tong (eds.), *Performance Anthology: Source Book of California Performance Art* (updated edition), San Francisco, Last Gasp Press, 1989.

Lyotard, J.F., 'The Sublime and the Avant-Garde', *Artforum*, April 1984, 22, pp.36–43.

McAdams, D.A., *Caught in the Act*, New York, Aperture, 1996.

McCoubrey, J.W. (ed.), *American Art 1700–1960: Sources and Documents*, Englewood Cliffs, NJ, Prentice-Hall, 1965.

McEvilley, T., 'Art in the Dark', *Artforum*, June 1983.

—— 'Diogenes of Sinope (*c.* 410 – *c.* 320 B.C.): Selected Performance Pieces', *Artforum*, March 1983.

McKinley, J., 'Quirk after Quirk in Side-by-Side Festivals', *New York Times*, 15 August 1999, Arts and Leisure, pp.3, 6.

MacLow, J., *The Marrying Maiden*, unpublished ms, 1960, revised 1967.

McNamara, B., and J. Dolan (eds.), *The Drama Review: Thirty Years of Commentary on the Avant-Garde*, Ann Arbor, UMI Research Press, 1986.

Malina, J., *The Diaries of Judith Malina 1947–1957*, New York, Grove Press, 1984.

Martin, R.A., and S.R. Centola (eds.), *The Theater Essays of Arthur Miller*, New York, Da Capo Press, 1996.

Mekas, J., 'The End of Civilization', *Village Voice* 23 July 1970, pp.45, 56–7.

Menta, E., *The Magic World Behind the Curtain*, New York, Peter Lang, 1995.

Montano, L., *Art in Everyday Life*, Los Angeles, Astro Artz, 1981.

Motherwell, R. (ed.), *The Dada Painters and Poets: An Anthology* (1951), Cambridge, Belknap Press, 1981.

—— *The Collected Writings of Robert Motherwell*, S. Terenzio (ed.), New York, Oxford University Press, 1992.

Mufson, D. (ed.), *Reza Abdoh*, Baltimore, Johns Hopkins University Press, 1999.

Myers, J., 'An Interview with Ron Athey', *TheatreForum*, Winter/Spring 1995, 6, p.61.

O'Neill, W.L. (ed.), *American Society Since 1945*, Chicago, Quadrangle Books, 1969.

'Our Country and Our Culture', *Partisan Review*, May–June 1952, XIX.3, pp.282–326.

Parnes, U., 'Jack Smith: A Partial Synopsis', *The True Comedy Planet*, 20 September 1989, pp.1–3.

—— 'Pop Performance in East Village Clubs', *The Drama Review*, Spring 1985, 29.1, pp.5–16.

Pasolli, R., 'The Genesis of *The Serpent*', *Village Voice*, 20 February 1969, pp.40, 50.

—— *A Book on the Open Theatre*, Indianapolis, Bobbs-Merrill, 1970.

Phillips, L. (ed.), *Beat Culture and the New America 1950–1965*, New York, Whitney Museum of American Art, 1995.

Poggi, J., *Theater in America: The Impact of Economic Forces, 1870–1967*, New York, Cornell University Press, 1968.

Poland, A., and B. Mailman (eds.), *The Off Off Broadway Book*, Indianapolis, Bobbs-Merrill, 1972.

Quadri, F., *et al.*, *Robert Wilson*, New York, Rizzoli, 1997.

Rabkin, G., 'Bizarre Survivor', *Soho Weekly News*, 11 November 1976, p.28.

Rainer, Y., *Work 1961–73*, Halifax, Press of Nova Scotia College of Art and Design, 1974.

Reische, D. (ed.), *The Performing Arts in America*, New York, H.W. Wilson, 1973.

Rockefeller Panel Report on the Future of Theatre, Dance, Music in America, *The Performing Arts: Problems and Prospects*, New York, McGraw-Hill, 1965.

Rockwell, J., review. of *United States*, *New York Times*, 6 February 1983, p.50.

Rogoff, G., 'The Theatre Is Not Safe', *Yale Theatre*, Spring 1969, 2.1, p.92.

Rose, B., 'Hans Namuth's Photograph and the Jackson Pollock Myth: Part One: Media Impact and the Failure of Criticism', *Arts Magazine*, 53.7, pp.112, 116.

Rosenberg, H., *The Tradition of the New* (1959), New York, McGraw-Hill, 1965.

Rosenthal, R., 'Performance and the Masochist Tradition', *High Performance*, Winter 1981–82, 4.4, pp.22–3.

Russell, M. (ed.), *Out of Character: Rants, Raves, and Monologues from Today's Top Performance Artists*, New York, Bantam Books, 1997.

Sainer, A., *The Radical Theatre Notebook*, New York, Avon Books, 1975.

Salinger, J.D., *The Catcher in the Rye*, New York, Signet Books, 1953.

Savran, D., 'The Wooster Group, Arthur Miller and *The Crucible*', *The Drama Review*, Summer 1985, 29.2, pp.99–109.

—— *The Wooster Group 1975–1985: Breaking the Rules*, Ann Arbor, UMI Research Press, 1986.

Sayler, O.M., *Our American Theatre*, New York, Brentano's, 1923.

Sayre, H.M., *The Object of Performance: The American Avant-Garde Since 1970* (1989), Chicago, University of Chicago Press, 1992.

Schechner, R., 'Interviews with Judith Malina and Kenneth H. Brown', *Tulane Drama Review*, Spring 1964, 8.3, pp.207–19.

—— '6 Axioms for Environmental Theatre', *The Drama Review*, Spring 1968, 12.3, pp.41–64.

—— 'An Interview with Joseph Chaikin', *The Drama Review*, Spring 1969, 13.3, pp.141–4.

—— *Environmental Theater*, New York, Hawthorn Books, 1973.

—— 'The Decline and Fall of the (American) Avant-Garde: Why It Happened and What We Can Do About It', *Performing Arts Journal*, 1981, part one, 5.2, pp.48–63; part two, 5.3, pp.9–19.

—— *Between Theater and Anthropology*, Philadelphia, University of Pennsylvania Press, 1985.

Schechner, R., *et al.* (eds.), 'The Living Theatre and Other Issues', *Tulane Drama Review*, Spring 1964, 8.3, pp.191–206.

Schevill, J., *Break Out! In Search of New Theatrical Environments*, Chicago, Swallow Press, 1973.

Schneemann, C., *More Than Meat Joy* (1979), B.R. McPherson (ed.), Kingston, McPherson & Co., 1997.

Scott, T., 'Stuart Sherman's Singular Spectacles', *The Drama Review*, March 1979, 23.1, pp.69–78.

Seitz, W.C., *The Art of Assemblage*, New York, The Museum of Modern Art, 1961.

Serban, A., 'The Life in a Sound', E. Blumenthal (trans.), *The Drama Review*, December 1976, 20.4, pp.25–6.

Shank, A.E., *et al.* (eds.), '4 Scenes in a Harsh Life: Synopsis of Scenes', in 'A Casebook: Ron Athey', *TheatreForum*, Winter/Spring 1995, 6, pp.62–3.

Shattuck, R., *The Banquet Years* (1955), New York, Vintage Books, 1968.

Sherman, S., *One Acts and Two Trilogies*, Imperial Beach, VRI Theater Library, 1987.

Simmer, B., 'Robert Wilson and Therapy', *The Drama Review*, March 1976, 20.1, pp.99–110.

Sitney, P.A., *Visionary Film*, New York, Oxford University Press, 1979.

Smith, M., 'The Good Scene: Off Off-Broadway', *Tulane Drama Review*, Summer 1966, 10.4, pp.159–76.

Sontag, S., *Against Interpretation and Other Essays* (1961), New York, Dell, 1969.

—— *Styles of Radical Will*, New York, Farrar, Straus & Giroux, 1969.

Stein, G., *Lectures in America* (1935), Boston, Beacon Press, 1985.

Steiner, G., *Language and Silence* (1967), New York, Atheneum, 1986.

Strasberg, L. (ed.), *Famous American Plays of the 1950s*, New York, Dell, 1962.

Tallmer, J., review of *Many Loves, Village Voice*, 21 January 1959, p.9.

Taylor, G., *Reinventing Shakespeare: A Cultural History from the Restoration to the Present*, New York, Weidenfeld & Nicolson, 1989.

Tomkins, C., *The Bride and the Bachelors: Five Masters of the Avant Garde* (1962), New York, Viking, 1968.

—— *Off the Wall: Robert Rauschenberg and the Art World of Our Time*, New York, Doubleday, 1980.

Trilling, L., *Beyond Culture: Essays on Literature and Learning*, New York, Viking, 1965.

Tulane Drama Review, Spring 1964, 8.3.

Tytell, J., *The Living Theatre: Art, Exile, and Outrage*, New York, Grove Press, 1995.

van Itallie, J.C., *America Hurrah*, New York, Coward-McCann, 1966.

—— *The Serpent*, New York, Atheneum, 1969.

Wagner, R., *The Art-Work of the Future and Other Works* (1895), W.A. Ellis (trans.), Lincoln, University of Nebraska Press, 1993.

Wehle, P., 'Reza Abdoh and *Tight Right White:* Interviews with Philippa Wehle', *Theatre-Forum*, Fall/Winter 1994, 4, p.60–2.

Wetzsteon, R., 'Theatre Journal', *Village Voice*, 6 March 1969, pp.39, 44.

Wilson, R., [Byrd Hoffman] *The King of Spain*, in W.M. Hoffman (ed.), *New American Plays, Vol. 3*, New York, Hill & Wang, 1970.

Wolfe, T., *The Purple Decades: A Reader*, New York, Farrar, Straus & Giroux, 1982, pp.265–93.

Yale Theatre, Spring 1969, 2.1.

Index